Letting the Soul Decide

A journey of more than one lifetime

Granville Stone

2

ISBN 9780952927723

A CIP record of this book is available at the British Library

Oh, the delight awaiting the brave warrior
Who dares to open 'Pandora's Box' and enter in
To explore the sub-conscious corridors of the labyrinth
And in the finding, subdue the Minotaur within.

Table of Contents

About the Book

An unbroken memory of the 'before life state', an enforced alignment to feelings and later, a thirst to seek answers, all contrived to become the alchemic mix that once set in motion did not allow me to cease the quest to uncover the mysteries of life.

There's no doubt to my mind that without being confined to a steam tent from birth due to a deficient immune system, I would never have retained the connection to the 'inner-life'.

I assume that in a 'normal' life the memory of 'life before life' fades into obscurity as new images flood the senses, even before birth - but this sensory blitz didn't happen. Using and therefore developing the senses in this physical world was limited soon after birth which must have led to a large portion of my burgeoning faculties becoming focussed on the finer feelings and images that I've since discovered perpetually stream from deep 'within'. It's a source I've grown to understand as the Soul, feelings that have been transposed into knowledge and then into wisdom after years spent tussling with trying to understand their relevance in the 'here and now'. This perceived wisdom, along with the ups and downs that gave it credence have been included in the hope it will serve to help others move towards a more peaceful and joyful life.

Sat sitting, being detached, entering the 'void' or 'zone', are just a few of the terms I've heard over the years for what people relate to as a way to explain their experience of 'the silence'. It's a state of being that was thrust upon me in the first six months of life, undoubtedly reinforced by several near death experiences endured in the same period – my psyche torn back and forth across the veil to ensure the memory of the heavenly realms remained – Was the same orchestration at work to ensure that I had a mother who refused to leave my side, to be ever present to give life saving stimulation whenever silence befell me?

From what I now understand, the Soul was responsible for this orchestration-, an overlighting all pervading intelligence that has apparently opened the gate to every round of life I've had since the beginning of time, gently leading me by the hand, knowing that one day I would open my eyes and 'see'. Its success in achieving this depended upon my cooperation in aligning to its wishes – or of ever wanting to!

The book begins with a description of how 'inner' journeys synchronised with 'outer' experiences to abruptly awaken me to the reality of a 'pre-life' world in my late twenties, an awakening that brought almost instantly, the realisation that I'd been channelling wisdom through from this source since birth. The book continues with an account of the development that opened me increasingly to 'otherworldly' experiences that deepened my knowledge of the hidden realms of being. The storyline focuses here and there on the tribulations of keeping 'inner' development balanced with an 'outer' life as husband, father and a career in construction management. Being prompted to facilitate and teach meditation helped in this task, providing the opportunity to try out emerging and realised wisdom on literally thousands of students for more than three decades, having them produce the College requirement for 'evidence of learning'.

Several Chapters include explanations, most of which are the result of wisdom gleaned from within, of how anyone can 'open up' to their Soul and choose to follow its whisperings which from my perspective and experience, always lead to a more demanding but infinitely more fulfilling life.

The book concludes in the present day where insights and visions for the future are shared with a view to providing a measure of inspiration and hope to those seeking explanations as to why life is often difficult to bear.

List of Figures

Acknowledgments

Gratitude is expressed to the following that have helped guide my footsteps through life:

My dear wife Katherine for labouring the many stages of 're-birth' I've gone through.

An unknown Sea Cadet Instructor for insisting I should always ask 'why'

The Salvation Army for a dish of 'mushy' peas on a cold winter's night – at five years old it was a taste of unselfish giving that I have never forgot

Captain Allison the College Principal and his wife who presented by example, an exemplary way to live

Isobel Finlayson, a sprightly seventy five year old, for introducing the basic principles of meditation

Eileen & Peter Caddy and the whole Findhorn Foundation for their pioneering ways of listening to and applying the guidance from within

Anthony Borgia, whose channelled words from the inner realms confirmed my intuition to become a major catalyst setting me off on the 'path of return'

Al Koran for his words of wisdom that led to me realising the power of thought

Geoffrey Freed and Clive, both doggedly reinforced the concept of living in 'the now'

Dr. Carol Brierly founder of the 'Prometheus Society' and its members who, over a three year period, provided the space to practice fledging attempts at presenting guided meditation and for teaching me the rudiments of Hypnosis, Psychometry and the many ways of Healing

Ruth White and her discarnate Soul Mate 'Gildas' for their direct feedback from the heavenly realms and for facilitating my first experience of 'rapture'

The Spiritualist Church community at Liverpool for the lasting friendships and the support and encouragement given to me during the two years spent studying their beliefs and allowing me to practice newly acquired abilities

To Cath Allen for the hours spent patiently proof reading this book and for adding her encouragement along the way

An array of 'Inner Teachers' who continue to guide me through the labyrinth of life in perfect synchronisation with my ability to understand.

Chapter One - *Turning within*

The final refuge

The novice meditator is constantly told to 'be still and listen' - this same advice was expressed in a reply to a letter I sent to a 'New Age' community back in 1975 enquiring if their doors were still open to visitors – It was not the response I wanted but putting into practice that advice in the years since has proven without doubt the wisdom contained in those few words, leading me eventually to the joyful revelation of the unlimited nature of being and oneness of life.

For most people in the western world, sitting still and listening to what seems to be nothing, is unappealing whatever the promised reward. Out of those that do give it a go, most become distracted or bored when results are not instantly evident; others run for cover as the heat comes on and subconscious fears rise to the surface. A few stay the course – the few that feel deep down it's the only way forward - perhaps having turned aside many times before to finally resolve to complete the 'journey home' to align with the greater life. I shrug my shoulders when people leave the meditation class after just one or two sessions because I know without doubt they will return someday to continue the journey in whatever way it presents itself. For those who stay the course, the ones that have through past failures generated the necessary motivation, they reap the reward - a pot of gold at the rainbows end!

The next task is waiting

Figure 2 - Spiritual tasks are often mundane

It was never an issue as to where inner prompting was coming from or leading to – after all I'd been 'connected' since birth - and before, though it took 27 years to realise it! I know without doubt that the ability to communicate with inner levels of being is part of human make up, often disregarded and only brought into conscious use when the well known milestone of development on every meditator's path is reached, the moment when an aspirant surrenders their mind to the dictates of its inbuilt Soul. It's something I'd no option but to continue to do as I took my first breath. Apparently I'd chosen my particular path like everyone does; Even so I still needed to wake up to the fact and play an active role, to consciously connect and share the knowledge with others to help make it real within this illusionary world of ours and most of all within my mind – I needed to pick up the mop and bucket and not step over it!

> **Provided 'stillness' is achieved there appears to be no restriction to anyone connecting consciously to what I've come to know as an aspect of my Soul and is to me, part of a universal network of mindstuff – apparently this 'intelligence' has always been around to connect to but remains at a distance, symbolically asleep, needing only a gentle kiss, an embrace, to awaken it – This process reminds me of a childhood fairy story.**

The stillness of meditation seems to be the refuge of many who are forced by life's ups and downs to seek out a lasting peace, but from the outset, its practice leads a genuine aspirant to become aware of any debilitating shadows which may deter many from continuing. With diligence, patience, and most of all, courage, meditation, under the Souls guidance, provides the means to work beyond such discomfort, to eventually release any negative influence to reveal joyful ones. From the moment I began to meditate and be indoctrinated into the stillness, the feelings of deep inner peace experienced provided a strong foundation and the motivation to continue. Perhaps I'd earned the grace in earlier lives or maybe run away from its practice many times but this time had the necessary resolve, helped along with more than a few prods in the side, to eventually 'find myself'. Within a year of beginning to meditate I'd opened 'Pandora's Box'[1], entered in, and had 'worked' my way through the fabled labyrinth of hopes, dreams and fears to be found there, emerging at the far side of the subconscious into the embrace of the Soul – the definite source of my life!

NATURAL MEDITATIONS

THE OCEAN HAS A MEMORY
OF 10,000 YEARS
THE COLLECTIVE CONSCIOUSNESS
OF A STAND OF TREES
SECRETS LOCKED INTO STRATA
WHISPERED UPON A PASSING BREEZE

CREAK-CRACK OF ATROPHYING LIMBS
TENSIONS START TO SURFACE
BURIED BENEATH THE ABYSS
THE ONLY EXPECTATION MICROSCOPIC
FROM THIS HIDDEN EXOGENESIS
EXTRUDES LAVA SMOKE AND HISS

INTO THE SOUL'S INNER SPACE SHINE SEARCHLIGHTS
SUN-BABIES, COSMIC RAYS
ILLUMINATING ALL WITH DREAMS
WITH ENERGY IMBUED THEY JOURNEY
SEEK THE SURFACE, THE FUTURE
WHERE THE TRUTH BEGINS

John Mallinder April 2010

Memories of reality – Before life!

As a child I responded to 'gut instinct' simply because the intellect didn't get in the way. Later, at the age of twelve, I must still have been responding to this inner prompting if the feedback from peers was anything to go by; Apparently ignoring convention, drifting off into my own world whenever the opportunity arose, it's no wonder I was extracted from class to have school doctors and the like test my hearing and speaking abilities only to realise that I was quite content to be excluded from conversation - that I was just a 'quiet' person. This behaviour must have been frustrating to teachers, to have me shut out all verbal attempts to gain my ear whenever engrossed in reading or any activity that drew my single minded attention. On countless occasions I felt the back of a teacher's hand or a piece of chalk after more gentle methods hadn't caused me to stir. For a child nowadays to behave in this way would I'm sure have them 'labelled' in some way!

Inner prompting was always responded to, from being urged to sit quietly in a nearby park before school to slipping away to spend time in a 'secret garden' I'd stumbled across. To the onlooker this behaviour, along with being painfully quiet, must have seemed akin to that of a sixty year old recluse. It didn't occur to me either, that reflecting on the meaning of life was such an unusual subject for a child only just breeching his teenage years. The latter was an illusion quickly dissolved when beginning to share thoughts with contemporaries. I owe those early critics a favour - even though they drove me 'underground' it didn't weaken my resolve to pursue such thoughts but strengthened it; by the age of sixteen an outline vision of heaven had formed within my 'old' young mind, a vision drawn out from the depths, from the memory of a very real pre-life existence!

Unknowingly at the time, the level of control exercised over the mind and the ability to move my focus at will is a state of consciousness that every meditator strives to achieve - and here I was, apparently using this ability that must have been developed over many lives – a fruit of past endeavour? This adhering to the prompting from within continued through teenage years, ever strengthened by a series of experiences which I can now see were 'orchestrated' to occur at just the right moment. I can also see that up to this time my intellect was kept in its place by life experience more than by personal intent. This is perhaps why I can still respond to gut feelings easier than most and why I've gleaned so much more from 'out of the ordinary' experiences that most others brush off or don't even notice – I've never lost the habit of listening and looking that was developed in early life – I've only ever strengthened it.

Positive thinking – Did it always work?

One of these 'orchestrated' experiences began at the age of sixteen after reading the book 'Bring Out the Magic in Your Mind', (Al), it described the principle and application of 'positive thinking', becoming a major influence throughout my life and providing the first real problem to solve – why did positive thinking work and more importantly – why didn't it?

As realised now, nearly fifty years later, things just don't ever happen by chance. The concept of positive thinking resonated with feelings that had guided my life up to that time - now the source of these feelings had pushed me forward to the next level of development. This particular 'book', which my father had pressed into my hands, described how thinking manifested form. As he let the book go he commented that a close friend had suggested it might be worth reading – could this very gift be the manifestation of a positive thought somewhere along the way? (One of many 'cyclic' thought processes that have provided much insight into the inner workings of life.) From what I now realise, Al Koran's book was one of many placed into my 'spiritual knapsack' for essential reading in perfect timing with 'awakening' and driven into my hands by an undoubted 'knowing'. (More on this later).

After eagerly reading and experimenting with some of the suggestions made I was left cliff hanging as to why positive thinking was only partly successful - though the small success I had did prime my enthusiasm to delve further, to find a solution to the failures, which in the event became a twenty year research project providing material for a large part of this book. In the footsteps of these musings, and perhaps entirely due to early experiences in life, I went on to develop an insatiable curiosity as to why an allegiance to inner feelings brought about positive outcomes that were infinitely more successful than just thinking positive, (albeit sometimes painful when choosing to heed them.) Had I stumbled upon the secret of life?

Looking back there was no burst of enlightenment to bring on that quiet, day-on-day reflection that dug ever deeper into the human condition but more a collection of inspirational moments, and not until writing this account did the realisation unfold that everyone's life is 'set up' long before birth as part of pre-life planning.

Born a 'blue baby' and needing a life saving blood transfusion meant that I was open to infection and had to be confined to a makeshift steam tent which kept me isolated from most outer world sensations. This six months of enforced confinement, the first of many seemingly 'stage managed' events in my life, no doubt helped to establish and reinforce the habit of 'being still' within a physical body – a habit that was deliberately practiced decades later.   The next phase of 'training' began at the age of two – left alone after elder siblings had gone to school and spending many hours alone each day before either parent returned from work. Delivering mail for the Post Office, mum's labours started at 5am, finishing after the 'second post' around 1pm, six days a week. Dads shift 'down the pit' stretched mum's day by two hours. I've no regrets with regard to this early initiation and in no doubt either that my attendance at nursery school at the age of four was in perfect timing with needs. On reflection it's become obvious why it was so much easier for me to sit the long hours needed to achieve the detachment that meditation practice demands than it is for most others – and of course I now have the added bonus of a clear recollection of having had a hand in planning my life experience prior to birth - how could I ever object or feel sorry for myself? (Everyone's involved in pre-life planning – if you're to believe the testimonials of a multitude of students I've taken back, with the help of specially designed visualisations, into pre-life memory.)

Not having the inclination to communicate with anyone in the early years of my life did lead to concern, however, my ability to sense people's moods from body language and feelings expressed or radiated, had by the age of four probably developed well on the way to becoming equal to that of any adult. This led naturally to me responding to peers the way they expected which served the purpose of distracting their concerns long before they took any serious action. Being 'led' into behaving in this way did have its positive side – super sensitivity though in certain circumstances this sensitivity brought about negative reactions in certain situations.

By the time it came to leaving home to go to college at the age of fourteen this sensitivity had developed into a knee jerk reaction of withdrawing deep within whenever I could feel aggression from those around me, sometimes spending days in silence - hurt to the core and only 'coming around' when those who had inadvertently caused my distress had 'kissed and made up' and were giving off better 'vibes'. It didn't seem to matter whether the aggression was directed at me or not. Many years passed before learning, through the practice of meditation, to embrace uncomfortable feelings, to be involved without reacting so severely, delving instead ever deeper into the psyche of the offending parties, reflecting on what was unturned and adding to my understanding of others.

Probably to re-experience the very 'peaceful' moments of the pre-life by entering deliberately into the stillness, I often found myself visiting the local park before going the last quarter mile to school each day, or alternatively spent hours doing makeshift gardening, especially during school holidays. I was just eleven when father discovered a semi-cultivated piece of land filling the gap between our garage and next doors – a place close at hand that I thought would provide a retreat. Exploring to see where I'd kept disappearing to he'd pushed his way through undergrowth and a pile of assorted rubbish that gravitates to corners of gardens, to be confronted by two very gangly looking potato plants growing in half light!

Discovering my personalised 'Garden of Eden' must have had quite an effect on him as I was instantly awarded responsibility for the whole of the front garden - this was definitely not what I wanted – now, instead of retreating to the peace and quiet of my retreat to hide from the hurt of the world whenever I could, I'd been thrust into the limelight with every passer-by insisting on giving a word of encouragement to this youngster who appeared to be so keen on gardening! The short lived retreat faded into distant memory as I had my work cut out trimming the hedge, mowing the lawn and keeping the incessant weeds at bay which left little time to lean on my spade to contemplate the meaning of life – The inner guardians must have been splitting their sides laughing - moving me out of the shadows into the daylight of the front garden foiled any attempt to return to my preferred lifestyle as a recluse which was definitely not meant to be part of my destiny. Looking back its easy to reflect on where 'inner' mentors have schemed incessantly to keep my life on track, forever presenting experiences to encourage the following of a path that has, in these latter years, become clear enough for me to 'see' the way to walk without having to be manipulated. Such interference, both material and subliminal, has led me into fulfilling various roles in life which has included over thirty years of teaching and the giving of presentations to upwards of five hundred people. One realisation I've had is that life continues to present new challenges and opportunities to grow because of conformance to the wishes of various inner world mentors, including a benevolent Soul that overlight's my being, an attitude definitely reinforced if not originated during early isolation or before. Whenever I choose not to conform to the dictates of the Soul I feel increasingly at odds with life until I do which led me long ago to stop seeking proof of the benefit of following inner prompting.

Feet on the ground, head in the heavens

My family, and just about everyone else I associated with as a child had some connection with the mining industry. Our home, the local dance hall and sports facilities, were all owned by the National Coal Board - 'the pit', was the common term we used for the NCB. This all-encompassing organisation collectively conspired to reinforce the prevailing Yorkshire attitude of being metaphorically and quite literally, 'down to earth' with sharp comments made to anyone stepping out of line. Without doubt this ingrained view of life sways me away from attaching importance to the knowledge streaming into consciousness from 'elevated entities' – Another pre-life 'set up'?

I've no doubt too that it was this background that kept the glamour of the 'travelling circus' from attracting me away from self development towards the many exciting and 'out of this world' experiences that profess to aid the achievement of 'nirvana' and perhaps the making of a million or two telling fortunes.

Moving into lodgings at the age of fourteen to attend nautical college was perhaps too soon for many but not for me - it was at last a chance to move on and away from what was becoming a very restrictive lifestyle. The attitudes that typified those that were part of my fast receding home life could best be represented when, after applying to sit the college entrance exam as a 'B' grade student, everyone expected me to fail! Leaving home at such a young age definitely felt like the right thing to do, I was after all, fully involved with the local Sea Cadets - an organisation set up to encourage enlistment into the Royal Navy, so why shouldn't I follow this through with a career at sea? Well of course I passed, the other five 'A' grade students failed which instigated much speculation among my teachers. No I didn't cheat – I was just good at mental arithmetic. (Well I jolly well ought to be!)

Again, life and my allegiance to follow through with whatever felt right, even though in direct confrontation to what I wanted, not only prevented me from becoming a recluse but forced close contact with a college full of people and a deep connection to the lives of three different families who provided board and lodging in the local community for the three years spent their. Re-joining the sea cadets ensured my evenings and weekends were also 'tied up' with people to interact with! It was at college, having gained a limited amount of confidence, that my maiden debate on the meaning of life was aired and summarily dismissed. As consolation, it was also the place that I first encountered unconditional love, providing the first experience of heartache when it came time to leave close friends behind, particularly the college principal and his wife who had become virtual surrogate parents after I'd been elected Cadet Captain in the final year. Another of life's 'set ups' that thrust a reclusive personality into the limelight presenting no option but to engage in continuous dialogue, forcing me to swim in the mainstream of life in no time at all. There were girl friends too, but none that 'rocked' my world - not until the one I met at home on shore leave after my very first trip to the Far East!

Such an emotional roller coaster I had never known. Euphoria at meeting and heartache at having to leave her after just three weeks leave. Eating and sleeping were out of the question for days after I'd rejoined the ship, followed by weeks of deep longing until we could be together again. After just three trips I'd resigned and returned home to begin working 'down the pit'! Although it would seem that my spiritual development had been put on hold, in truth it hadn't and this period in my life became just as an important as any other - an opportunity to balance my emotional life and focus more intently on others in a completely different way.

Meeting Katherine was the first real encounter with love which had a tremendous transformative power on my life. Because of the limitations of infancy and the arms length affection displayed by my family, perhaps it wasn't surprising that feeling love, showing love and being loved in return turned my emotional world upside down - The accompanying feelings were both delightful and dreadful -

opening me up and making me feel extremely vulnerable at one and the same time.

For the first time in my life I was confronted with emotions that became mixed up with the underlying feelings that I'd relied upon from birth, pulling me deep into the depths of the emotional world as a consequence. It certainly felt right to allow myself to be vulnerable in this way but brought almost unbearable discomfort in its footsteps that took years to adjust to. Not until meditation had become part of a daily routine some years later and had led me through a series of 'opening' experiences, did I relax my fear to step fully into this unknown land, trusting my feet would find firm footing.

It was the only way forward - to allow thoughts and fears to rise to the surface, to be expressed and then released. It formed the next part of my journey with no way around, only through, and this fellow wasn't for turning!

Working through and coming to terms with these 'new' emotions, which people usually come to terms with during adolescence, awakened deep feelings of love and brought a whole new wave of understanding – now I knew what all the fuss was about. Yes, my isolated childhood had indeed forced me to seek comfort within the inner realms of being but had also kept this sweet secret of life, this thing called love, hidden from view as a consequence – until now.

Marrying my Soul Mate, having two children and returning to college to study surveying in order to redirect my career were enough to handle at this time, and as a down to earth sort of person who was boringly practical, I would have lived out my life in domestic bliss if it wasn't for the fact that I'd been picked out for special treatment and wouldn't be given any opportunity to gather moss! That special treatment began when reaching the ripe old age of twenty-six when my life again turned within – Actually, it turned upside down and inside out!

A catalyst for change

Another fateful book, 'Life in the World Unseen' (Benson), was the cause of this latest change, and dramatic it was, perfectly synchronised to appear at just the 'right' moment, (though unaware of it at the time) - Just as my life was settling into routines and was in danger of becoming comfortable! Obviously the time was ripe for inner guardians to throw one or two spanners into the works and this particular spanner came in the form of a Sunday newspaper article, an abstract from a new book which described Heaven! The passage, as brief as it was, confirmed my conclusions - The reaction within me was nothing short of cataclysmic and despite the paper's sarcastic opinions, a third world war couldn't have stopped me obtaining a copy!

By the age of eleven I had begun to reconstruct from memory what heaven was like - I've always had an insatiable need to understand everything about life and by the age of sixteen had fitted together a complete scenario of life beyond life but had no means of confirming that these 'daydreams' were reality - they had sat for as long as I could remember as a figment of my imagination.

This make believe 'heavenly realm' was a place in which we rested between lives, a place I had memory of but no means to prove existed, not even to myself – at least not until reading this latest book that proved to be life changing!

The book left in its wake the shocking realisation that everything I'd ever 'fabricated' about my inner world was true - what else had I mused about without taking too seriously?

From that time up until today I've continued to update the 'knowledge' flowing from within, limited only by my ability to understand what is 'seen'. The early insights providing an inroad for further attunement sessions and, just as the Aquarian Age water carrier symbolises – I now know that this unending stream of wisdom is available, not just to me, but to all who look within.

> **Just as a seed needs water, light and nutrients – our being also needs the living stream of light for it to 'grow' and more importantly, to continue to grow.**

Several weeks passed before the book arrived and after reading just a few pages feelings of wonderment overtook my life compelling me to read it from cover to cover virtually non-stop. It was indeed a life changing experience. Essentially the information was channelled through the author by a discarnate entity called Monsignor Benson, the authenticity of which I'd no problem accepting, after all, wasn't I a 'Channel' too? He described in detail, via the author's consciousness, heavenly surroundings that matched exactly the conclusions I'd reached.

None judgemental love

In an instant the ideas streaming through consciousness during quiet reflections since childhood were confirmed. They were clothed in truth. Heaven did exist – but there could be no rejoicing??? Perhaps contrary to what people would expect, this realisation brought with it an avalanche of guilt with regard to my thoughts and behaviour. The inner guides were no longer at arm's length as vague figments of my imagination, but had become very real entities watching every move I made, listening to every thought - how uncomfortable is that! In a drive to make myself appear whiter than white and feel more at ease with these entities breathing down my neck I began to let everyone know every thought I was having. Not a good idea for someone wishing to climb the career ladder - and not particularly good for my home life either when having to admit that most of the important decisions in my life were driven by inner prompting! I didn't care -

there were far more important considerations to take account of – my afterlife!

My presumption was wrong. In time I realised that benevolent beings who have access to such inner pathways, have only love as their motive and our best interests as their objective. Always the key that allows such access is love – totally non judgemental - To me, 'love' is the most beautiful and perfect of all the cosmic laws that I've so far become aware of! The positive effect of this epitome was that it had a domino effect on every other morsel of 'knowledge' that I'd perceived up to that time. The 'Heavenly Realm' was no longer a remote concept conjured up in my head from a vague memory but had become reality in the twinkling of an eye, a reality relayed to me by discarnate entities – guardians of various degrees upon elevated levels of being.

Every idea I'd ever had about the afterlife suddenly became fact. More important than that was the very real sense that I had a 'hot line' to the inner realms of being and that all I need do to gain answers to any of the mysteries of life was to 'tune in' and ask. The only limitation to this process was of course my ability to understand the concepts being presented. Though I'd had the ability to 'be still' and 'tune in' since childhood and had received impressions in my mind that I'd never questioned, now, after reading 'life in the World Unseen', I was motivated to glean and understand every morsel of knowledge those impressions carried until feeling there could be nothing more to be imparted – though I know now that such a day will never arrive!

Literally lifetimes of investment

Drawing from my passion of pondering on the meaning of life and the wealth of insight already made available to my consciousness, it's 'seen' that thousands of years and many lifetimes are invested in our development from the moment we are released into the creative atmosphere of Earth. All the effort geared to bring forth the day when we choose the path of return to re-unite with the God Self's representative – the Soul. It came as no surprise to realise that inner 'guides' were pushing me at this time with added enthusiasm, to achieve in the present life a breakthrough that had without doubt been eons in the making. It seems my Soul, as always, was calling the shots and I was choosing to follow without restraint, especially now. Yes, even when my thoughts were full of other stuff, 'Big Brother' intervened to ensure that all that preparation would not go to waste! Intuition was without doubt leading the way forward as a very powerful undercurrent within my life – proven time and time again in the years since to be standing patiently at every crossroad to give directions. Perhaps I'm not the first to wish I'd begun to take note long ago?

Just a few weeks before reading the book 'Life in the World Unseen' (Benson) I'd read another called 'The Magic of Findhorn', (Hawken) that had a few passages similarly attributed to having been channelled from 'above'. I'd received this earlier book from a book club as the 'book of the month' and having initially discarded it because the subject matter seemed to be 'strange' and disjointed, I now found myself revisiting certain passages with zeal. The book took on a whole new meaning - presenting a concept that didn't describe heaven but talked instead of creating heaven on earth aided by channelling from within to provide day to day instructions on how to do so!

At the time I didn't realise what a phenomenal change my life was going through as a result of reading these two books (not forgetting either, the one passed onto me by my father years earlier). My thought processes were turning on their head and a hungry search began for more 'channelled' reading – mostly to compare what was written to the insight already imprinted upon my consciousness. A side effect of this 'digging' was to stimulate the opening of whole new chapters of knowledge begging to be verified from an alternative source to enable me to 'own' its inherent wisdom.

The 'Magic of Findhorn' (Hawken) related the experiences of Peter, Eileen and Dorothy, co-founders of the Findhorn Foundation, (a 'New Age' community located in the far north of Scotland), and the various and diverse ways they communicated 'within'. These different ways of channelling provided a challenge to my intellect to understand and fit them into my very limited portfolio on the subject at the time. The 'internal hot line' was working overtime trying to 'fill out' what seemed to be an overwhelming amount of new concepts being presented.

I was surprised to receive a response when writing to the Findhorn Foundation. The Magic of Findhorn (Hawken) had described in detail the organisation and its residents and left me with an insatiable thirst to know more about a community that owed its very existence to following 'guidance'. It was also heartening to hear that literally hundreds, if not thousands of people of all ages, creeds and nationalities were, like me, responding to the inner voice of God in a multitude of ways. From this enquiry came an explosion of information with my bookshelves filling rapidly with 'channelled' books from many different authors, including several from the Foundation's own printing press.

Within a few months I'd become well and truly launched into a totally new way of life, a way of life that people at 'Findhorn' had been living and demonstrating for years! A deep yearning to visit the Foundation was growing. I wanted to connect with them, to taste their way of life, to perhaps live it for myself. Daydreams abounded around the idea of being there, but even with a well established attitude to achieving needs, affording the cost and using up the two weeks holiday allowed by my employer to visit Findhorn instead of with my family made it seem impossible to turn the yearning into reality. I knew I had not only to be positive but to remain so in order to sustain the vision to turn the daydreams into reality - Was it enough?

Scotland and the Findhorn Foundation - The Pilgrimage

Yes it was - out of the blue, and literally within days of casting my desires into the heavens, the employer I'd worked several years for asked for volunteers to transfer to a project soon to start in the north of Scotland - just half an hour away from my blessed 'Findhorn' - wow! Was this the greatest miracle of my life? Nowadays I've become accustomed to expect needs to be met, *especially needs that align with the path that our Soul wishes us to take* – ('Expect a miracle' is one of the main guiding principles at Findhorn.)

Unbeknown to me at the time, Scotland was where I would take a deliberate step on the 'journey home' and would learn the importance of being still - to meditate. It was also the place, as a result of entering the stillness at least once a day, where I would deepen the relationship with my Soul and to top it all, the Findhorn Foundation was just around the corner – a community it seemed that was full of kindred Souls, many opened up to inner guidance in much the same way as me and with whom I could share my growing pains with!

There's a well known saying quoted by 'New Age' groups *'when you begin the journey within, hold onto your hat'* – and it had proven true for me! No sooner had I resolved to seek out the Findhorn Community that things began to slot into place and within days I was moving north. It appeared to the outsider, and those close to me, that I was abandoning a young family, deserting them to go roaming into the wilds of Scotland on a whim. To me it was a pilgrimage, a journey to find myself, something I had to do no matter what the material, emotional and intellectual cost. I could offer no excuse other than to say to my dear wife that 'it felt right, that I had no alternative'. You can guess the reaction. My hat definitely got a battering but I clung onto it as though my very life was at stake – but there was something even more valuable to nurture – my Soul!

The job in Scotland was to oversee dredging works in preparation for a new 1km bridge spanning between Inverness and the Black Isle – to be followed up with responsibility as Engineer for the structure itself. It turned out to be one of the most enjoyable and fulfilling projects I've ever worked on, serving to keep my feet on the ground during the unfolding life changing events that were sending my consciousness into the heavens – and all played out in the silence and beauty of the highlands of Scotland – how perfect!

Well versed in 'looking' into the meaning of events I'd been aware for some time of the symbolic meaning of the work I did and its synchronicity with spiritual unfolding – riding the emotional waves (Merchant Navy), exploring the sub-consciousness (Coal Mines) and latterly, building new foundations (Steel Mills), all ran in sequence and in parallel with personal development. Now I was ready to build a bridge across to a new level of awareness on the far shore!

They were, to begin with, lonely days in Scotland, made all the more so by a constant barrage of emotional stuff at having to leave my family for several weeks at a time. An inner cleansing some would say - the only comfort to be derived was a sense of doing the right thing that came from the feelings I'd had as a 'blanket' wrapped around me since birth; feelings that were now being clung to as the only means of survival. I had no choice in the matter either - when at times I ignored these feelings and began to give way to conformity I became extremely uncomfortable and agitated as though part of me had been taken away!

At twenty nine, now living and working in Scotland, albeit temporary, it was obviously 'contrived' to have an elderly lady 'pop up' to teach me the basics of meditation. Even though I'd begun to accept the appearance of such people in 'perfect timing' with my development it was still a surprise. I'd questioned people and read extensively on the subject but never expected to progress with this whilst living and working in 'Inverness' of all places - but here she was, advertising on the door of a community centre! Scotland never fails to surprise me, the place is overflowing with progressive people and groups that appear to be just as 'connected' as anyone – How wrong could I have been!

The poster advertising a chance to relax and meditate stood out like a neon sign and couldn't help but be noticed by people passing by, except that no one else must have taken it seriously - I was the only one to attend. Because of this the five lunchtime sessions ended up as 'one to one' tutoring designed specifically for a beginner to meditation like me – there seemed to be no limit to the miracles that life has in store!

This personal tutoring came to an end when increased responsibilities at work prevented attendance – another 'set up' but this time forcing me into doing something for myself? I didn't need much persuasion as by this time the practice of meditation had well and truly smitten me, how could I turn my back on a sense of peace that was beyond comprehension – my first taste of a peace that did indeed pass beyond all understanding.

Repeating the simple exercises of meditation in the quiet of my temporary flat brought the same feelings of peace that my blessed tutor had succeeded in encouraging and easily provided the motivation to continue. Being away from home for up to three weeks at a time was an ideal opportunity to spend most of my free time practising 'stillness' without being disturbed. I did so want my young family by my side but this episode in my life was undoubtedly meant to be and I had an obligation to my God to use the opportunity as best I could. Connecting within developed my ability to help others by promoting a better understanding of people in general and those close to me - so it was again with perfect timing that soon after unfolding and establishing a new direction for my life that my family joined me in Scotland for the whole of the summer making it one of the most memorable and fulfilling periods for us all.

Early autumn saw the family return to Yorkshire in time for the children to begin the new school term. Once again I found myself alone in the quiet of a large house and having had to temporarily

suspend meditation sessions whilst the family were with me, I resumed its practice with added zeal for up to three hours a day.

As feelings of peace deepened so too did an awareness of other more subtle levels of being. These feelings were not due to being on my own - such solitude and the resultant feelings were well known and embraced as an old friend. No, these were new sensations, like the subtle feelings around at Christmas or at an airport where long parted lovers meet. They were, as I grew to understand years afterwards, the result of connecting by a direct line to my Soul, to the 'God Self' within, feelings awaiting everyone when they 'go within' with intent to re-kindle a connection that was 'known' at the beginning of time; More on this subject later.

Having a familiarity to 'the source' since birth, being introduced to meditation strengthened a feeling that there was yet something even more profound to uncover and reinforced a resolve to continue the inner journey until this 'something' happened - and it did!

Right from the start of exploring this new experience called meditation I was confronted with having to let go of any and all desire in a process that could best be described by using the analogy of a stairway, and a frustrating one at that - two steps up and one step down, with heart rending yearnings to 'become' holding me back and a total release or abandonment as I let go taking me forward again! An end to this process only came when realising the attitude of mind needed, one which enabled me to climb the remaining steps in one great leap.

The profound peace I experienced when first beginning to meditate became the carrot to get me started with the Christmassy sensations keeping me going for a while but I became increasingly frustrated because the 'pot of gold' I knew was out there just did not appear and disillusionment was threatening to take over – an inner conflict began!

How many times in past lives must I have been determined to see things through only to lose interest at the eleventh hour? Now feelings of self disgust at my lack of resolve were arising to overcome this lethargy. This time I wasn't going to give in, no matter how long it would take, nomatter how frustrated I got. I just 'knew' that to continue was going to lead to the most important breakthrough, of not just this life, but of the whole of my journey since turning my back on paradise. To be fair I did have insights to keep me going, accompanied by subtle feelings that just wouldn't let me stop which I knew could only be satiated by some sort of break through. Like an explorer, a new frontier of experience awaited me, had fired my imagination and held the promise that I would discover a world of experiences that I'd read were life transforming, - if only I could keep going.

What I know now is that this very build up of frustration was a necessary part of the awakening process! I needed the impetus, the will power, the energy, to make the final push to reach the summit, but paradoxically I also needed to somehow learn how to stop pushing at just the 'right moment' to allow my consciousness to 'free wheel' the last mile! This was the eye of the needle, the great chasm, the step into the dark, and which I know protects that sacred inner space from any would-be usurper.

This latter phase into this 'inner kingdom' continued for many weeks, I continued to spend up to three hours a day 'in the silence' and still experienced nothing! Eventually, I reached the end of my tether - it was make or break time. All the frustration was heaped into one great push. - I decided to dedicate a whole weekend to meditation, visualisations, affirmations, prayer - anything and everything that I'd learned or had perceived as inspiring over the previous months was to be thrown into the pot during this weekend of weekends. - I was determined to remain anchored to the spot until something did 'happen'.

There I was, laid flat out on a camp bed in the lounge of a three bedroom house in the far north of Scotland, (the camp bed was the only bit of furniture I'd kept after my family returned home). I began the meditation marathon soon after breakfast on a Saturday morning, the door was locked and to the outside, the house appeared empty - as intended. I remained motionless. To anyone looking through the window I must have looked like a corpse laid out waiting for the hearse to arrive, (symbolically I was)! Four hours later I was still waiting - a quick dart to the loo and then back to the morgue. This weekend was to mark the death of self to make way for Soul!

Initially frustration had re-asserted itself as I returned to the 'battle front'. On one side the physical body, stiff and screaming for exercise, food and the like; on the opposing side - nothing, just a hardly perceptible knowing, a deep inner knowing that wouldn't allow me to let go of this inner quest.

Was it the frustration, the fatigue of battle or did the brain finally get the message that my body wasn't going to go anywhere until it had produced the goodies? Whatever was happening internally, after six hours of non-stop meditation I had the sensation that my body was gently rocking.

This gentle rocking, a vibration of sorts, radiated out from the solar plexus area of my stomach to affect my whole body - Somehow I'd hit upon the right attitude within a moment of perfect stillness to cause the Chakra triads of the upper and lower body to combine their energies, to become the alchemic mix that instantly balanced my being and caused the inner doorway of the heart to open.

This balancing had, at long last, allowed energy to flow unabated directly through my being from the source; immediately following this whole body vibration was a feeling of expansion, which in its early stages felt as though my body was being inflated. I later came to understand that I had entered the 'void'. At last a result to quell the months of frustration! - An experience that has proven since to have pushed me beyond all doubt about the need to keep my feet firmly on the pathway home.

After several more trips into the emptiness of the void and I had become familiar to the new sensations. Of course this experience was more than just a taste, it was real, I could feel it - I now know what 'to be' is but after all the years since still find it difficult to explain it to others. I had reached an immeasurable position where I'd begun to oversee my brain's activity on the way to becoming its master. Before long I was achieving this expanded state of awareness within a few minutes of beginning to meditate, followed soon after by an extension of awareness into what seemed to be unlimited dimensions – a 'beingness' in which I was still fully aware of my physical body though completely detached from its senses. I can only describe the feeling as totally blissful, timeless and formless - a void without dimension and 'ever present'. I felt more alive than ever before and the essence of anything brought to mind when in this awareness, became instantly 'known'.

Darkness pervaded the whole experience and had it not been for the accompanying feelings of joy the experience could have been interpreted very differently. One or two students have backed away from practicing meditation after having experienced this total and all encompassing darkness within the void – the fear it stimulated far outweighed the soft caresses to be experienced in this, the world of the Soul.

It was a state of being I was tempted to indulge in whenever the opportunity arose, with feelings of euphoria lingering long after a session came to an end. I couldn't continue in this way, obviously – no doubt observed 'from above' as yet another comfortable armchair was pulled away from under me that ran the risk of bringing a halt to my progress

To the outside world it may appear as coincidence but I've come to know, since these heady days that the most important events in my life are 'set up' to occur at just the right moment. These 'right moments' have conspired over the years to present experiences that have forced an adjustment to the way I think to a point that leaves no shadow of doubt that a perfect divine order permeates and acts upon the whole of life.

Still in Scotland, another challenge presented itself when responding to an advertisement for volunteers to join the Samaritans – once again, I was spurred on by inner prompting. As a result of the childhood experiences related earlier, I wasn't particularly good at communicating feelings to others despite the 'guides' constantly pushing me into social circles – but now a practical opportunity to overcome this inadequacy was presenting itself.

As always in my life, a decision didn't need to be made. My attunement within was a very real pact with my Soul - 'thy will be done', was the gist of it. The advertisement was the confirmation of the path I needed to follow at this time and was more of an instruction to join than a request. 'Helping' in this way not only benefited the community but would also help in a very powerful and newly emerging drive 'to find and understand myself'.

After four years voluntary service with the Samaritans my eyes had opened wide as to how other people thought and reacted to life and provided a major realisation of just how very much alike we all are - especially when looking through the heightened perspective, through the eyes of the Soul. A couple of months or so after settling into this role I became uneasy at the large number of distressed people needing the service. It wasn't long too before realising that resources were far from adequate to deal with those needs. Many experiences occurred whilst 'on duty' which stirred something deep inside me, a disturbance that I needed to do something about - but what? The people causing these heart-wrenching feelings seemed to be the more sensitive and thoughtful types of society who were easily hurt and retreated at the slightest sign of insincerity, (perhaps not surprisingly, a behaviour I'd taken years to come to terms with). My early childhood had taught me well – generally when speaking to these, mostly distressed individuals, I had to ensure I didn't jump to conclusions but to use increasingly the skills I'd developed in meditation: to 'look' and not to react, and definitely not to judge!

I began steering my life towards endeavours perceived as being more effective in helping people step back from 'the brink'. This is where the practice of meditation particularly helped - having experienced over-whelming feelings of peace by its practice I became motivated to develop a set of visualisations I knew would help those in distress. In my zealousness, almost from the outset of beginning to meditate, I wanted everyone to experience the same feelings of peace that I had done, but in reality, after facilitating taster sessions, I knew I had to step back and allow each and every individual to follow their heart, and their path, at their own pace – just as I had been allowed to.

Though the Samaritans could as a service offer support and practical assistance which steered many from the edge, there were many in distress that needed more - they wanted answers that made sense and if they didn't get them, suicide was to be the only solution. I'd volunteered as a way of learning more about myself whilst helping others but it seemed to me from the outset that many of those seeking help were threatening suicide if I couldn't get through to them. (I suspect that the timing and the type of problem presented by these distressed Souls could have been an inner plane 'set up' for my benefit and it wasn't long before it became apparent why.)

I was put on the spot time and time again - working with the Samaritans was the first occasion I'd been forced to rely on intuition alone. Attuning to the Soul of those I was trying to help, connecting with their inner guides, tapping into their 'overlighting' advice and relaying back what was perceived – and all within an instant whilst remaining sincere was quite a task! Such people, of whom I'd no doubt were in a heightened state of awareness due to their situation, seemed to have gone beyond the fear of death[2] and needed what I've come to regard as 'Soul communion' to make sense of life. It was definitely a time to put into practice what little I had learned about heaven and earth and the motive to 'live'.

Chapter Two - *House groups to further education*

The first meditation group

This period provided the motivation, and guidance, that led to the formation of the first ever meditation group. I'd tried out a few taster sessions and 'knew' I needed to keep going - to try out learned meditation techniques on others with the help of a new friend, a Resource Person for the Findhorn Foundation called Alistair McKay. (I'd asked on my first visit to the Foundation for the names of any local contacts.) Alistair had not only spent two years practising Transcendental Meditation but was also walking the same inner path, and yes, another miracle, he lived and worked within walking distance of my temporary home in Inverness - no wonder I knew I had to continue on this quest with so much dropping into place.

The initial feelings of guilt and self-condemnation at leaving everything behind subsided with the realisation that the journey to Scotland had proved to be exactly the right thing to do. In the event I had reconnected to my Soul and that had to take first place in anyone's life. This reconnection was the same link I'd had since birth but was now rapidly becoming a conscious connection and infinitely more lucid and interactive.

Soon after becoming 're-established' I began reviewing childhood conclusions of heaven, earth and everything else between, exploring with fresh eyes the many ideas presented to my consciousness from this fountain of wisdom deep within, a flow that increased markedly due to my participation and was now aided with a conscious belief in the integrity of its source.

Increasingly, people in need of help were invited to join meditation sessions with the results quickly proving that meditation could be developed and used as a means to help people relax – a monumental task for the distressed, and more importantly to some, the sessions provided answers to long sought after questions relating to the meaning of life. (At the time I assumed my Soul was the only source of this knowledge). We met in each other's homes in and around Inverness and later, at home in the north of England, after my time in Scotland ended. After each session an account of the evenings work was recorded with a copy of the outcomes given out at the following meeting. Many questions arose during the sessions stimulating feedback that always led to more questions and much contemplation to unearth the answers – behold the age old method of relaying knowledge!

Inner connectedness brought through from pre-birth and developed with the help of meditation practice, had evolved into a sort of 'knowing presence' by this time and was proving invaluable for giving 'feedback' on a continuous basis when talking to distressed people and to those who, like myself were heading 'home'. From the responses it was realised they were getting the answers they sought, but doing this when on duty with the Samaritans was breaking 'help line' rules. – We were supposed to listen and not comment, especially not with answers that were often radical. To me these people were in a no man's land and making a connection to their Soul was the only thread by which to pull them back and I wasn't going to stick to any rules if it meant a life could be saved - but no confrontation ever arose and after four years we gracefully parted when another door opened.

A communion of Souls

To me, Soul consciousness seems to be limited to those who have stilled the mind sufficiently to allow 'universal' mind-stuff to flow through it – a state of mind that people suffering from severe distress also seem able to achieve quite by accident?

Over many years of listening with intent it seems that at times the mind of a distressed person becomes remote, distant, numbed by life experience and therefore stood aside in some way to allow the Soul through, if only for a short period, but in a state that allows communion with other Souls to also take place.

Unbeknown to me at the time, the help line service was assisting me to take advantage of this state of mind certain distressed individuals had entered by providing the arena that effectively 'allowed' me to connect, to link directly with them in a sort of community of Souls; and even though the connection to a distressed person may be subconscious they still tended to respond in ways that are always proven to have been stimulated by this universal affiliation.

Entering this common hinterland of the Soul was crucial to ensure that the right words were said, heart to heart This appeared to be the only way forward, as in many instances, the severely distressed had long since cut themselves off from wanting to live. Indeed the detachment of meditation had opened a way for me to meet them in a place where the severely distressed could always be connected to – and to anyone else if receptive. This 'higher consciousness', the realm of Soul, avails a connection to every Soul, including the 'lost Souls' who remain 'earth bound' after their round of life has come to an end, (more on this later).

Communication was not the only obstacle to overcome, before a Soul connection could be made, individual belief systems and conditioning presented a formidable frontier to work through, barriers that appear to be common in many people's minds. The only drawback was that vulnerable people had a tendency to slip back into a suicidal state of mind if any form of pressure was brought to bear that challenged these entrenched beliefs and behaviour patterns. Communion with their Soul was one thing, getting through the intellectual barrier was another.

Miracles everywhere?

One of the results of turning within was the stark realisation that I was the person responsible for attracting day to day experiences, an awareness brought clearly to mind because of the type and number of people entering my life since beginning the inner pilgrimage. I had begun to bump into kindred Souls in every direction I turned, strangers for the most part who were listening and offering advice and encouragement like long lost friends – Souls in communion with Souls, and on purpose! From these encounters I had an abundant source of fellow pilgrims to confirm raft after raft of dialogue emerging from within which helped to make my inner journey easier. Living and working in Scotland for a while provided the ideal 'space' to begin and establish this personal renaissance. With my recently reinforced belief in the afterlife the stage was set for countless miracles to happen, of which the excursion to Scotland appeared to be the first – or was it? I realised years later that it wasn't the heightened state of awareness encouraged by meditation practice that had increased the number of miracles in my life - other's lives are just as blessed, no, it was simply that I'd become the observer of my life and aware of their unfolding for the first time – I'm sure there must have been many occurring in my life up to this period.

As my time in Scotland drew to a close I had begun to open myself to all and anything that life presented, knowing that as each set of experiences were embraced and the knowledge they conveyed absorbed, they would make way for a new wave to enter, in an ever ascending spiral towards who knows where????

> **To attain a still mind I've had to work through, embrace and understand everything that I am and in the process, come to know others as well as I know myself, to realise that we are all walk the same path, that we are all 'as one' – connected!**

Over the years, it's become easier to 'see into' and know others hand in hand with a depth of sensitivity that has allowed perception of the inner worlds with ever greater clarity.

This blossoming awareness also unfolded a perception of 'other' entities which, before this period, their existence hadn't entered my thoughts other than those associated with UFO's which I'd come to accept given the age and vastness of the universe and a sighting first hand that I and fellow shipmates had recorded when sailing across the Indian Ocean. In this respect it was the shockwaves after the reading the book 'Life in the World Unseen' (Benson) that encouraged me to look deeper into these 'other worlds' which provided an almost instant response to my probing.

Overnight these other worlds moved near with a gradual unfolding of how they fitted into an ever growing portfolio of 'life'. The myriad forms of the inner worlds ranged across the seven major life streams of life, from personal mentors and guides to group and planetary entities which, over three decades later, I'm still sorting into place.

The sheer volume and effect of life changing coincidences occurring in my life over this period left me with no doubt that inner guides were and always are at work - they obviously know me better than I know myself as their arrangement, via the Soul, is tailored exactly to meet my needs.

In parallel with these developments I began to consolidate 'inner connections' by deliberately seeking for and listening to the 'still small voice within' and was soon able to put words to the arising feelings. As with anything in my life I needed to understand the full spectrum of communication within, why others heard voices or wrote down words automatically or even went into a trance to speak with 'the voice of spirit'. I needed to glean an overview of the process before being able to explain the phenomena to others and I was being driven by ever more searching questions being asked by those joining the meditation group and later, by college students.

Years later, having satiated this need I can say with definite authority that the insights welling up into my awareness are visions that are available to any 'receptive' human consciousness, the depth and width of knowledge 'coming through' limited only by an ability to understand what is being 'given' – and of course having a belief in such stuff in the first place! Inner 'teachers' were and are always on hand to help in this process - people I've come to know more clearly as 'Guides' or 'Elders'. Without interfering with my choices they have presented opportunities that have had the effect of mixing and matching life experience to help me interpret these visions apace with a growing understanding. Yes, to do this I had surrendered free will in favour of the greater good of God somewhere along the way, and had chosen to allow these inner teachers to organise my life, making the path easier for me to follow with the reward of a much reinforced and enhanced inner connectedness and progress.

Continuing 'development', which included experiences I knew were deliberately 'placed on my path', led to the attendance at various gatherings during the late seventies/early eighties. This tour of traditional and New Age organisations broadly based on self development always seemed to provide the answers to the latest set of ideas passing through my mind - a synchronicity that I've also become accustomed to expect. This period also helped me develop discrimination, adding to my keen sense of knowing what avenue to follow, what book to read, what person to take notice of. I even began to discard, or retain in my mind for further consideration, information given in adjacent passages in many of the books that 'landed' on my bedside table – books that others might have thought brilliant or conversely, rubbish.

Facilitating house groups, in co-operation with other like-minded people, attention was increasingly focused on providing, from the very first meditation, an opportunity for distressed individuals to experience a little of the peace they earnestly sought. It was hoped this would motivate them to attend further sessions or at least encourage the adoption of a way of life that attracted opportunities to experience the peace always to be found when being still. Steering the way forward for a diverse group was like finding a route through a jungle. From the beginning I had no pre-conceived ideas as to how to achieve this goal and drew increasingly on an ever strengthening connection within – a process encouraged by the fact that whenever I tried to orchestrate a session it always felt as though something important was missing. Again, there was a strong sense that being forced to live by my wits in this way was 'meant to be' – Yet another cunning way for inner guides to reinforce a more detached way of living?

Because many people were attending the meditation groups every week it became important to present an increasing amount of new material to maintain interest. The guided meditations from pre-prepared visualisations were often augmented and then eventually replaced with in depth descriptions of any visions or insights that spontaneously came into awareness during the sessions. Though both ways of presenting helped to reinforce feelings of peace and wellbeing and promote development towards self realisation, the latter always provided a more holistic experience for the group - the outcomes highlighting the contrast.

Though gaining the confidence to relay visions as they were being conveyed to my awareness took a few more years to fully adopt they are nowadays a permanent feature of every session having proved without doubt to be the most productive with regard to group and individual progress.

Confirmation of the success of this process came from the many testimonials and notes made by those taking part; they had been 'shown' or had become aware of the things that helped them move on, with many students saying they had perceived the same vision, often in advance of the narrative that was given, which added to the confidence that I was indeed a 'channel' at such times.

As always in my life, as one discovery is made another mystery arises to be looked into and this was no different as these spontaneously arising visions began to draw me into another level of consciousness as I began to delve deeper into who and what was providing them – I was no longer content to group them under the general heading of 'guidance'.

'Channelling' provided source material for ever more effective guided meditations and the motivation I needed to continue, reinforcing a 'knowing' that inner guides were hard at work. The visions arose at exactly the right time and appeared to fulfil the needs of the whole group to provide the opportunity for students to share the same vision. This confirms to me that collaboration is constantly taking place at higher levels of being between all those present and their individual and collective mentors upon the inner planes. Many levels of intelligence seem to be involved during any particular session with everyone connecting within the same 'field of consciousnesses' to glean what they need, except perhaps the odd student who may have a barrier raised. This phenomenon perhaps explains why the creative pursuits of artists and musicians are infinitely enhanced by their receptiveness to inspiration 'from above'- they have access to a universe full of creative minds!

The vision presented at each session must be indelibly printed upon my consciousness as it's easy to recall afterwards and relate the essential symbology and inherent message it carries. There are more global visions to be perceived which are available to anyone's consciousness whenever they 'tune in', proven time and again whenever I attend an RP gathering to share such visions with like minded people from around the world. What is revealing is that 'sets' of visions appear to 'hang' around for a while and are universally available to anyone able to still their thoughts. This suggests to me that such visions are a perpetual teaching process encouraging the world's population to develop at an equal pace - Even though most people are consciously oblivious to them I've no doubt the essential influence they carry is fed into everyone's consciousness subliminally. Whether we choose to toe the line is another issue.

If it feels right, it is right!

On a personal note this period marked the beginning of a determination to perceive the way forward each day instead of fearfully blundering into the future – to proceed with the things that 'felt right' and turn away if they didn't. This simplified my life no end with much more time becoming available to do other things, especially at work where clear choices were cutting to the chase and providing the time to stand back and approach tasks in a holistic way. It was as though I were finding my way through a minefield and changing direction whenever the path I took felt uncomfortable – looking back over a day's work often filled me with wonder at how the pattern of work Id followed fitted in precisely with needs.

Perceiving the way forward in my life was a 'tuning in' process not dissimilar to tuning into a student's experiences to derive meaning to their narratives. To me there are many different meanings to any particular symbol or scene and by choosing only the meaning that felt right it was more likely to resonate the truth with the student concerned - a success that emerged only after many years of trial and error – my consciousness needed to learn how to link into the various intentions, and levels that gave rise to the symbols.

In a similar way I began to disregard emotional fear by responding to the more subtle feelings arising from within, inner promptings that had proven their worth many times by bringing about positive changes in my life. Instead of shying away from experience that confronted my fear of public speaking I deliberately chose to go with the requests that arose and even, on occasions, to seek out opportunities that I knew would be testing. It's what led me into teaching formally and on occasions to present meditation workshops to audiences in excess of 600. From my new perspective it seemed that the whole world was changing, like I'd gone on holiday with all my senses flooded with new and exciting sensations to explore and learn about even though it was scary at times. I was learning to become an observer of my life, to listen, and to react only to feelings. I began to disregard emotive situations and not respond to them – Knowing the difference between an emotion and a feeling from deep within became crystal clear.

Because of this clarity I developed an understanding of the way the 'source' expressed itself through the Soul and into my life, drawing down an ever expanding library of wisdom in the process. It's a source I now understand to be an aspect of God that radiates through every person's Soul – that to me, the Soul acts as an eternal 'go between'. Of course I became more interactive with my Soul and began taking note of how a pathway was presented from moment to moment for me to follow, a day by day series of experiences uniquely designed to suit the person I was and was becoming. This led to an understanding that as my subconscious was purged of conditioning, the covering hiding the Soul was likewise removed, making it ever easier for me to perceive its essence and to become 'at one'.

Motivated by the desire for answers, my journey of self-discovery has turned out to be one of remembering who 'I am' and consequently, expanding awareness into a cosmic soup that I tend to refer to as 'universal consciousness'.

The essence of my Soul emerged from within like a long lost friend. As I became more proficient at being 'still' through the practice of meditation, sensations of returning home to somewhere very familiar and wholesome filled my awareness whenever 'tuning in'. It's a relationship I know everyone is destined to rekindle at some point (if they haven't already), as they realise that the journey of life is one of uncovering knowledge that is and always will be available when entering the sacred space within. My understanding of this link has grown apace with the time and effort I have accorded it. Nowadays, linking into this flowing stream[3] of knowledge, has led to the point where it is perceived as a network that all conscious beings appear to be connected to though we humans appear to take little notice of its interaction within our life. This cosmic network is the nearest definition I presently have of a concept of God, a God that as far as I am concerned works in and through the whole of life.

Feelings of joy were much enhanced by adopting the new attitude of embracing all and any 'situation' that arose - no matter how uncomfortable it seemed to be, or became. I do have to stifle a tendency to chuckle at those who are struggling to overcome what I can see from my present vantage point are the pains of rebirth – an awakening that is joyful to any onlooker who has themselves 'gone through the mill' and can 'see' another sheep is about to enter into a level of consciousness were there can only be tears of joy!

I realised at this point in my development that visions radiating from the source try to hold the whole of creation in perfect balance and continuously attempt to restore imbalance if given the opportunity. All that's necessary it seems, is for me to stop interfering, to 'go with the flow', to allow these visions to restore my life, and if everyone does the same, I've no doubt that the whole planet would be restored to its ideal state.

To me, meditation is about working towards and eventually allowing the self to become part of this universal flow and in so doing, manifest in my life a little of the 'Golden Age' that is awaiting everyone. This vision of perfection seen through the eyes of the Soul can be the only true prophesy, drawing humanity ever closer to its acceptance as a gift being pressed upon them by the principle that is life.

The 'Establishment'

For the next ten years house groups were focalised wherever and whenever requested with the notes from the gatherings constantly reviewed and updated throughout the period. Certain visualisations and meditations were more successful than others and became part of the formal document needed by a Further Education college that allowed me to facilitate meditation classes – ('Creative Meditation' became an accredited course with the Open College Network in 1995)

The opportunity to present meditation at college came after an invite from one of a group of people attending a session at a friend's home – she was a department head at the F E College and opened the next door for me to walk through.

Having a wealth of material to hand from which to prepare a syllabus was in perfect timing for this next stage of development. Again, it wasn't what I would have chosen but proved to be exactly what I needed - to stand before a group of strangers and teach a run of the mill subject was a challenge in itself but to teach meditation in the heartland of 'down to earth' Yorkshire people was testing to say the least! A year after getting my feet under the classroom table the course expanded into two classes a week with a third class held at another college just around the corner from home.

Having learned to take full advantage of every opportunity that might be presented, particularly those that felt right, I was well prepared to cope with the flood of emotions that twenty or so distressed students bombarded my psyche with when 'opening up' to them – or in my case when 'tuning into' them – It was especially difficult during the first few 'getting to know you' sessions but I survived to tell the tale as we humans always seem to do when adhering to inner prompting.

At this time it also became clear that the term 'Creative Meditation' best suited the overall presentation and content of the course. This embellishment to the subject of meditation will become obvious in later chapters.

I was advised by friends within the 'new age movement' not to get involved with formal education because of the red tape and restrictions that would be encountered – or they thought existed! Personally I saw it as an opportunity to bridge the gulf between the alternative and conventional sides of education and it felt right to plough on, whatever the difficulty.

True to my friends' fears there was indeed a whole raft of red tape, and even those in education expressed doubts as to my capability -

haven't I heard this before? These negative responses only served to spur on my resolve to succeed as I had at this point in my life developed an almost immovable stubbornness when it came to following intuition, so I began to systematically work my way through the various requirements - Schemes of Work, Lesson Plans, etc, etc., were prepared and developed for the meditation class in the same format as that of mainstream education. Educational jargon was difficult to understand at first and the records tedious but once I'd entered the routine stuff onto a computer it became a whole lot easier – yes, it was the mid nineties and computers had begun infiltrating every workspace by then.

It became apparent when undertaking teacher training two years later, (another mop and bucket placed in my way), that many of the principles being taught had already been adopted into the portfolio I'd put together for the college course even though most were masked by the way they were described. Role-play for instance was used extensively to practice teaching skills until we had achieved the required level of ability - I'd been encouraging students of meditation to use role-play within the imagination to see themselves acting out experiences they had previously avoided to make it easier for them to face the experience back in life. Role play was also used in meditation to familiarise students with abstract concepts such as 'entering a cave' to ease the process of 'inner exploration'.

It seems to me that life is geared to bring about the eventual realisation that it's all just one big 'set up', a role to be played out. (William Shakespeare seemed to realise. I've reached the conclusion that nothing, absolutely nothing within this physical world is real, that the only reality to be clutched onto is a feeling that urges me ever onwards towards the goal of total oneness within universal consciousness, a consciousness that always reacts with overwhelming feelings of love in response to any contact made.

'Creative Meditation' evolved to include the presentation of short explanations in conjunction with progressive meditations. These were mainly geared to help the distressed and for those who care for them in the hope that a little understanding of the reasons for suffering would be gleaned and that all students would attain a level of consciousness that realised that life can be lived with fewer tears and more joy, whatever the circumstances.

All the preparation and 'opening up' processes that had taken place thus far in my life were now being put to the test within the public arena and bringing to fruition my long held vision of helping people steer away from self destruction – *before* they got to the edge! Having to produce 'Evidence of Learning,' a college requirement for all subjects, helped to bring a sense of reality to the subject to prove beyond doubt to students and faculty alike that meditation practice actually makes a difference to peoples lives!

As a part of encouraging self awareness I've always insisted that students and perspective teachers of Creative Meditation record results of guided meditations, both to provide a record for later reflection and to allow an interpretation of the symbology to be given until they themselves become able to interpret the results.

Over the last thirty five years I've possibly read and interpreted thousands of narratives - the ongoing review of these notes providing feedback and the means to assess and fine tune the effectiveness of the guided meditations being presented.

After twelve years of formal teaching, 'Creative Meditation' became well and truly established with scores of students achieving 'Open College' accreditation to level 3 - all returning successfully into the hectic lifestyle much of the world presents these days, with more than a few going on to facilitate groups using similar resources.

Even with all the formality of a college setting, each individual Lesson Plan included time to talk, to allow an attunement to higher consciousness to take place, to provide the Soul, inner guides and teachers the opportunity to inspire and prompt conversational content that became the cue for me to slightly modify the affirmation, visualisation or meditation that followed if prompted to do so. Even the often noisy corridors and traffic outside was a useful challenge for students to listen to, embrace, and then disregard when encouraged to enter the silence.

> **From observation the effectiveness of meditation is due to the way it opens up the subconscious labyrinth of the mind little by little in a way that is in perfect accord with each person's ability to grow and realise potential.**

Running parallel with this outer work was the continuation of my inner development. An ever growing 'connection' began to manifest itself in the joy of being involved in group activities, especially with those of like mind. I've come to understand that interacting with others creatively reflects the creative process of the universe, a process which is often referred to as Synergy[4]. The principles of synergy were developed for teaching to Creative Meditation students in their third year to encourage the expansion of consciousness from the personal to the interpersonal level – this expansion appears to be occurring at many different levels of society today; One area I've been extensively involved with professionally since the mid nineties is described as 'Partnering', which applies many of the principles in project management.

Chapter Three - *Stress!*

The hidden causes of stress – an overview

What follows is a brief explanation of what stands in the way of Soul consciousness and needs to be looked into, understood and embraced should an aspirant wish to move into the freedom that lies beyond the subconscious.

According to the father of psychology, Sigmund Freud, and his school of thought, 'the unconscious contains some memories, impulses, and desires that are not available to consciousness[5]'. Freud believed that emotionally painful memories are diverted to the unconscious where they continue to influence our actions even though we are not aware of them. A 'Freudian slip' is said to be an unintentional remark emerging from the unconscious.

In traumatic experiences, such as car accidents, memory lapses are common; years may pass before a full recollection is made and only then if the individual is able to face such memories.

After a day's activity my head is filled with impressions, reactions, unresolved conversations, etc, etc, which are pushed into the recesses of my brain if I don't have an opportunity to 'unwind'. After a day or two, if not cleared, these repressed leftovers begin to show as physical symptoms - my elbows began to itch, and later, if still not having the chance to relax, skin rashes begin to show – an obvious signal that tells me to take time out or risk suffering ever more serious symptoms.

Becoming aware of how my mind reacted to these 'stored memories' and caused me to feel uncomfortable became the motivation to regularly take time out to be still, to review and respond to each and every experience that had left its stain of unfinished business within

my subconscious – a process that effectively dispersed the residue –
until the next build up of subterranean flotsam!

Many people find it difficult to understand the mind/ body relationship
and haven't even given a thought towards uncovering the cause of
the distress they suffer other than to seek help for the symptoms.
Like me, the cause of the stress could simply be down to not taking a
break when the body needs it – I need to be continuously mindful to
avoid such pitfalls developing.

The psychological mechanisms that cause reactions to stress have
been researched for some time, e.g. In the 1950's James Olds and
Peter Milner carried out a series of experiments leading to the
conclusion that brain stimulation causes reactions in the physical
body. Although such stimulants could be positive or negative the
results show that various parts of the brain activate different bodily
functions.

Present day research comparing scanned cross-sections of the brain
before and after its stimulation show a marked increase in activity.
Further observation shows a relationship between types of
experience and particular areas of the brain that become more active
as a result of repeating brain stimulation.

Ekman, Levenson and Frieson [1983] carried out a series of studies
that have shown arousal differences for different emotions, in
particular that the emotions of anger, fear and sadness, produce a
significant increase in the client's heart rate compared to emotions of
happiness, surprise or disgust.

At first I thought my life was fairly unique because of the difficult
experiences I'd gone through but it soon became apparent that most
people had either suffered or were suffering debilitating levels of
stress. It is often said by inner guides, when asked about how much
suffering we are to endure, that 'everyone is pushed to the limits but
never beyond - it would be counterproductive to have someone end
their life prematurely because they are unable to cope' – an answer

which leaves me with more questions. From the Souls perspective this physical vehicle is regarded as expendable in the grander scheme but paradoxically, also the vehicle that is to be transformed into a body of light to enable us to make our transition into eternity once we have become its master and have surrendered all that we have become in willing service to God.

For the severely distressed who can't sit through a lengthy meditation, a stage by stage method was developed to include regular breaks for discussion and for recording insights. This form of meditation is more akin to a relaxation session and just the same as in more progressive meditations, encourages the remembrance of enjoyable events or holidays to help in the letting go of anxieties – at least in the interim period, to allow an opportunity for insights to 'arise'.

It's at this point where the Soul may step in and begin to lead the students individually and sometimes collectively, into deeper and more relevant experiences. For ease of understanding I often refer to the persons Soul as the communicator and not to an array of various personalities – to me the Soul is the true channel for communion upon the inner planes as it stands as a mother/ father figure over all our affairs until such time as we become 'at one' and are able to discriminate between the various 'intelligences' to whom a connection may be made.

Emotional and physical symptoms of stress are common these days as a result of a reduction in the work force, placing more responsibility and perhaps the fear of losing their job on the shoulders of those who remain – I've been on both sides of that situation several times. Those out of work are also being pressurised indirectly by the news that, for example, only well qualified young and healthy people will find employment! Being unable to cope but fearing redundancy should their employer find out could trap people into a 'no win' situation and will bring on a rapid heart rate, chest pains, sweating, etc. These symptoms of fear, shock, etc., were first recorded just after the second world war, ['Symptoms of Fear in

Combat' Shaffer, 1947], symptoms which I've noted in many of those who join the meditation class and which abate after attending just a few sessions.

Releasing repressed memories

From experience with those who attend the sessions seeking for a way to relax, the main route was through developing exercises that encouraged the meditator to look at and embrace any and all experience that makes them feel uneasy. With the few who couldn't do this the cause of the uneasiness remained as a very real barrier to further development. Those who choose to develop the art of meditation beyond just wanting to relax soon find as I did, that meditation's objective of complete detachment takes them through stages of 'facing' even the most difficult of experiences until completely embraced and subsequently dispersed – from the results this appears to leave the student relatively able to explore a whole new way of being. This barrier to the greater life can only be dismantled by entry into the deep recesses of the unconscious, a journey that is often symbolised by a movement through the fabled labyrinth of the Minotaur, to face and overcome the fears and phobias that give life to this beast within – a journey that leads to the core of our being that when completed, brings us into 'oneness' with the Soul.

Every student is encouraged to review the outcome of their meditation in the hope they will learn to interpret and understand its content. Those who have the motivation to do this are rewarded with a strengthened 'connection' to their Soul with direct feedback soon to follow. This feedback is perceived in many ways, sometimes referred to as the voice of God.

Meditation practice is proven to be effective with groups of any age, background or level of development.

Using the imagination to open the inner doorway

The ability to use the imagination like any other quality we have, takes lifetimes to develop but thankfully, these days, children are encouraged in its further development and use.

Once students of meditation have progressed beyond what seems to be an unending stream of distractions passing through the mind and are able to use the imagination to some degree to re-live enjoyable scenes from the past they are then led into enhancing that enjoyable scene using their 'inner senses'. Just as in this outer world of ours the inner senses of sight, taste, touch, sound and smell can be brought progressively into play, bringing an increasing amount of reality to the imaginary scene and providing an opportunity for 'things' to pop up that were just not part of the memory of what was there. This is where I've found the aspirant needs to allow their imagination to 'run' for a while, and where a measured belief of another reality may help if the intellect gets in the way.

These unexpected appearances when reflected upon later seem to be the beginnings of one of many forms of communication the carnal brain may use to relay what the Soul is presenting from a more subtle realm – objects, symbols, colours, the spoken word, visitations or unusual landscapes, all 'drummed up' by the imagination in the brains effort to make sense of what is being relayed to it by the loftier faculties of the Soul. In this way, from the simple exercise of re-living memorable experience emerges the benefit of not only distracting nagging thoughts, (which brings in its wake relaxation and feelings of wellbeing), but also an opportunity for the Soul to communicate and the lowering of self made 'barriers' so that repressed memory, particularly those associated with uncomfortable or traumatic incidents can be 'aired'.

Not surprisingly, because the Soul is being handed more direct responsibility for personal development, almost always, anything 'popping' into the re-membered scene appears to aid the unfolding process; On many occasions there's an appearance of a long departed loved one to give encouragement in some way, brought into the experience by the Soul because it's 'seen' to be a way of helping the aspirant embrace and thereby dissolve many of the barriers to further exploration of the self.

Care is taken during this period to ensure that no one is overwhelmed with the recollection of too many painful and disturbing memories. Any such overload may lead to emotional reactions that could be counterproductive by halting progress for a while.

Anyone achieving even a limited state of relaxation during a meditation should, from experience, be able to recall and reflect upon stress causing experiences and as a consequence begin to reduce its effect on their life. As I became more experienced in teaching meditation it also became obvious that I could adapt this successful process by having students use their imagination to role-play 'difficult to face' experience on an imaginary theatre stage, which, over the years has proven to be almost universally effective. Any deeply buried sub-conscious memories may be 'brought out of the cupboard' once aspirants reach a level of development where painful memories can be confidently embraced and subsequently healed as they are released - the emphasis being upon embracing any and all memories that arise. It's an open-ended approach with particular usefulness when difficult or painful memories emerge. In such cases students are encouraged to repeat certain visualisations until the associated discomfort eases or disappears entirely.

Visits into the sub-conscious memory are gradually increased as and when students are able to embrace the emotions they're confronted with. Care is taken here to remain 'tuned in' to ensure no one is pushed further than they feel comfortable with. 'Inner guides' usually move closer to their charges at these times to feed collective insight and to help ensure the greatest benefit is derived from the experience.

Chapter Four - *Connecting within*

Embrace and release

There appears to be no time limit for unloading subconscious memory - its content and the emotional intensity suffered obviously vary from person to person, as does a person's ability to embrace any emotion that may arise. No one should concern themselves that progress is slow – any movement forward after lifetimes of inertia is truly celebrated by the heavenly hosts.

One effect of being still is the eventual awareness of an ability to 'overlight' the memory banks of the mind. This was not a memory game but a gradual moving into an overview of who I was from the perspective of the Soul - the 'I am presence'. This view allowed the deliberate 'tuning into' and the 'drawing out' into conscious memory of past experiences that were causing present life discomfort. To me this ability marked the beginning stage of every meditators goal – 'detachment'.

In this way the stillness of meditation allowed objectivity to develop to the point where I could see the way forward, where I could choose to face the fears and/or guilt that past experience was consciously and subconsciously steering me clear of. It wasn't that I decided to do things differently, I simply held back from doing anything until it 'felt right' – this developing attitude was also a source of exasperation for many of those I worked with. It took several years of trial and error before finally realising that everything worked out exactly right if only I could flow with and not ignore inner prompting, prompting that I began to see was emanating from very subtle but powerful feelings that I had begun to take notice of.

> **Act when it felt right, step back when it didn't - simple, but very difficult to do when in the habit of making things happen!**

Why did being still and adopting a detached attitude of mind work? In a nutshell I put it down to falling into line with the dictates of my Soul and as the Soul is an expression of universal mindstuff then I was establishing an attitude of 'letting go and letting God'. I was learning to effectively allow peace and harmony to be restored in my life though I didn't know that at the time, I just felt amazingly peaceful when being still for even a few minutes.

OK, so I'd achieved some measure of peace by sitting still but it wasn't long before the 'honeymoon' ended – I was left in no doubt that a small dispensation had been 'given' to allow me to taste the fruit and honey of what was to be in order to generate the necessary motivation to return to that utopia of mind by completing the journey 'home'.

From direct observation and feedback, the period and intensity of this awkward phase of the 'awakening' process varies from person to person and is determined by the depth and width of past experience and the reactions they have to it - until the majority of it is re-membered, embraced and released. Our past and therefore our conditioning appear to determine the volume of 'stuff' that needs to be processed when practicing the art of becoming 'still'.

Joy instead of dread!

An increasing awareness of self brought with it the stark reality that I had a lot of groundwork to do and I needed to look deeper into the workings of my brain before I could effectively help others. Undoubtedly, being still opened the door to the inner recesses of consciousness, released hidden memories into full awareness, and in turn stimulated emotional and mental reactions which, if embraced, were discharged into the cosmic recycle bin but a lot more stuff came into mind as well?

The more I developed a still and watchful attitude through meditating regularly, the more my attitude and response towards others became highlighted and magnified – standing equal with every other side effect of meditation was an increased awareness of whenever I'd said or done something to hurt others. Consequently, and what I know now to be part of the 'grand design,' the arising deep-seated feelings of concern at my behaviour became more than enough motive to put effort into changing it.

Aligning to the 'I Am' presence

From the outset, meditation, in its very quiet but powerful way, changed my life by presenting heightened feelings which, if I wished to hold onto and develop further gave me no choice but to look at every morsel of behaviour and adjust it accordingly. Feelings of joy were enhanced along with every other feeling a human being could experience which I'd hitherto ignored or had been oblivious to except in times of crisis or enforced change. All these new sensations ganged up to push me towards what became a sort of personal epiphany.

> **The sparkle in dew, bewitching bird song or a starry night, - perhaps this new reality was a religious or mystical initiation or a new heaven on earth emerging? – No, it had always been there - I just hadn't bothered to notice!**

The effects of my change of heart had a dramatic affect on day to day experience; it seemed as though everything in my life had taken on a new glow. New people, new experiences, more responsibility and more joy - I didn't need any proof whatsoever that meditation had been the cause, though I had no proof to give to the outsider – except for the long beard, multi coloured jumpers, needing to sleep less, able to do three times more work and preferring a vegetarian diet! - my dear wife breathed a sigh of relief once I'd passed this stage but has spent most of the time since wondering what was to come next!

Before making these tentative steps towards enlightenment, I had blamed bad luck or others for bringing about mishaps or uncomfortable situations, (gremlins?) I'd never given a second thought to the idea that I'd anything to do with causing them! With a developing awareness I realised that I was indeed the cause, that it was the way I thought that attracted, like a magnet, every experience into my life – every last one! Distinctive feelings arose at this time to reinforce the attitude that I should embrace and not avoid unpleasant experiences in order to help neutralise what some would call 'bad karma' and in so doing reduce their attraction into my life.

I was to realise later it was my fear of things going wrong that cast an image of that very mishap into the 'ether' (Astral Plane), for almost instant manifestation. As I focused on this new way of being, the mishaps and associated discomforts lessened and it became a tongue in cheek challenge to 'open' myself to experiences that would previously have been avoided because they had previously made me feel uncomfortable, pouring as much love as I could muster into them. 'Let them do their worst' was part of my newly developed response to adversity, stopping short of doing myself harm, this attitude help me get over the initial feelings of fear I felt! It was hard, but by gum it did me good as wave after wave of sediment emerged from the depths to be washed away by love, leaving me feeling lighter and less burdened! I had it seemed, begun in earnest to purge myself of unwanted reactions at the physical level, continuing the process that I had begun with the imagination and which had now worked its way into life. There was an unusual side effect to this new behaviour. After each successive wave of experience and subsequent acceptance, my heart awoke a little more to feelings that I'd never felt before. It seemed to be a mixture of heartache and euphoria at one and the same time - I was, it seems, loving myself better.

Time and many more experiences increased an awareness of what was happening. I began to understand that generating enough courage, not only to face but also to embrace experiences that were causing me grief somehow cut through and dispersed associated emotions of fear or dread. These emotions were not only dissipating fear but were also allowing joy to enter increasingly into my life – I was lowering self made barriers. The joy arising partly from a feeling of release from the perpetual round of emotions associated with 'going there' again, but mainly from an increased sense of an awakening to ever deeper feelings of love towards others and towards life in general.

From relaxation to meditation

Published in 1975 'The Relaxation Response' written by H. Benson, N.Y., Morrow, compares meditation with relaxation techniques and concludes that they both produce the same end results, which is not surprising as the initial exercises of meditation are intended to promote a relaxed state before meditation proper can begin.

Relaxation from my point of view is an important habit that has its place alongside exercise, healthy eating, etc, etc., all helping to reduce illness caused by stress. Meditation on the other hand I see as the gateway to the Soul, a practice that can only begin once a person is able to relax sufficiently to allow the Soul to take charge of our life.

Out of the meditation sessions presented to students emerged a pattern of achievement that highlighted a success in reducing uncomfortable reactions which had previously caused distress. To provide evidence for this success (initially a college requirement), and to make it easy to collect the data, simple graphs and tables were designed and developed to be filled in at intervals. Most importantly, these results provided a means to measure individual progress which helped students realise that positive change had occurred in their life.

It is a succession of realisations such as these that motivate the meditator, eventually leading them to become permanently hooked into self development and inner exploration. Even the most sceptical of students to these often 'new' experiences become motivated to look at, embrace and release 'buried' events that help reduce present day distress when confronted by the evidence only they could have produced! As mentioned earlier, students are encouraged to write a brief account after each session which are followed up by discussions and an attempt to reach a conclusion with regard to interpreting what's been experienced. Reading through and adding insight to these responses continues to help fine-tune my skills of interpretation whilst also providing students with an opportunity to do the same. This feedback also helps create a communication link which students come to know and trust as emanating from a connection channelled directly from their Soul.

As a point of interest and another sign of the changes taking place within society, when I began recording students progress it took approximately a year, meeting once a week, before they began to realise an 'inner connection', These days it takes just three months for new students to achieve the same level of development!

A year or two after beginning to meditate I began making assessments as to its effect upon my life by reflecting on the way day to day experiences were changing - the law of 'like attracts like', informs me that my experiences reflect the way I think and as my thoughts re-focus so too does my life. This understanding brought an acute awareness of particular trains of thought and the associated life experience it attracted, providing a strong motive to change or enhance some of those thoughts; This awareness also brought the realisation that I could 'read' other people's general thought streams from the impromptu happenings in their life.

Increased awareness came into play when interacting with others in the teaching role – At a certain point it was realised that I could assess the amount of 'baggage' a person was bringing into the session by reflecting on what I had said to them. That when really 'connecting' to someone, inner prompting leads me to respond in a particular way that has a bearing on what a student needs to know. I've observed with great fascination how most people do this, especially with those they have a rapport with, though it appears to be a mostly subconscious act. Great words of wisdom are heard from those you would least expect, including children – without doubt, they have connected within to bring forth the golden nuggets of truth from the great universal mindstuff - from God, via the Soul.

Generally speaking, I'm aware that we seem to have a limit to how much repressed memory we can recall and embrace at any one time – that we need to be patient with ourselves - and with others.

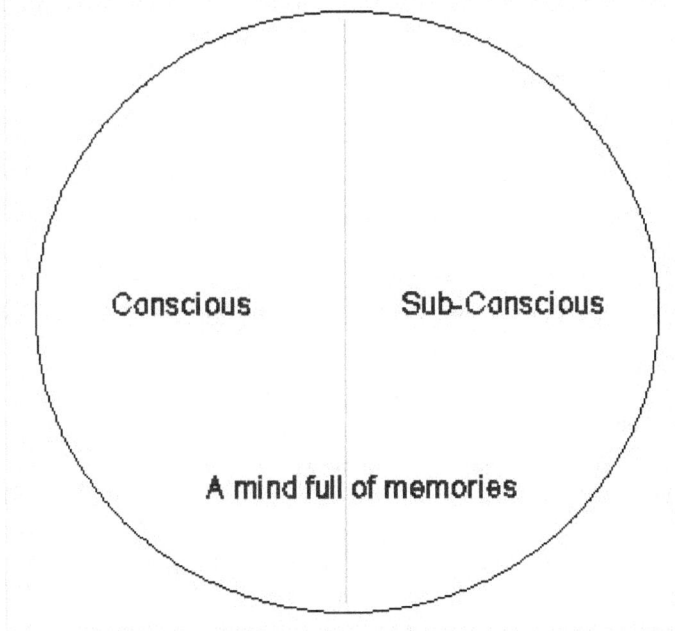

Conscious   Sub-Conscious

A mind full of memories

Figure 2 - Conscious /Subconscious memory

Because of the possible reactions that may occur as a result of progress with meditation beyond the 'beginner stage' I've found it important to take extra care with certain individuals until it feels right to move forward again. In doing so the journey towards a greater awareness of the Soul continues unhindered without the risk of 'surprises[6]' that could cause a person to back off or withdraw from meditating altogether.

An integral part of deep meditation is for students to be given the opportunity to measure their emotional state, making observations and assessments from feedback to determine the levels of stress they suffer in certain situations. The self realisation exercises mentioned earlier include questionnaires and self assessments of their reactions to stressful experience which, when reviewed, help heighten self-awareness providing an opportunity to reflect on and embrace any emotion brought to the surface.

These questionnaires are repeated at intervals and provide the added bonus of highlighting and bringing a sometimes mind numbing realisation of the changes that have taken place.

From such assessments, paying attention to a particular reaction helps students to tune into the cause with the purpose of uncovering the experience that brought about the reaction. All the questionnaires were developed from personal experience - I knew that 'tuning' into and remaining with a particular reaction helped to promote the awareness of its cause and a wealth of knowledge about how and why it affected me.

Comparing my experiences with those of students it's easy to see that we are all overflowing with conditioned responses and that one person's severe reaction to an experience may be another's enjoyment – (the amusement park ride I shared with my Daughter many years ago comes to mind.)

Reinforcing good habits

Psychologists inform us that it's often easier to establish relaxation as a habit if there's some form of associated reward - 'Premack's Principle' (David Premack, 1959), states that 'any activity in the hierarchy may be reinforced [made more likely] by any activity above it and may itself reinforce any activity below it'. According to Premack's Principle the practice of relaxation should increase because of the reinforcing effect of the more enjoyable sensations achieved following a relaxation session. The same principle applies when following instructions to use the imagination to recall an enjoyable past experience - the feelings of peace and contentment experienced help draw students into establishing a habit of taking time out to be still and of course this same enticement eventually leads them into the depths of a meditation experience.

If choosing to progress, when a more permanent state of relaxation is achieved there comes into view a whole raft of new challenges waiting to step in from the sidelines. This gives me the impression that the inner mentors are helping to reinforce the link within and strengthening our resolve by opening us up to more testing trials. Some would interpret this as a test of faith. From my perspective it's the beginning of the mind's battle to hold onto its imagined supremacy which only ends when it is finally subordinated and 'put aside' to allow the Soul to lead the way – the mind brought into use only when needed.

It's obviously a natural trait when given free choice for people to err towards experiences that feel comfortable or enjoyable. Practicing meditation techniques over the years has increased my awareness of just how many experiences I've automatically avoided because they didn't fit into either category - I was effectively blocking out a great deal of opportunity that could have contributed to my development. Experiences were being consciously and subconsciously attracted or rejected, manipulated, avoided, or changed to fit into outcomes determined by my conditioning. Most of these negative reactions happened at the speed of light! - only after developing a watchful eye could I even begin to see what was going on and start to put the brakes on certain knee jerk behaviours.

See how the energy flows!

When first achieving a state of detachment it seems that I had managed, albeit briefly, to open up my body to the free flow of life giving energy. I've since become aware that this was the beginning stage of a process of aligning my being in accord with universal needs as dictated by the Soul.

This incoming energy, invoked in deep meditation, empowered all the centres of my being – the good and the not so good and in the years that followed I had to embrace and release every 'speck of dirt' that got in its way to enable the energy to flow unimpeded and back out to the cosmos through my heart centre.

In Yoga teaching these centres are referred to as 'Chakras'. Awakening my heart into activity required years of effort, of balancing the creative energies of the upper three chakras, with the empowering energies of the lower three; the love expended in this process bringing together these two complex and differing sets of energies - my heart centre the fulcrum or pivot between these upper and lower triads. By embracing my experiences instead of avoiding them I was effectively integrating these two sets of energies and encouraging my whole being to balance itself and 'open up' thus allowing a connection to be made with the inner levels of being. Since that time my consciousness has been open to a flood of inspiration from above which has brought understanding into every facet of my life whenever 'looked' into and continues to do so - My heart has become the gateway to the mystical realm of Shamballa!

Those who lack the necessary will power to 'just sit' shouldn't be concerned. In the early days of my development the phases of relative peace experienced during and shortly after each meditation session soon began to contrast dramatically with the rest of my life and it wasn't long before reaching the stage of feeling almost bereft whenever I couldn't find time to experience 'the feeling' again – I could hardly wait for the next opportunity to 'enter the silence'.

This new way of responding to life, prompted by feelings emanating from within soon confirmed that each experience in my life was indeed attracted into reality by thought and by continuing to focus on being still I became acutely aware of how particular sets of thoughts brought about certain events. It was by this route that I moved into a habitual frame of mind that was watching and listening for most of the time – I was becoming an observer of life. Being detached in this way allows me to be more 'in tune' with life and not at its beck and call - to be in the right place at the right time (from my Soul's viewpoint of course).

Moving into the attitude of 'not thinking' about tomorrow or even the next hour unless there's a need sounds irresponsible to many and did to me in the past but I now regard it as a dynamic way of living that is generally synchronised to all other aspects of life. I've no doubt that because I've become aware of and have experienced the chaos my thoughts have created it's helped me to move into this new way of thinking. In the same vein I've refrained for many years now from planning events; holidays and the like are not 'set in stone' but allowed to unfold with bookings made 'on the hoof' and destinations fixed in perfect timing with the needs of the time. Initially a scary process is now one of the many ways of being that have helped bring a real sense of freedom and wonder into in my life.

This way of thinking has also influenced my thoughts on what the future holds - whenever asked to speculate I usually respond with an open ended and unconditioned view - a disappointing answer for most as they would of course wish to know about things relating to their fate or fortune.

Visualisation and affirmation

> **It was years before realising just how important it was to become aware of hidden memory, to understand what made me tick and begin to set myself free from debilitating reactions to experience.**

Meditation naturally draws an individual to the source within, stimulating an expansion of awareness at the same time. Some students may become overwhelmed by this and need to follow step by step visualisation exercises to allow a tempered introduction to changes in awareness - Exercises that are designed to encourage the acting out of essential scenarios within the imagination to help sponsor a familiarity with inner sensations can often be surreal. If fear is uppermost in a person's mind as they enter into the depths of meditation then fearful apparitions will manifest to meet such expectancy – the law of 'like attracts like' acts universally across all planes of being. It's the same with dreaming – if we go to sleep with fear in our mind then fearful visions will fill our dreams.

This expectancy is always the cause of a minority of students becoming frightened during a meditation - how would anyone feel if they began to perceive say a ghostly figure showing itself unless they had achieved, and could maintain, an objective frame of mind? – It's for this reason that increased awareness needs to be tempered with an understanding that only graduated experiences along with lots of explanations can provide.

Inner appearances can often be more real than any in this physical world of ours with many students having had frightening paranormal experiences long before they joined our meditation group. In these instances much time is spent giving reassurance and helping them to realise that the power to exorcise ghosts, whatever their origin, lies in the simple act of radiating a feeling of unconditional love. These passing impressions are instantly reabsorbed into the cosmos by this infinitely more powerful and all encompassing embrace – this is one of many tasks awaiting inner plane travellers who wish to be of service to humanity.

The vast majority of experiences that students have during a meditation are filled with wonder and awe, with many being self critical for not having explored the inner world long ago! Joyful experiences await all who have the motivation to stay the course and any initial negative experience is soon forgotten.

Something that always surprises me is how easily students face fears that have caused them pain and discomfort for years or even lifetimes once encouraged to enter into a relaxed state – achieved by simply looking at an image of the self reflected back from a mirror or some other medium. The exercise provides a taste of objectivity that is also a powerful affirmation towards releasing repressed emotion with a side effect that leaves them with feelings of peace that most have never experienced before.

Affirmations help to speed up this self healing process and can be customised to help make inroads into very difficult areas of repressed memory. If repeated regularly as a statement or mantra, specific affirmations help to steer attitudes towards accepting change. An example of a simple but effective affirmation, which can be applied universally, is by repeating the sentence 'I love and accept myself' - affirmations that many religions include in their meditation and prayer routines have been written with specific needs in mind.

Even the slightest success in this endeavour has a marked effect upon a person's life. The quoting of school and family mottoes, company slogans, and even nursery rhymes, all contribute to an individual becoming aligned to the intent, to becoming 'at one' with the quality described. To my mind one the most powerful collection of affirmations is in The Lord's Prayer, and probably because I've repeated it so often is the reason why it's so effective in my life.

With an enhanced awareness I realised that at the same time as thinking about something – anything – an image of that thought formed upon the inner screen of my mind. No doubt a developed ability everyone has but most, including me, take for granted – or I used to. The only problem with visualisation is that I knew it was also the driving force of a chain of events that brought such a 'mind picture' into physical manifestation provided that certain conditions were met. This realisation, in the early days of beginning to meditate added further motivation to not only watch my thinking but to also try to keep my mind free of all thinking until called upon.

Many students seek to learn how to meditate because they believe it can help them cope with how they feel, many having had an experience that has left them traumatised, bewildered, or generally struggling with life - the cause of which, long since been forgotten. People with deep seated anxieties find it difficult to relax let alone be able to still their thoughts sufficiently to visualise a normal life.

Diverting the attention of such people by having them visualise going to the theatre with friends has become an effective way to side step these anxieties whilst at the same time provide an opportunity to observe and disperse the cause. - This works in a similar way to when we first begin to meditate with the fleeting images of our mind eventually clearing because we are refraining from adding further energy to them, in this 'stage play' visualization the energy also drains from any deeply buried experience when its 'presented' to our consciousness whilst in a relaxed state of mind.

Side effects of becoming empowered

Awareness that we have to some degree the ability to effect change on our environment placed added responsibility upon my shoulders, not only to achieve stillness but to remain so to reduce the possibility that any stray thoughts did not cause imbalance in the life around me. As for any thoughts that were repressed and active within my subconscious, still attracting uncomfortable experiences to stir up my emotions I could do nothing until full memory of each and every cause of these subterranean disturbances had been brought into full awareness, embraced and released. - These were the specks of dirt that were the hardest to shift but the more I moved into the stillness the more aware I became of them and more able to be disposed of. It wasn't that I'd suddenly developed a unique ability to be creative it was just that I had, for the first time in my life, begun to take deliberate steps to get out of the way, to stop interfering with what could otherwise be a balanced life brimming with peace and harmony and endless possibilities.

To help me reach the still calm centre, I needed to constantly repeat affirmations and undertake visualisations to establish and maintain thoughts at a certain level of positivity in order to keep on releasing repressed memory. The flotsam rising to the surface because of these repeated self cleansing commands was often difficult to accept – e.g.: I was increasingly put under pressure to stand out in the crowd in order to confront my fear of public exposure but as soon I began to accept wholeheartedly and embrace what seemed to be an unending stream of such experiences, they suddenly tapered off. The same sequence of release unfolded with every experience that I was reluctant to undertake until the time when the 'magnet' of undesirable subconscious thoughts must have been substantially weakened because I became noticeably less agitated and according to those near to me, began to exude an air of calmness.

I'm left with no doubt that had I not 'got around' to embracing these repressed thoughts the day would have come when the itchy elbows and rashes that often accompanied them would have developed into something more serious. With many people, instead of the nervous energy manifesting as skin rashes and the like, they suffer from what are commonly referred to as 'panic attacks'. The symptoms of these are similar to those suffering from shock except the symptoms don't go away after a few days and may affect a person for many years; that is, until the sufferer begins to look for, becomes aware of, and embraces the underlying cause.

Experiences I found difficult to embrace and had a tendency to keep at arm's length became increasingly empowered to eventually force their way into my life – at that time I was effectively strengthening such unwanted experiences every time I focused attention on them and making me more aware of them as a consequence.

Of course I decided I'd better embrace whatever came into mind and not only that, but go head first into any that I felt a resistance to, staying with the discomfort until it lessened with the result that I could enter into such encounters with increasing ease. This new way of thinking strengthened an overall command of my thoughts and therefore emotions, allowing a freedom of expression I'd never before experienced. It turned into a sort of game - whenever becoming aware of my reluctance to take part in something, I deliberately threw my whole self into it, and kept 'with it' until all signs of resistance and associated discomfort had subsided. This behaviour became an effective means to strengthen my command over the 'inner beast' and its increasing empowerment caused by the ever increasing energy flow I was invoking. This was a major change to earlier years when only undertaking things I didn't want to because there was no alternative – I was now choosing to do the very things previously avoided!

Intuition tells me this way of 'coping' with life is in unison with the Soul, confirmed by the obvious regulation by an 'unseen hand' of the number and intensity of uncomfortable experiences that were being laid before me each day – or not, if it was seen that I needed a break. This practice of stepping forward eventually developed into a sub conscious habit and established, once I'd dealt with the 'backlog', a permanent reaction to any new fear that arose, to be dispatched before they had got comfortable within my subconscious!

This new attitude also helped move me towards adopting the stance of an observer in everyday life, and not just within meditation. Being able to enter into any experience that is 'put my way' starved my intellect of any possibility of repressing them – thus far anyway!

Believing without doubt that human evolution includes many return visits to the material world, I have the opinion, having gone through the mill many times, that there's a 'built in' tendency for humanity to overcome difficulties. I think people get thoroughly fed up with the same old scenarios of worry, fear or guilt and begin to pull away from them in a sort of emotional tug of war, letting go eventually and facing the consequences that usually turn out to be a lot less painful than ever imagined.

I was no different to anyone else in this respect and finally chose to, once and for all time, to put fear behind me by engaging in the very thing I feared. Such changes in heart were not just down to an increase in awareness brought on by meditation practice, they were and are, from what I now sense, partly due to a general shift in human consciousness and a popular consensus that it's better to overcome fear than be forever controlled by it. There are television programmes these days devoted to showing people challenging their fear – perhaps I should try bungee jumping?

Scraping the bottom of the barrel

It took about three years of diligent 'listening and watching' before I really began to scrape the bottom of the barrel and clear the backlog of experiences that had been repressed - and years more before learning how to keep the barrel clean. I had indeed been spared from a sudden inrush of nightmarish memories by the benevolence of my Soul.

My personnel endeavours certainly helped when it came to working with literally thousands of stressed students over the years, helping them to visualise a way through their subterranean nightmares and as I did so, led me to the conclusion that successfully 'seeing' the self, facing/confronting uncomfortable experience in the calm of relaxation, dramatically reduces the symptoms of stress. This was also confirmed by the evidence provided by students of meditation which overwhelmingly indicates that re-visiting and acting out difficult experiences within the safety net of a relaxed body within an imaginary scene has a positive effect on their life and makes similar experiences, whenever they crop up, easier to cope with.

The outcomes of all graduating students confirm that once they had become comfortable with these new ways of revealing and embracing previously hidden memory, they became more able to move on in life, dispersing for good the debilitating fears that had previously held them back. Several have gone on to facilitate their own meditation groups, others have begun new careers - all are leading a happier life.

Chapter Five - *The collective spirit*

Universal consciousness – Uncovering the Soul

The psychologist Carl Jung, introduced the idea of the 'Collective Unconscious', a term which seems to embrace many of the principles of 'Universal Consciousness', a term that is often used to describe a state of consciousness achieved in meditation.

> **The next natural step on the path towards enlightenment, following on from understanding and coming to terms with the causes of stress, was the journey through the subconscious – a journey that was to pass beyond its symbolic labyrinth to reach the open arms of the Soul.**

All that I was hoping for at the outset was a feeling of peace and knew meditation would achieve that from the moment I closed my eyes and began to be still. From the Soul's perspective I had at last set out with deliberate intent to embrace the monsters of my subconscious.

As the shadow of the subconscious cleared, my Soul began to show itself. It had always been there, awaiting re-discovery, buried in the mind stuff I'd amassed over many lifetimes. Mind stuff that had, with all its limited thinking, been causing reactions within my body but now at last were being dispersed by love!

It was at this level of development that I began to perceive the presence of a higher intelligence working with me - not a take-over bid but more a feeling of being 'overlighted'. Reading about, and in particular, listening to other's accounts on this phenomenon left me with much confusion that took years to sort and sift through with the help of much insight from above. From this emerged an understanding that each person has at least one guide, usually conscripted from those in the human race who have evolved beyond 'physical rounds', having chosen to become mentors upon the inner planes of being. These guides come into the awareness of anyone the moment they begin look within to seek answers - In truth they have always been there to connect with. They work in unison with our Soul who acts as the go between for any communication; – whenever tuned into the Soul I am connected to the universal mindstuff which I am aware is linked to all the levels of being.

In group meditations, overlighting teachers associated with those taking part often 'meld' with the group to give invaluable assistance, helping to 'open up' their charges to understand many of the concepts being introduced. Latterly I came to understand that guidance is constantly available to all and that everyone becomes an unwitting teacher drawn into the 'Soul to Soul' network as soon as they open their heart to helping others. It was through a gradual increase of influence from my own guiding lights that has led me into becoming linked to this inner network. I have also learned through these blessed contacts, how to be spontaneous and pace instruction at a level to suit the group as a whole, with added explanations and practice, allowing the Soul to take the lead by remaining 'open'.

Beyond the mindstuff

Once 'personal baggage' is well on its way to being dispatched many students choose to continue with inner exploration - a natural choice once an inner connection is perceived and established, a path I know everyone will follow eventually - to me its evolution! I realised early on that even a brief glimpse of the inner life brings a flood of remembrance and joyful sensations I'm sure no one could turn their back on indefinitely. I've become reliant upon this very reaction in students new to meditation knowing, after years of observation, that those attracted to the practice of are on the verge of opening fully to the golden rays of sunshine breaking out from within the cloudy sky of self - it takes only a brief encounter to set them on the path of return – a path that leads 'home'.

It's amusing and fulfilling to observe the inevitable transformation take place when someone makes 'first contact' with the most powerful and infinite part of their being - Amusing to hear of the previously impossible hoops they have suddenly become able to jump through and fulfilling because the resultant reverberations gladden my heart at a very deep level, reinforcing the age-old adage that we are indeed 'one'.

The holiday is over - back to work!

Becoming aware of, embracing, and banishing the cause of the uncomfortable emotions usually brings hot on its heels another wave of reactions - a phenomenon well known to teachers of meditation - reactions caused by conditioned thinking - yet another layer of the subconscious onion to be peeled! These are not the repressed memories brought to the surface to be banished by love but knee jerk responses to experience that people prefer to hold onto because they provide a sense of security and see no reason to dispense with them. Like a young child wanting to keep its dummy, losing preferred behaviour patterns hurt, often leaving us feeling vulnerable at every stage of their purging. This second wave is an open ended stream of what, from my understanding, is a combination of personal and transpersonal memory emanating from a storage facility akin to that of the hard drive of a computer and which circumscribes the earth in much the same way as the earth's magnetic field. This field of self preserving influence is what I generally refer to as the Astral Plane.

> **Using the analogy of a computer's hard drive, from my perspective, this 'pre-programmed' memory perpetually determines our tomorrows until we intercede to eventually hand over the direction of our life to the Soul.**

Usually described as the causal plane because of the effect it has upon our life, and collectively upon humanities, the Astral Plane loomed large once I'd cleared the decks of repressed memories – it was always there influencing my life but now I'd become consciously aware of its presence. It stood as a very real barrier obstructing my goal of reaching the objective of Soul unification. Symbolically, the dragon slayer (the growing influence of the Soul), was confronting the dragon (the physical body), the latter having got used to pleasing itself, was and is a formidable beast that began to fight for what it considered to be its very existence as I handed its guiding reins to my Soul to continue the process of letting go.

Having had control over my affairs for so long, the mental/emotional aspect of my being represented here by the dragon, had grown accustomed to being in charge and sought outcomes that maintained its existence. From this period any successful outcome resulting from giving into the desires of the dragon were purely coincidental - the endless pursuit of wealth and a thousand other things only ever provided temporary fulfillment and had done its job, had led me to develop the necessary frustration and rejection of the material life that drove me deeper within in search of true and permanent happiness. Perhaps it's the frustration every individual needs to experience before developing the motivation to redirect the energy of the beast to more noble causes – a frustration often heralded by a series of the infamous 'Dark nights of the Soul'.

Surrendering personal power

Finally, I reached a point of development where the experience of meditation and its associated feelings of wellbeing spilled out into my life to outweigh perpetually sought after worldly sensations – a process that naturally led me away from being interested in the material world's attractions – well almost. My earthly garb, my beastly body realigning to the wishes of my Soul, began to lose its hold with long held desires becoming weak through disuse, and emotional reactions lessening as I moved further into the 'silent cloak' of my Soul. Without so many distractions in my mind I began to 'see' clearly the full force of the Astral Plane, to become the observer of its un-tempered influences acting upon me and humanity as a whole. And now, benevolent guardians, having 'seen' and interpreted the tell tale rays of my aura as a sign of readiness, were leading me into the next round of development. To stimulate further development meant that a little of their protection would be removed to allow the magnification of the remaining mental, and consequently emotional reactions to be experienced. (From present perceptions the same thing is beginning to happen to the world at large). Such exposure brought back debilitating reactions that I thought were long gone - this secondary onslaught, can only be overcome it seems by the symbolic death of self – a totally habitual attitude of letting go.

The habit of embracing everything thrown at me had thankfully become part of what I was and as I later realised, the only way to move through the sticky miasma of the Astral Plane that was now revealed to my consciousness. It seemed never ending at the time but at the height of my frustration and heartache a sort of mystical 'turning' took place deep within my heart. I can poorly describe it as a deep heartache being suddenly taken away and replaced by a surge of love that filled my whole being. With hindsight I realise now that it was the birth stage of the alchemic reaction referred to earlier in the book, taking place deep within my being as the upper and lower energy centres (Chakras), were brought together and balanced by the love I was expending in trying to overcome the seemingly insurmountable influences of the Astral Plane. This self generated love became the force, and the only force it seems, that could finally open the hearts gateway into the realm of the Soul, instantly releasing all the 'trapped' energy that was causing my heart to ache, and taking me into an infinite wellspring of love that is to me the essence of God.

Traditionally, this transformation and subsequent empowerment is said to be reserved for those choosing to offer up their whole being in willing service, having purposely resolved to face the annihilation of self. From present day observations it appears the population as a whole are being forcibly 'encouraged' in this way, having no choice but to make the best of embracing whatever the psyche presents to their consciousness irrespective of how they can handle the much magnified emotions that are now arising – I believe that skeletons are being pushed out of our individual and collective cupboards whether we like it or not – its time, or more to the point, it's the end of time!

The beast[7] is being taken in hand when we willingly choose to be of service by responding to inner prompting or in other words, acting according to how we feel and not letting our body, emotions or mind decide, other than as a back up or expression of those feelings.

When I made the choice to 'let go' matters little now - the frustration suffered in the to and fro of intellect versus inner prompting did its job – I no longer resist, I have learned to habitually let go - to 'go with the flow' even though I do moan from time to time. This flowing process led to the opening of the fabled 'Pandora's Box'[8] - a box, which according to legend, carry's a warning - promising to release all manner of ills upon anyone daring to open it! In reality this opening, is from personal observation, thinning the veil between the inner world and this outer world of ours, empowering and bringing into awareness all manner of repressed thoughts – good and bad. If not become aware of, embraced and released, these increasingly empowered thoughts may cause some individuals to become very uncomfortable indeed.

Interpreting the images and symbols that emerge in a student's meditation experience, helps me to confirm and monitor their movement along a unique path of development, a path that provides the most efficient and beneficial route towards releasing untoward thoughts. In this way the destructive elements of the Astral Plane are hopefully held back until students have well and truly 'dealt' with personal stuff and have achieved the necessary strength of personality to help in the mammoth task of embracing and dispersing their quota of a global storehouse of impressions that are associated with and attracted into manifestation by their psyche. Perhaps a third of all students begin to show noticeable changes to their life soon after being guided through the exercise of opening 'Pandora's Box'.

None of the changes are negative, and the overall impression I'm left with is that they are journeying towards a life of joy that had previously been stifled by fear or guilt, that opening the box is from experience another way of helping to remove any congestion blocking the Chakra centres. During such a visualisation, the 'box' may appear in one of an infinite number of guises, each one relating its unique story of the resistance 'built up' to protect the aspirant from hurt suffered over many lifetimes on the journey towards enlightenment. One common outcome of this exercise is the appearance of walls or fences preventing further progress that is usually an indication of a long entrenched attitude of self preservation. On repeating a similar exercise the fence may have been replaced by a stream or bridge, which when eventually crossed, symbolises that access to the higher realms of being has been accomplished.

> **Interpreting student accounts presented quite a task in the early days and only after spending literally days attuning to and eventually gaining insight of each description did the common factors begin to emerge.**

One or two students have difficulty opening the box at all which to me indicates a resistance being vulnerable – when 'looked into' it is usually found to be the result of past experiences that have caused a person to withdraw from life in some way. Generally, those with high levels of repressed guilt or fear produce boxes that are more robustly constructed and conversely, those who have a tendency to be open and receptive find the box lid ajar with nothing inside or have a 'see through' box. In time I've come to the conclusion that Pandora's Box holds no hidden agenda to those from the latter group and to those who are 'closed' – a gradual and gentle introduction is made towards the freedom that comes to anyone who realises that repressed memories hold nothing to be afraid of in the light of the present day! Reflecting on the results of this particular visualisation when repeated at regular intervals is one of the ways measurements can be made of a person's progress towards 'awakening'.

Chapter Six - *The Souls takeover bid*

Frustration

Meditating heightened the perception of the cause behind my day to day experiences and at one point caused me to become increasingly irritated and dissatisfied with progress whenever I slipped back into old ways. Just like anyone trying to achieve perfection in their particular art or craft it motivated me to do better but even though continuing to develop and practice new visualisation exercises, to role-play and reinforce different ways of response, there was still a tendency to seemingly back track – I was obviously doing something wrong, or was I?

I read somewhere that we need to fail one hundred and forty four times before we succeed in a particular task. It seemed to be true. My failure to change the way I responded to certain situations became so frustrating I thought I'd never get anywhere towards the intended goal of detachment. For several years I held the belief that any real progress in this endeavour would have to wait until my next life where I could perhaps be given a 'better set up' to enable success!

From previous chapters it will be obvious to the reader that the art of meditation is about getting to know the self, an increasing awareness that along with stepping side, allows the Soul to rise to the surface and show itself. The ancient practice of meditation used movement and sound within strictly secluded surroundings to help the individual distract their attention long enough to enter the stillness and to remain there until such time as awareness expanded into the 'void'. It seems to have been easier for our ancestors – I assume they didn't have to deal with a developed intellect like we have today – an intellect filled with thousands of distracting thoughts and worst still, many convincing arguments that turn us away from what may be thought of as hocus-pocus! When at last I entered the void many years ago now I had thought that there would be no more to do, but although it was a major milestone of development it turned out to be just another carrot to move me along the self development conveyor belt!

Achieving stillness did result in thinning the veil shrouding my Soul and although measuring this with regard to my development became less important due to moving ever nearer to a state of detachment, I did need to provide students with a means to measure their progress to provide sufficient motivation to continue on the journey within.

It would seem that all I had to do at the beginning of my journey was to realise potential - a simple answer but not one that meant anything to me until I'd spent years on the path and had achieved a level of development where I could reach the that same conclusion! Greater clarity and a sense of purpose did enter my life almost from day one, but paradoxically, so too did the aforesaid frustration as many old behaviour patterns rose up from the depths driven out by the incoming 'light' that I was invoking and which needed years more work before being cleared! I knew that hiding in a 'cave' somewhere to prevent my interaction with life was not an option – in my case I knew it would restrict the opportunity to develop, to face the very experiences that would put me to the test and hopefully enable me to let them go – especially since I was the sort of person who would enjoy being a recluse. It's the same advice I give to students - to face full on whatever their Soul presents through life experience as the shortest route to enlightenment – don't step over the bucket, use it, and if another bucket appears, use that too!

'Allowing' life to unfold

As if by divine mandate, and on cue with a rising frustration, the Soul began to percolate out into consciousness with its own way of being, providing me with the ability to let go easier – or was my growing ability to let go allowing the Soul access into my life? Either way it proved to be one of the most difficult things for me to succeed with but the frustration of never seeming to succeed eventually subsided as I developed the 'letting go habit'.

> **One of the startling revelations of quietening down my thought processes was a heightening of awareness - not just in my relationships, but to the whole of life.**

A major realisation at this time was that my resistance to becoming involved in uncomfortable situations was lessening - I was not only losing the fear of any 'situation' cropping up but was also beginning to welcome the challenge instead of holding my breadth as I went headlong towards them! I concluded that because of this 'open' attitude, I was no longer 'attracting' uncomfortable situations into my life - or was this another paradox - was a change of mind reducing the type of experience attracted or was it a disregard for the discomfort such experiences brought?? The fact that I began to enjoy social outings previously avoided became one of the many proofs that I was feeling more comfortable with life – and I didn't need to get tipsy to do so.

An experience that perhaps highlights one of the internal battle being fought at this time was in regard to a fear of visiting the dentist. Of course the day had to come when such fear needed to be overcome as part of the ongoing endeavour to steer the 'beast' into line.

The mere suggestion of going to the dentists, even glancing at an advert for toothpaste or of hearing a noise associated with such a place was enough to bring on a cold sweat - Such reactions I've no doubt caused by the after-effects of the gas and air used by the dentists during childhood visits.

On my next visit, intending to once and for all overcome my fear, the experience ended up being a fourty minute ordeal in which I spent the whole time frantically struggling to keep re-playing 'Tchaikovsky's 1812 overture' within my head - Although not feeling much discomfort at first the experience needed unstinting will power to stay focused and relatively calm. I'd long since abandoned the idea of being put to sleep in favour of a gum numbing injection and so was fully awake whilst the dentist spent most of this time grappling with what my experience told me were stronger than average teeth; after the first ten minutes the dentist mounted my chest with his knee to both gain a better purchase on the tooth whilst at the same time trying his best to stop me following him around the room! Then, just as I thought he'd managed to loosen the roots there was an almighty crack, following by an uncharacteristic comment by the dentist. He spent the remainder of the time digging out the roots left behind - the tooth had shattered during removal, and by this time the painkiller was beginning to wear off. I've chuckled many times since as I remember the scene coming to an end with him completely exhausted and dripping with sweat and me lying completely prostrated on his couch similarly perspiring but 'happy' - I'd made a major inroad to overcome my fear of the dentist's chair and after several more visits my fear had gone, along with most of my teeth!

I have to smile at what is generally termed 'divine humour'. On this occasion I'd thrown down an invisible gauntlet, feeling brave enough to face my fear 'no matter what', and of course, as always, someone up there responded with the 'so you b****y well think so'! As I've grown in experience I've learned to temper my challenges to life with any achievements expressed 'tongue in cheek', knowing full well that another round of hurdles could well present themselves.

It's natural to steer away from experiences that we fear but sooner or later, I needed to face every one if I wished to progress and so continued to accept life's invitations as and when they cropped up. Nowadays I trust that whatever is presented to me each day is meant to be and step through any fear that might arise to help speed the day when this second round of inner cleansing is complete.

Most of those I've given counsel to seem to be subject to the symptoms that arise from avoiding experience which ironically, often leads to many more years of discomfort, cold sweats, rashes, disease, etc. which when looked at and released not only brings relief but has the knock on effect of making the world a better place for everyone else too - if my observations of the Astral Plane are anything to go by. The alternative is to suffer an increase in trauma that forcefully opens the inner door to cause our eventual surrender in some less palatable form. Either way, sooner or later, each individual will face the cause of their fear, hopefully revisiting the source of fear by choice, embracing and dispersing it forever.

Perhaps the greatest benefit of heightened awareness is the uncovering of a Soul previously shrouded by the thoughts my brain constantly churned out or had hidden away. – Always the Soul waits patiently for the day when its charge cuts through this sticky miasma - the two becoming one - the symbolism of marriage revealed?

The physical body - the shroud that conseals the Soul

Rebirth!

Figure 3 - Our protective shell

To help explain this uncovering process, I've represented 'Soul' consciousness in Fig 3, as existing in the core of our being, surrounded and sealed off completely by a self-made protective coating that represents the everyday 'Self'. As this barrier of 'Self' is embraced and let go of, the unlimited potential of the Soul is revealed.

The density and thickness of the outer coating cannot be measured other than to say that the 'Soul' has immeasurable proportions whereas the 'Self' is limited by how much we have 'constructed' in our resistance to the 'greater life'.

Peeling the onion of self - Don't let the tears stop you!

It was by continuing to develop the ability to focus and be still that 'allowed' subconscious memory to 'rise to the surface', dispersing the cloak of forgetfulness that had been blocking my awareness, a process depicted in fig 3. This self-created barrier to the subconscious thinned more effectively once I'd begun to reinforce an ability to watch and not re-bury emerging memories. Initially, many students of meditation do the same as they push the emerging awareness of uncomfortable memories automatically back into the depths of the subconscious - having students record or share these recollections does help in the process of preventing this. Like peeling an onion, when I first began to bring repressed memories into my mind the least buried layers began to pop into awareness first with deeply buried memory emerging only after years of meditative reflection. Looking and listening with a still and receptive mind during regular meditation sessions uncovered more and more layers. Most students, when first trying to meditate complain that their mind is overloaded with images as soon as their eyes are closed. If only they would persevere, this initial flood and any subsequent 'waves' of images soon abate to be replaced with feelings of deep peace and contentment.

Be still and let the storm pass

The deeper memories moved into awareness only after I'd established a balanced a rock solid attitude that was steady enough not to be disturbed by whatever was unturned - an attitude that could look at distressing or glamorous reactions to experience objectively without being distracted from the purpose of 'looking'. Surprisingly it was my 'knee jerk reactions' to life – reactions that occurred at the speed of light, that were the most difficult to prevent because I first had to become aware of them! After choosing to spend many more years in quiet reflection I eventually began catching hold of and slowing down all reactions to experience where they could be embraced and released. Dreams also played a major role in this cleansing – (some are shared later) - and not to forget the greatest ally of all - the Soul, who was all the while coming into clearer view. The Soul has always provided the inner knowing and a sense of direction at every step of the way, leading me to develop an increasing faculty to understand, embrace and disperse if necessary, every experience that had been cast into the recesses of the Astral Plane by my busy body of a mind. All I ever had to do was to listen and adhere to the Souls whisperings!

God consciousness?

Paradoxically, I need to explain a little of a concept that is essentially indescribable! Fig 4 shows symbolically the various stages of shell dispersal and our relationship to 'infinity'. The circumscribing circle represents my idea of the 'collective consciousness' (God), the smaller circles representing individual consciousnesses at varying stages of development with regard to the dispersal of the shroud to awareness formed by conditioning, fear or guilt. The varying thicknesses are drawn represent a measure of how much a person is holding onto such traits. The sketch also suggests that as an individual lets go their awareness expands 'back' into the collective consciousness automatically. Apparently, we have only ever shielded ourselves from this greater awareness because of life's distractions! It can be surmised from the sketch how we would automatically connect to others as we let go of our conditioning shells.

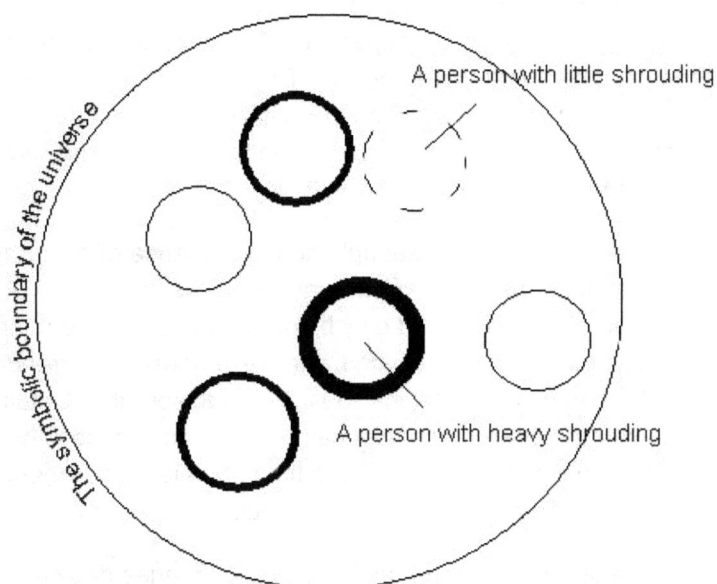

Our protective shroud and its relationship to infinity

Figure 4 - Relationship to infinity

Ancient Wisdom - The 'Knowledge'.

Further insight into hidden aspects of life can be gained by anyone researching 'Ancient Wisdom(11)' – Dion Fortune's book (Fortune, The Cosmic Doctrine), includes much of this wisdom and the Laws that underlie our universe. Annie Besant's teachings also include much of the same wisdom.

These 'Laws' explain the 'set up' and maintenance of everything within the influence of the known universe. The application of these laws within our life is limited only by our understanding and use of them; a limitation that is reduced when we choose to surrender to Divine Will and allow our consciousness to absorb them intuitively - to step into the stream of what I call 'God consciousness' through the act of 'becoming still', to connect to the subtle feelings emanating from within - channelled through the Soul.

There are sections in most bookshops and libraries dedicated to 'New Age' publications. Many of these books include references to and the application of various aspects of the Ancient Wisdom – but I would add that 'new age' books should be read with discrimination to ensure that only the wisdom they contain is gleaned. I tend to shy away from recommending books, preferring instead each person find their own using intuition as the guide. Although I've listed some of the books that 'fell onto my lap' – to me none that I've read have truth written all the way through and uncovering the bits that are is a challenge waiting for any reader once they have developed a consciousness finely tuned to feelings.

Chapter Seven - *The bigger picture*

The Astral Plane and beyond

From the explorations made into the inner realms of being over the years and to provide an introduction to the concept of what may be perceived by anyone Fig (5) shows the most influential of these realms as far as we are concerned - the 'Astral Plane': a Plane that collects and stores for later discharge into form the more powerful and lasting thought impressions created by humankind. These range from dense debilitating thoughtforms indicated at the inner levels towards those that are more inspirational and uplifting at the upper levels. This knowledge became apparent only after raising awareness 'above' this upper level where observations of the Astral Plane could be made.

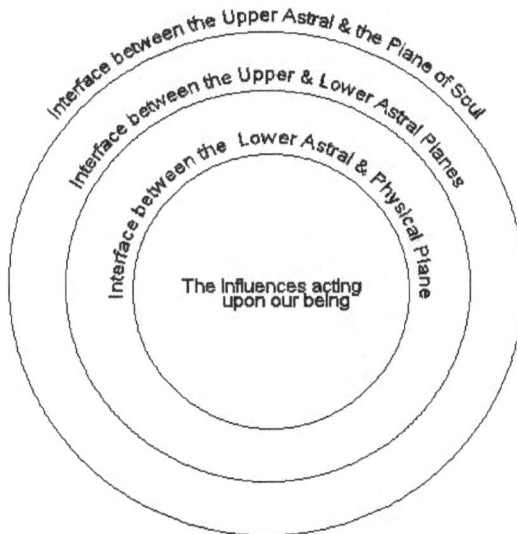

Figure 5 - Inner plane relationships

The Astral Plane is symbolically shown in Fig (5) as two spheres of influence surrounding our being with the densest and most debilitating layer closest to it. This sketch could also have the Earth at its centre with the upper and lower atmosphere representing the two main layers of the Astral Plane. The objective of meditation is to detach consciousness from this dense inner layer to effectively be out of reach of its influence. It should be added that ascended beings are constantly monitoring this layer, adding and maintaining their uplifting visions to help raise the spirits of those who are 'trapped' within its cycle of cause and effect or 'Karma'.

Observation of the Astral Plane and the intensity of stored thoughts in its denser levels left me in no doubt as to how humanity, in normal consciousness, is cajoled in every aspect of life until the day we hopefully rise up above its influence. It is here, where the Law of 'Like attracts Like' overloads those who suffer from afflictions such as depression - a negatively orientated consciousness attracting the infinitely more debilitating influence contained in the dense clouds of thoughtforms of the 'greater' Astral surrounding and permeating the Earth. These outer influences may pull individuals and groups of people into unbearable depths of despair and towards unbalanced behaviour patterns. The Astral losing its power only when sufferers raise consciousness above and beyond personal maladies. There's apparently no quick fix by a Master Soul clearing this debilitating atmosphere this time around – the job now rests squarely on humanity's shoulders. These benevolent beings are not abandoning us, as they remain always closer to us than our breath, they are ready to support and encourage at every turn and occasionally, by the grace of God, to stretch out a hand to lift us instantly into the sunlight in answer to our (positive) prayers.

If we live our life as an individual or as part of a belief system of a group that maintains principles that are beyond and above the negative thoughtforms of the Astral Plane then any experience of its debilitating layers will be limited.

Responsibility for Earth

It's obvious to me that paradise came to an end as soon as humanity's intellect evolved to a point where it became able to interfere with the prevailing and harmonious 'set up'; a set up brought into being by more lofty Souls the day we began to flex our creative muscles. Just like dropping an increasing amount of dirt into sparkling spring water the perfect expression of paradise began to mist over long before today and is now, to the uninitiated, completely hidden from view. This state of affairs apparently exists because it was ordained that 'humanity would have dominion over the Earth', that it would be humanities workshop - a place to learn to be co-creative, (or destructive). Until we collectively choose to take full responsibility for Earth we are apparently destined to suffer the consequences of our naivety (or deliberate intent), with action taken 'from above' only if it's 'seen' that we are on a course towards self destruction!

It seems we will have to put up with this less than perfect world of ours until such time as we get our act together, come of age, and re-align our collective will to that of Divinity's - 'growing' to assist the humanities guardians in their endeavours rather than interfere.

The 'interference' caused since we earth dwellers began to think has apparently led to a 'build up' of oppressive thoughtforms described above that have not only got in the way of perfection but have 'hung' around to make it very uncomfortable for everyone – especially those who are struggling to keep their head above the emotional waters of life. The 'Astral Plane' is laden with this debilitating atmosphere, its location often conceptualised as surrounding the Earth but is 'seen' as the denser outer layer of a multi layered sphere with the infinite universe at its core, a core deep within our being and not out in space. – Anyone who unwittingly tunes into the Astral's debilitating levels will be subjected to the oppression stored there unless able to remain detached from its negative influence that would otherwise attract its effect into their life, (an effect commonly referred to as

'Karma'.) It would be ideal if we could all project love into this Astral miasma to banish its potential negative effect upon our lives forever!

Thoughts of a more positive nature

The 'Astral Plane' is often referred to as the 'Causal Plane' because of the role it plays in 'hanging onto' human thoughts which impress their blueprint upon the malleable substance of the Etheric Plane, (a sub atomic field permeating the physical world from which all physical matter precipitates). This blueprint, just like any architect's drawing, is faithfully followed, not by human hands, but by the Nature Kingdom whose covert beings within the Etheric Plane bring together the necessary elements in a process that always attempts to manifest human thoughts into concrete form at this physical level of being.

It's for this reason that learning to be positive, to take deliberate and determined steps and 'see' a particular goal always worked better for me, a process that became even more effective when aligning my will with that which was 'meant to be' – to Divine Will, by responding to the whispers of my Soul.

On this inward journey towards enlightenment, like every aspirant before me, the Astral Plane presented a formidable barrier to be overcome. Yes I had opened Pandora's Box, progressed through the labyrinth of self to uncover repressed memory and had solved the cause to most of my reactions to experience - but now this was something else. Deliberately entering the miasma of the Astral Plane presented the first conscious taste of an 'otherworldly' life, a subtle and very real life force that turned out to have intelligence of a sort and to be responsive to the creative thoughts of humanity – and to mine if I so desired.

The beings of this otherworldly life are generally classified under the heading of 'nature spirits'. (Do *you* believe in faeries?)

This took contemplation to a whole new level and it wasn't long before realising that many levels of beings existed within this medium, with 'Deva's overlighting the assorted nature spirits and Angels overlighting the Deva's, in a chain of hierarchy under the stewardship of the universal mindstuff emanating from the source, from God. It is a mindstuff which, with regard to our planet, is being increasingly influenced by humankind as we exercise our creative muscles.

It has been brought into my awareness that at the beginning of time, the fabric of the Astral Plane was a blank canvas that was originally painted with visions of perfection that 'brought into being' a host of nature spirits that had no option but to do what they were programmed to do and always will - to manifest the visions within that 'space' into form to create what was then, a perpetual paradise upon Earth. Eventually these perfect visions were despoiled as humanity began to 'think creatively' and blur the visions with ones that are less than perfect.

Here was the challenge - to progress on my inner journey through the Astral Plane all I need do was to become detached in mind and body and not create thoughtforms of any description whatsoever, whilst at the same time respond to the inner prompting of my Soul – *is that all!!*

This was a journey into and through very real and tempting thoughtforms with equally powerful nature beings standing by to 'precipitate them into form' and I needed to move through them without becoming tempted or ensnared! There were two alternatives at this time, one was to generate a feeling of all encompassing love, embracing whatever presented itself on the journey through the Astral Plane to help bring them into line with deific will and thus gain mastership over them; the other was to become completely detached and remain so until not thinking had become an ingrained habit and therefore no longer attracted these unsavoury or conversely, delightful beings.

The illusion of suffering

In the event I used a combination of both, developing a way of feeling and sending love whilst retaining a detached state of mind. When confronted with debilitating feelings I embraced them, when they were fanciful and glamorous I simply watched until they went away – most times anyway! Sounds easy but in the outworking took years to achieve with many failures to learn from.

The revelation that this life was one of many on the way to becoming a co-creator didn't lead to a sudden burst of excitement. On the contrary, my reluctance at birth to fully engage in this earthly plane continued for many years. If anything, it made matters worse when thinking for too many years that life was a big 'set up' - a means to an end, and fully understood why the affirmation 'I will endure' was uppermost in my mind when entering this present life.

It dawned on me eventually that I would need to feel some enthusiasm and try to 'enjoy' the challenge of life if I were ever to graduate its classrooms – blood, sweat and tears are not enough it seems! Nowadays this pessimistic attitude has thankfully passed and I'm learning that life can be enjoyable too – the only set up involved it seems is the one expressing from the illusions of my mind!

It's down to individual interpretation as to what a positive thought is, mine is in the way they affect people's wellbeing, that positive thoughts have better outcomes than those that are negative. Observing the way positive thoughts affect others once established within the psyche of the group, and become well and truly anchored upon the corresponding level of the Astral Plane, I've no doubt they add to the general store of good influences acting upon humanity by cancelling out much of the 'not so good'; What to me appears to be even more effective than this though is for individuals and groups to perceive and draw down the perfect and undefiled visions from deep within that fulfil all needs.

Rising above the Astral Plane - World service

The process of 'symbolically' rising up through the Astral Plane to gradually become its observer, to 'see' the clumps of influential thoughts 'hanging around' in its atmosphere, is an ability that required an habitually detached and non judgemental state of mind. The only motive for this expansion of awareness was a continuing desire to become 'at one' with my Soul. This 'gift' of 'seeing' the influences that have, and still are being created by humanity, with of course the attendant understanding, awaits all aspirants on the path as an insightful side effect.

Becoming detached went hand in hand with aligning to the needs of my Soul though several years passed before realising just what those needs were and the 'work' I'd become increasingly involved in. For as long as I can recall I've been listening and responding to inner promptings and had continued to think that such guidance was always to steer my development or those I interacted with, but I was wrong as my personal development had shifted to become interpersonal somewhere down the line! Looking back, I probably wouldn't have been as useful had I been fully aware of the work being asked of me and possibly overwhelmed too if I'd been called upon to jump directly into what were to my mind not so long ago, realms beyond comprehension.

In the event I've been taken by the hand and introduced to this work one step at a time over many years through a series of experiences that my intellect can now understand and fully engage in.

These inner projects involve the release of those who have become habitually 'earthbound' - specifically, individuals who have not moved on to their 'allotted place' when their life has come to an end but have gravitated instead to a world of make belief created by people with similar beliefs and expectations. These imaginary worlds exist within the thought sensitive membrane of the Astral Plane. These are very real worlds to whoever resides within them and are not dissimilar to the realms occasionally visited by students of meditation who become mesmerised when discovering what they believe to be 'Shangri-La' - a discovery which can sometimes delay the journey through their personal sub-conscious labyrinth of hopes, dreams and fears when believing they have arrived 'home'.

During these inner sojourns much insight was imparted as to the practical application of 'thinking' in everyday life and how the simple act of extending feelings of love helped raise the awareness of these 'trapped' humans by causing stubborn belief structures to 'soften'. Initially, the work that came my way was that of embracing 'clouds' of negativity whenever they came into my awareness. These clouds were and are the menacing thoughtforms hanging around within the Astral Plane which spontaneously 'pop' into my awareness to be 'exorcised'. I'm sure most people who have a mindset that is orientated towards 'doing good' undertake similar work, albeit often subconscious.

These bundles of negative thoughtforms, ready to tip their unwholesome cargo into manifestation should just one more negative thought be added are instead pulled back from the cliff edge by an act of love. In all events, I've been 'taught' to embrace whatever shows itself with love to bring out the very best solution as 'seen from above', and definitely not to interfere with the complex loops of learning often attached to such incidents by engaging my ego – not even with the best of intentions!

From these beginnings, several others from an ongoing meditation group joined me in the 'work' which quickly developed and extended after we had attracted an overlighting Angel into our midst - a 'go between'. Through this benevolent being we were collectively guided at weekly gatherings over a two year period to project our feelings of love directly into the various imaginary worlds which were effectively delaying human transition; it was a love which manifested in ways that always seemed ideal within the scene that unfolded - e.g.: a bridge, ladder or stairway appeared to allow free passage, and on one of these journeys into the inner realms, windows formed to allow the greater light to shine in. During some of these 'rescue missions' thousands of people were observed to be moving upwards and out of their enclosures, and in every experience the residents of these make believe worlds expressed relief and much joy at seeing apparitions that were far beyond and above anything they had ever seen before, a joy that flooded our own hearts along with gratitude and humility for having been of service in this way.

Practical manifestation – is it magic?

From the experiences described above along with many others it was realised that connecting within was providing insight into every aspect of existence, stimulating ever deeper explorations into the multi dimensional structure that is behind it.

Just one particular aspect that drew my early attention concerned what I presently understand to be the inner workings of manifestation - to me, a deeper explanation as to how visualization and the more effective affirmation of knowing needs will be met enters into our physical reality.

Clues to the beginning of this 'coming down into form' can be found in previous paragraphs that explain how certain trains of thought or beliefs often create artificial worlds that are as real as this world to their human creator but this world of our is denser than those worlds and fortunately for us, thoughts need 'go betweens' to turn them into physical substance.

In our physical world these go betweens are referred to as 'Etheric entities' or nature spirits, beings with limited intelligence who life purpose seems to be that of forever attempting to create form from human thought by 'clothing' them with elements with human emotion providing the force by which they are 'pushed' into form. As with any creative pursuit, if a person's thought streams are forever changing and not settling into clear images before or during the 'making stage' the outcome is poor – Nature Spirits are just not energised into action! The 'human creator' needs to become focused and have clear thought streams for elementals to begin the 'dressing' process. Even then there's still no guarantee of success as the thoughts need to be released to allow the 'filling out' process to be completed. Passion or compassion provide this force but so too can any heightened emotion including fear and guilt! Once emotion is aroused all the factors are in place to bring the thought to 'life' once it has been released into an 'air of expectancy'. Concepts too are brought into their equivalent state of existence within the mental atmosphere of the intellect but because of their fluidity need to be constantly refreshed with ever developing thoughts!

At the sub atomic level, any thought in the process of gaining form, appears to the sensitive's eye as a collection of glistening, gossamer like fibres mimicking the form and the final stage of release is its creator accepting the form as reality that allows human senses to become fully aware of its presence - manifestation can be as sudden as receiving a package through the post within minutes of knowing a need is to be provided!

To summarise: to manifest form 'see' the need clearly, empower the need with emotion and complete the circuit by giving undoubted thanks – the latter releases our mental hold on the image to allow it to condense into form. Positive minded people tend to be more successful with this concept.

With respect to the above, exercises have been developed in meditation sessions to have students provide evidence indicating how positive and negative attitudes affect outcomes. This evidence provides students with the opportunity to realise thoughts that affect not just their mood, but also the world about them - the weather, physical objects, even the ground they stand on – that their thoughts today do indeed attract the experiences of tomorrow.

One of the ways developed to provide this evidence, which anyone can experiment with, is to write down a list of what you would expect to happen as part of your daily routine - Everyday things such as what you would normally eat for breakfast or, in what way would you expect certain people to treat you when you first meet, arrive at work, etc. Alongside each item on the list provide a preferred alternative – it's an exercise that produces in some astonishing and life changing results. One student wrote in jest that 'they would love breakfast in bed' – she was knocked for six when the very next day this was fulfilled by her daughter, unprompted, for the very first time ever!

It wasn't just the results of this exercise that produced changes. Most students began a new line of thinking which I guess will without doubt continue for the rest of their life..... and beyond!

Conditioned or inspired thinking?

Apparently the belief in the seed becoming a plant is so ingrained in our conditioning that we hardly ever doubt new plants will grow from them - the result of an evolutionary process taking thousands of years to unfold. For this outcome to be different the belief of every gardener and farmer in the world would need to differ, and that difference, whatever it was, would need to prevail for many generations before noticeable changes began to occur in our reality because of the changes taking place in long established thought forms. Before humanity developed the ability to think independently there was apparently no choice but for all of us to align our thoughts with perfection – a vision set up at the beginning of time to manifest what we would describe as paradise. Should our collective thoughts be aligned with this powerful vision once again, nothing could stand in the way of its manifestation within every aspect of our lives – this could, and has in the lives of the Saints who have gone before us, be brought about in anyone's life if their thoughts are permanently aligned to the same vision. Entering the silence shows the way to achieving this and marks the beginning of a journey which can start right now and though not showing the fruits of our endeavours instantly, does begin to unfold within the thought processes and eventually within our life.

An example that demonstrates how thoughtforms build up over time is one concerns the fear of spiders. If the fear is life-long a very clear thoughtform is established within Astral Plane matrix which attracts spiders into existence every time the individual concerned hears a mention of, reads about one or see's images of them, by instantly visualising a spider and manifesting its appearance according to the intensity of the fear associated with their visualization - it's no wonder that spiders creep out of every dark corner in lives of those who are terrified of them! Visualisation is the short cut to precipitating long stored fears into reality, it's also the short cut to dispersing them if we are able to embrace any feelings of fear that arise with love.

And of course we have planetary influences magnifying every thoughtform that is 'held' within the Astral storage from time to time just to remind us that they're still around and which also require our loving embrace before their banishment is accomplished.

> **On the way towards detachment I had not only stopped adding to conditioning thoughtforms but had also reduced my personal store thereby helping to lighten the load not just for me but in a small way for others too – This latter effect led me to understand that as more and more people achieve a similar level of consciousness there will be less debilitating thoughtforms affecting the rest of humanity.**

It can be deduced, that in the course of evolution, as humanity developed the ability to think creatively, the Astral Plane filled with thoughtforms from which the resulting negative images began to build and have an increasing and debilitating influence on human experience and behaviour - thoughts of millions of people over thousands of years clogging up the system long before our present era. Fortunately, due to the intervention of Master Souls, (evolved humans), we are saved from suffering most of the effects of these thoughtforms by having the Astral Plane spring cleaned from time to time. Jesus and other master Souls before him are credited with embracing and transmuting the debilitating thoughtforms of human minds that had accumulated within the Astral Plane up to the period of their visit, clearing the backlog of negativity in an all-encompassing act of love. This last 'cleansing' took place at the beginning of the Piscean Age (as symbolised by the Fish), and it is at the beginning of every Age - the old must pass away for the new to emerge. It is also said that the collective human consciousness is now able to carry out the same task - to cleanse the negativity of the past two thousand years, to take up the mantle of responsibility and clear away debilitating influences in a global show of love as the present New Age of Aquarius (the Water Carrier), takes over. If we do indeed succeed in carrying out a collective cleansing - has it begun?

Time to receive the keys for Earth

It's prophesised in these latter days, that as the collective human mind becomes aware of its role, the Master Souls will step back and allow to a certain degree, the results of our thoughts to manifest in form without restraint. In so doing we are enabled to realise our creative potential, the good and the not so good, and will hopefully be spurred on to take full responsibility for the way we think and act! Is it by chance that the present worry about global warming, a terrorist attack or monetary collapse is in some way the start of this 'end of days' scenario? Is it stimulating the change that was prophesised so very long ago, at the beginning of time, and bringing humanity back home to receive its inheritance?

THE ANGEL

A TRANQUIL LAKE
CONTAINED
WITHIN A BOWL OF STONE
RISING PURPOSEFULLY, FORMING
BUT IS IT A HUMAN HEAD
MADE AS IT IS OF A RAINBOW OF SWIRLING STARS?
MORPHING INTO CRYSTALLINE ELEMENTAL FORM
A LAND-LOCKED OCEANIC
SHE STARES WITH COMPASSION
THE EYES, SEARCHLIGHTS INTO MY SOUL
THEN SHE SUBMERGES

I HAVE SEEN AN ANGEL
WHY CAN'T THIS MEMORY SUBSIDE?
BECAUSE THE LESSONS ARE STILL BEING LEARNED
BECAUSE WE LIVE UNTIL THE LAST BREATH
ONLY THEN DO WE REMEMBER
DREAMS DREAMT BEFORE WE WERE BORN
IN A TRANQUIL LAKE
WHERE ALL OF OUR LIFE'S JOURNEYS BEGAN

John Wolf 2008

Chapter Eight - *The wisdom beyond*

Choosing to be born - Life before life

I've reached the conclusion that it must be referring to decisions agreed prior to birth about the life experience that is to follow because, although I can make day to day choices, the underlying current to my life flows in specific directions until certain lessons are well and truly learned. For the majority of people 'going through the mill' this conclusion must seem to be at best farfetched and would be for me too except that the shadowy memory of my pre-life and the 'choices' agreed back then have been refreshed in crystal clear clarity since.

Choosing the circumstances of birth is apparently something we're all involved in and for those who cannot accept in faith what life presents can relatively easily gain proof first hand by choosing to be led through a process of remembrance within a guided meditation. Alternatively, there are practitioners who offer hypnosis as a way to remember but caution would need to prevail as to the level of consciousness they are taking you to for the information, or are working from.

Though I had familiarity with my pre-life existence, I still felt a little trepidation when first entering into the unknown lands that seem to stretch into infinity. Meditation sessions gradually removed this as I crossed the imaginary dividing line between this realm and the various realms of heaven time and time again. The visits to these hitherto invisible realms has become as easy as passing from one room to the next with the world of my pre-life becoming clearer and easier to comprehend as the years roll by

In my quest to understand everything about everything I've become aware that one of the main principles applied by inner realm teachers is their tendency to only answer questions and not to freely give out 'information'. This makes sense from what I've realised through my own experience of teaching - that students learn more easily if I answer questions on a particular topic and not fill their minds with information they find difficult or can't understand. In this vein it has been made plain from inner mentors that if I need answers I'd better ask!

It was this asking, or more correctly, after years of yearning to understand certain aspects of my day to day behaviour, that eventually led to a constant flow of wisdom that's augmented from time to time with vivid dreams to provide the answers I've sought.

Becoming increasingly aware of how I fitted into the grand scheme of things had a tendency to make me feel intimidated but this attitude was dropped when realising that letting go of every behaviour pattern, even those recently acquired, and allowing myself to act out feelings, made it easier for me to become a more effective channel for the wisdom flowing through from the source; and of course this openness came hand in hand with feelings of joy!

First grade planet Earth

Apparently, physical existence is unique, dense matter of a frequency that's at the formative boundary of the known universe, a testing ground for developing and flexing creative muscles, mostly without restraint (though some experiences appear to be set up). 'I will endure' were the words that came to mind when passing through the birth canal into my present life – Given the life I've had so far it certainly could be seen as an endurance test but I'm moving more towards enjoying life as understanding floods my being and consequently lessening any resistance I have to new experience, even though my senior years approach.

A simple way that I've found that helps students clarify pre-life experience is to have them begin by remembering events of the previous day or two on a regular basis. Once established it becomes relatively easy for them to extend memory backward in time until eventually the important events of their life are recalled. Of course the discipline of meditation helps. Dion Fortune's book (Fortune, Through the Gates of Death), describes the process in detail. In a similar way, a meditation exercise was developed to help students go back to birth and before. Even the most doubting of students had second thoughts after experiencing scenes that were later confirmed to be true by older relatives - details such as how the mother felt during pregnancy, the colour of the midwife's uniform, even the décor of the labour room have been related after such sessions! In cosmic reality, and in the depths of a still mind, all past events are in the present and are accessible at any time - though confusion would reign should we not have the coordinates of our chosen destination provided by the Soul's whisperings.

Many times I've taken students on trips of remembrance to the gateway of birth and beyond to unfold life purposes, to help release aspirants from feelings of fear and guilt that have passed over into the present life from experiences they previously had no conscious memory of. Though many will say that the imagination is playing tricks, those who have had long standing dread instantly removed from their life would say otherwise.

Banished to Earth it seems

Memories of pre-life decisions about my life-to-be were not recorded in my carnal brain, how they could be if medical specialists are to be believed when they say the brain doesn't function properly until the foetus is well developed. - But I'm not talking about memories within the mind of flesh but the overlighting intelligence that moves with the Soul from life to life. This hidden memory can be recalled after learning how to raise awareness to the Plane of Soul, above the confusion of the lower Astral Plane, to a level where the memory of my life choices and the reasons for making them are plain to 'see'. (Though such memory could not be accessed until I'd first developed a physical brain and had then by choice, stretched the inherent consciousness to embrace and become 'at one' with Soul consciousness.) The following was just one of many excursions made into the inner levels of being, each 'journey' driven by a need to understand a particular aspect of the inner life and its affect on the present.

On this particular past life journey, into a life that preceded this human evolutionary round, I found myself immersed in a swirling mass of consciousness interlinked with that of many others. This wasn't a confused mass but a sort of intellectual club within which I felt distinctly out of place! Even though the experience lasted just a minute or two it left impressions that took months to fully understand. In time the feelings and sensations recorded filtered through into understanding, a process of interpretation that has quickened with practice over the years.

The difficulty I had in 'fitting into' that alien environment was due to an unbending requirement to conform - being in such a 'club' required all its members to follow rules dictated by the whole and I was having none of it! Like almost all my human contemporaries I brought the same rebellious nature 'through' to these earthly rounds where I've had the freedom of choice to comply, though the responsibilities put my way have led me have since to become infinitely more cooperative. From what I perceived in my brief re-visit to the far past, the punishment for self-determining individuals was to be extradited to planet Earth, to be exposed to the raw and untamed elements only she could provide. It was a promotion of sorts, handpicked people from around the galaxy converging to take part in the 'Earth experiment' - but from the point of view of the place I'd left, I was a criminal being exported to the colonies!

These deliberate incursions into and through the Astral Plane 'barrier' provide a certain level of knowledge which in itself becomes the reward to any yearning heart as they breach the upper layers which hold the records of the ages. Intuition and experience leaves me in no doubt that anyone having less than a pure motive for plunging into this Astral matrix runs the risk of getting tied up in its seemingly endless strands of illusion, entrapping them long before any true knowledge is reached - those that have pure motive can drink their fill to overflowing from these inspirational upper layers as any attempt to distract them from their quest is disregarded.

Using an inbuilt ability to 'share consciousness', (undoubtedly passed through from 'pre-Earth' days), enables visits to the Astral Plane every time I close my eyes, there to observe and look into the latest influences acting upon my life and in these later days, an expanded view to see the influences acting upon humanity too. These visits initially served to give ongoing insight into the Astral Plane's workings leading to the realisation that, along with every other human being, the first part of my personal history, stretching back to the beginning of these earthly rounds, was spent falling into the Astral's ever thickening soup of desire and the remaining part finding my way out! - Perhaps why it's often called the path of return - the way home.

> **For me the journey within is a process of realising my potential – Probably because of the many lifetimes I've just existed until becoming so weary of life that I've at last turned within to begin the search for a greater meaning? Whatever the motive, since childhood, I've had the drive to follow a path, perceived a little at a time, that I know is leading me towards unlimited possibilities and the eternal peace that I've been given the grace to taste.**

Getting comfortable with the Soul

The success of passing through the Astral Plane and being able to 'tune into' the infinite and 'higher' levels of consciousness relied totally upon generating and expressing a feeling of love - not for a specific person but for the whole of life, for all and everything that came marching into my awareness. In meditation, once I'd successfully balanced the upper and lower aspects of my being in the stillness, the 'released energy' opened the doorway of the heart to spontaneous moments of 'shared consciousnesses within the upper realms of being. In one exercise I was impressed with the concept that the earthly material plane is indeed seen as the schoolhouse for creativity and an 'opportunity' to experience elements at their most basic. For me, up to this period of development, the earth was a place to 'grin and bear' - a place I'd initially developed an aversion for, but somewhere along the way I had stopped blaming others for my demise!

This enjoyment blossomed when realising I had an overlighting and non-judgemental intelligence closer than my skin acting as 'big brother', helping to lift any age old fear and guilt, providing a sense of comfort and support that would always be there whenever surrendering to the Soul's embrace. This 'brother/sister' led me to realise that my true self was never a frightened, guilt ridden animal struggling to survive, an animal increasingly being driven by a developing intellect focused on self preservation but a multi layered being, a permanent chip off the old block of God that could 'steer' the beast from within if I would take up the reigns of the Soul. In its expanded view of the cosmos my Soul had set me up for this round of life in the sure knowledge that I would eventually let go and follow the 'magnetic path of return' (love). Though I'd escaped overlighting rules when 'evolving' from the group mind of my pre-earth experience, I was now paradoxically, volunteering for new rules that would lead to a similar sharing, not of minds though, but of hearts – seemingly the only means of avoiding pain and suffering, rules that required that I totally let go and allow 'oneness' with my Soul and by association, with the whole life throughout the universe.

Having awoken memories and insight through regression, in dreams and voluntarily during meditation, was it no wonder that I now travelled aboard the train of self-exploration with added intent and resolve? And of course the more I explored the depths and widths of the greater self the more I realised that the gates of entry and exit into life are an illusion!

A very real self-made barrier concealed my true self but thinned when focussing on an ever increasing flow of feelings surging through my being from deep within simply because I'd bothered to look and then chose to connect to them. From experience of thousands of accounts this self made barrier blocks most from making such a connection – new students to meditation often making the remark they haven't 'seen' anything after sitting for thirty minutes through a guided meditation. To the surprise of these students the response is always the same - 'there's nothing to see only feelings to interpret – that feelings are expressed in symbology upon the inner landscape of the imagination during a meditation or in dreams and occasionally, attracted into life experience once the brain has had time to make the appropriate 'adjustments' that allows consciousness to record them.

Of course there still remained the need to understand the symbology of the experiences students were recording but, after a couple of years of laboriously working through trying to understand their weekly experiences certain rules began to drop into place. Nowadays, after working through literally thousands of similar experiences over the years has led to a level of fluency that allows me to interpret dreams and meditation with relative ease.

The problem for most when first 'sitting' to meditate is that of the mind being filled with a constant procession of images and thoughts. However, the initial exercises to distract the attention away from the mind and its many images soon moves the students to the next level of awareness; this new level takes them into the depths of the subconscious to where another set of exercises help students cope with whatever is 'uncovered'. As previously blocked out memories are looked at and embraced, headway is made through the subconscious to the 'far side' of the Astral miasma. As the term subconscious suggests, no one knows what will be revealed in this subterranean labyrinth until its passageways are traversed. The labyrinth is filled with 'buried' past experiences that often cause unexpected reactions in day to day life and in order to take back conscious command, each aspirant needs to become aware of and embrace whatever is 'uncovered'.

At a certain level of attainment each aspirant moves along a unique path of 'return' - in a direction determined by past experience. This part of the inner journey has of necessity to be undertaken hand in hand with the Soul. If it's traversed by force, i.e.: by the use of drugs or with help from certain forms of hypnosis, as it may result in a breakdown of a person's ability to discriminate between reality and illusion. The level of attainment is the point when the seeker is able to remain objective and centered whilst being progressively exposed to experiences that had been too painful but now needed to be looked at, embraced and released in order to 'clear' the subconscious passageways - There seems to no other way to reach the inner kingdoms of God.

Meditation was the medium by which I had been prepared and had become acquainted with the Soul which allowed this stage by stage cleansing take place and in its achievement awarded me with the ability to overlight all the thoughtforms of the Astral Plane to observe their 'workings' whenever the need arose revealing yet another gift to be added to my portfolio of human abilities - that of seeing with the 'third eye'(12) – the fabled eye of the Soul. The graduated overview highlighted all the Astral Plane thoughtforms of the past that were stored within the labyrinth of my subconscious at a pace that I could face, embrace and disperse them. My personal history had created these and until banished, continued to attract unneeded and unexpected experiences into my life. I'd already got into the habit of looking at and embracing every fleeting image that presented itself upon the inner screen of my mind which served me well when entering this subterranean labyrinth.

The need to sit down to meditate has waned since attaining an ability to stay 'in tune' - a bit like being connected to the world wide web, sending and receiving messages at any time - the wireless network in my case being the spiritual network that we are all tied into consciously or subconsciously.

Feelings are not emotions

It's generally accepted that the ordinary turns into the extra-ordinary when feelings are aroused by a work of art – paintings, poetry, music, etc., become timeless. Over the years I've realised that feelings lie at the back of the whole of creation and that the initial, barely perceptible impressions experienced in meditation become vivid and animated when 'looked into' with objectivity. To a meditator, feelings are definitely separated from emotions, the latter arising as a reaction to experience, the former becoming ever stronger as we move towards expressing the transpersonal feelings of our Soul - quite a conundrum to solve within existing relationships if one moves forward before the other. Achieving detachment does provide clarity of direction in this regard, a direction which may change from moment to moment and is often seen by observers as a change of mind and not the far simpler explanation of an adherence to feelings emanating from the Soul.

Throughout the thirty years or so I've focalised meditation classes I've 'held' the vision of bringing together a group of like minded individuals who were able to meditate, with 'world service' as the objective, an ambition I've only recently had success with. Looking back I can see that to be effective I needed to thoroughly understand the group mechanisms involved in this endeavour and to learn through trial and error how to steer a group towards being of service in this way; It involved learning how to give each person the space to attune to their Soul, to channel its light which in practice led to the group shining its collective light brightly into the heavens to eventually attract an Angel which is now overlighting the building and the area in which we live .

Our meditations have increasingly been filled with inspirational detail since this benevolent being graced our meeting place - the community building in which we hold our week on week gathering has gone from strength to strength with activities and events filling its rooms every day.

It is for everyone

Everyone has the ability to 'tune in' to the Soul and hear its voice translated from feelings in many different ways - one is through the increasing number of 'inspirational moments' that occur to provide a taste of what's in store and the sure motivation to continue.

As a prelude to meditation, students are always encouraged to relax to aid the attainment of the objective frame of mind needed to look calmly at any repressed memory that may arise which would otherwise cause distress. Successfully working through and clearing the way through the subconscious each aspirant is rewarded with an habitual detachment along with a developed a level of sensitivity which some would say is the gift of clairvoyance.

At progressive stages of development a Clairvoyant could define themselves as a Psychic, Medium, Mystic or Seer - all are demonstrating the potential that we all have to perceive the influences acting upon ourselves and others. To progress beyond the level of a mystic we first need to ensure that what we 'see' is not of our making

The drawbacks and rewards of sensitivity

One of the drawbacks to undisciplined sensitivity is the picking up of everything 'out there' and if feeling under the weather some of this mental flotsam, if opened up to, makes for a very uncomfortable existence; on the positive side more uplifting emotions can often be perceived in such places as the arrival terminal of airports or during Christmas festivities and the like. For those aspiring towards enlightenment, who have 'opened themselves' as a necessary part of the growing process, there's a need to remain detached in all encounters, to become a steadfast observer - the eventual goal, to overcome the heaviness of the Astral Plane and climb another step on the stairway towards home.

In this respect of this I became involved in an 'incident' that tested such resolve when approaching a 'Miners Union' picket line back in the 70's, the aggression radiating from the group manifested as a dark and threatening cloud. No, they weren't magicians; my imagination perceived it that way after my brain got to work interpreting the general emotions being given off by the group.

The emotions were so strong they had an immediate effect on my psyche with the typical symptoms of a panic attack beginning to erupt as soon as I focussed my attention on them – a rapid heartbeat, sweating and an overwhelming urge to turn away! Previous to my new found awareness I would have had no alternative but to find another way into work; instead I chose to continue walking towards the chanting mob, to embrace[9] my fear and the emotions being directed towards me. As soon as I did my racing heartbeat settled and the crowd barring my way calmed down and moved aside to allow free passage – and not another word was said!

Scores of similar experiences have left me without any doubt that embracing such emotion resolves the situation, (so far anyway), that love is the power behind this transformation, drawing in and bringing back into perfect balance whatever imbalance may exist.

It's become an automatic response, when driving along a busy motorway, or at any place for that matter where a residue of disturbing emotion has been 'left behind' after a traumatic incident, to react with an attitude of love - it's my attempt to water down or neutralize the emotion knowing that it will help others not become so weighed down when passing that way. The effectiveness of this 'cleansing' has been confirmed many times when revisiting the same spot.

Similar residues can be 'picked up' at beauty spots, deposited when visitors are suddenly confronted with a view from high up. These places have a countless number of impressions left behind over many years which are constantly being reinforced by those who have a fear of heights; impressions which even the least sensitive person will perceive when nearing the edge and have trepidations they normally don't experience. A few visitors will embrace what they are sensing and help as I try to do to help 'clear' or heal the area, others will marvel at their ability to perceive and strengthen the impressions by 'visualising' them! There's a negative aspect to this latter behaviour given that, as in any situation where creative thoughts are constantly reinforced, the thoughts begin to take on a life of their own with crude entities coming into being to carry out the wishes of their human creators – entities some people refer to as gremlins.

The practice of meditation also strengthened an ability to discriminate between the different 'energies' perceived as I went about the normal course of my life - some of these were not debilitating impressions to be embraced but instead, to be observed as they provided a source of learning e.g.: the myriad of impressions that human beings constantly create.

Chapter Nine - *Re-absorption of negativity*

No one knows the hour nor the day

It's well known that adopting a vegetarian diet increases sensitivity by gradually lessening the density of the body. In its less dense state the body is much more sensitive to its surroundings, sometimes becoming too much so and out of step with a developing consciousness. This uneven development can often lead to extreme agitation, especially when at locations where traumatic events have taken place. This oversensitivity is quickly brought into balance after a change of diet or when a level of detachment had been attained.

I adopted a vegetarian diet nearly fourty years ago, which is perhaps why my first meditation session some two years later made such an impression - there's certainly no doubt in my mind that the objectives of meditation were enhanced because of the food I ate. This extra sensory ability could become a glamorous floorshow tempting many a traveller off the path for a while, but those with the resolve to disregard such temptations continue without hindrance and develop ever greater gifts than that of just being a sensitive. - 'First find ye the kingdom of God and all else will be added unto you' is a biblical quote that comes to mind - there seems to be no end to the discoveries awaiting the patient explorer who doesn't become sidetracked.

Meditation leads every aspirant down the road to understanding the self; part of this process is becoming acutely aware of behaviour traits and their causes. Gaining this awareness for myself and having the motive since childhood to seek for answers, set me on a deeper path than most to uncover the mechanisms at work, mechanisms that dissolved behaviour traits once full awareness of their cause had come into mind. It's the 'work' that followed hot on the heels of walking through the subterranean levels of my subconscious.

From the removal of irritating habits to bringing harmony into the most difficult of conflicts, visualization - seeing an outcome on the screen of the imagination, can also be used for negative ends but 'energy' used in this way acts against the perpetrator - more on this later.

Visualisation is an inherent human ability that an increasing number of people are learning to use, or I should say learning to use it effectively as everyone I know already does do but most use this innate ability subconsciously – if consciously used when bringing to mind those things we are in need of, as described earlier in the book, it gives added impetus, and success, in meeting those needs.

Another way to use visualization is by observing the changes in our 'Aura'.

The 'Aura' can be seen radiating from our body by our mentors within the inner realms of being and by anyone with a developed sensitivity; from this viewpoint the aura is an indicator of the level of energy we are 'allowing' to be channelled through our being. Any variations in the radiations seen in a healthy body highlight blockages to the energy flow and with further 'looking', reveals the stream of thoughts that are the cause of such blockage. If we have an 'unconditioned' consciousness this energy flows freely and the body remains healthy but I have yet to meet anyone who is without such conditioning, particularly with regard to aging – myself included!

Meditation regards all conditioned thinking as unhealthy and if a particular train of thought is held onto for 'too long' the thoughtform it creates begins to 'fix' the thought into form. If for example we are given responsibilities we 'think' are too much for us to bear, there's a tendency to approach such responsibility with a lack of enthusiasm, 'seeing' all sorts of difficulties in the way – reasons that will manifest in our reality if we don't change the approach. It's said that one common side effect of an 'imagined' (or visualised) overload of responsibility is backache.

Everyone is aware that fear is by far the most debilitating of all the emotions and if a group collectively visualise the images causing them to suffer these emotions then corresponding thoughtforms are created, along with their attendant elementals, which have the potential to affect an unlimited number of others. One example is the fear of earthquakes which has probably been floating around the 'airwaves of human thinking' for thousands of years and no doubt is the cause of the terrible fear some suffer even when the slightest tremor is felt.

Some thoughtforms are hairs breadth away from tipping into form, waiting for the next straw to break the camel's back. Knowing when the next thoughtform will pop into existence to tip a major event into form is just as unpredictable as the six billion or so minds producing such straws!

Hence the biblical prediction for 'the end of time' states that 'no one knows the hour or the day' - How could they when global changes of any kind rely on humanity's collective thinking to throw the switch? Though world effecting thoughtforms can be 'seen' hovering on the inner planes of the Astral by anyone who is sensitive and 'sufficiently still', just how close or distant they are to precipitation is largely unknown until shortly before their manifestation into form.

Planetary thought forms – The influence of the media

Some thoughtforms may never discharge into form, destructive or otherwise, they are embraced and dispersed by the human creators or by one of many groups dedicated to keeping the earth in balance long before this happens. Not to forget the Divine hands that are always around to limit the harm we may bring upon ourselves should a discharge stall or prevent human development – this way, time is allowed to pass in the hope that humanity will eventually cancel out such negative thoughtforms with positive ones! Alternatively, it may be seen to benefit mankind by allowing a measured discharge of negative energy.

The media of the present age brings both benefits and drawbacks with respect to the creation of thoughtforms. By informing or misinforming it is realised that the general public can be manipulated - a process known these days as 'Spin Doctoring' - a method used throughout the ages to influence the mass mind this way or that. Its power comes from the 'knock on' effect of the emotionally charged thoughtforms created by the general population during such a process which continues its influence long after the original 'publicity' has come to an end. Apart from political purposes it can also be used for good when applied during an ongoing and widespread crisis by giving out information that helps to cool down 'a situation'.

With regard to mass manipulation, one particular story that lingers in memory was related in the 'channelled' book, 'Our Son Moves Among You' (Long). The story describes the actions of a priest in ancient times who deliberately used the thought streams of hundreds of neophytes he had conscripted. With the help of drugs he led them into aligning their beliefs with his commands. With this obedient 'mass mind' following his every instruction many astonishing feats of apparent magic were performed that soon had the remainder of the population eating out of his hand. It was a time in history when human consciousness was in its infancy with the more evolved elite, from another era, acting as guardians – all except for this particular High Priest who used his knowledge of the laws of manifestation for personal gain.

On a positive note, there are now many groups around the world creating thoughtforms that are aligned to the Prime Vision that is guiding humankind to its peaceful destiny, thoughtforms whose effect upon our lives is infinitely greater than any thoughtform we have ever created.

Seeking help from 'above'

The Astral Plane can be a meeting place for mentors and guides from the upper planes of being to interact with their charges during sleep, in deep meditation and for most, during the rest periods after each life as it 'hosts' what is often called the 'Summerland' - a realm created to provide a staging post, a place to unwind and take off the burdens that have weighed us down in life. The Summerland differs from other 'pseudo heavens' insofar as it exists to heal and release us from past experience that may be holding us back and, until we take up the reigns of creativity, provide all that we need for the next round of development, whether back here or within the higher realms of being. The medium of the Astral Plane can also be used to 'set up' thought forms and archetypal images that help lead humanity ever onwards on the path of evolution, sprinkling its perpetual influence over humanity through dreams, visions or intuition to guide us along a more 'productive' path. Projecting awareness to this meeting place, to meld consciousness with these lofty guardians or to read its symbols is within the possibility of every aspirant who's able to put aside worldly attachments.

Increased awareness on the inner planes of being brought the understanding that my emotional body has a corresponding expression within the Astral Plane and, as already mentioned, the only way to gain mastery over its influences, (the thoughtforms invading my subconscious), was to embrace and release every image and its associated reaction as and when they emerged. This way of quelling reactions had to become a knee jerk habit to every emotional experience before my consciousness could truly view the Astral Plane objectively – hands on, but out of necessity, kept at arm's length. The unexpected consequence of attaining this ability was that of experiencing depths and widths of feelings I'd never experienced before, moving me to tears of joy or heart aching sadness in an instant should I be so moved!

Tracks in the snow

We're all involved with the struggle to overcome the shadows within ourselves - to raise consciousness above the debilitating layers of the Astral Plane at least to the more inspirational levels. In so doing each of us helps relieve the pressure of negative thoughtforms on the rest of humanity making it easier for those without the strength to follow in our footsteps. It's a process that is making our earthly home ever lighter and more joyful to live in and is helping to restore the paradise that existed at the outset of humanity's journey through time – but first the work.

There is a positive outcome intended behind us falling time and time again into the heavy sea of emotions of the lower Astral, it increases our resolve not to return there, to let go of attachments to particular ways of behaviour and to move further towards an attitude of objectivity whenever emotive situations arise. In my experience, this wasn't the restraining of any reactions to experience that often occurs with, for example, members of the armed forces, but one that fully led to me recognising and embracing uncomfortable 'situations' and enhancing the connection to deeper feelings emanating from my Soul that had previously been hidden.

In the past it was like trying to swim with my clothes on, tending to become weighed down, sinking into the murky depths because I didn't know how to let go and get out of the mire of emotions, hanging onto the clothing instead of casting them aside. I needed to become aware that what I clung onto through fear of losing the protection they provided could be removed, that I could become involved as an objective observer and allow my body to float to the surface – or alternatively sink into the depths if it was meant to be. There was nothing to fear, as the more clothes I cast aside a strange thing happened – I became lighter, freer, happier.

Observing my thoughts progressed to observing my life, all the while lessening the opportunity for debilitating emotions to cause imbalance and chaos, embracing instead of reacting to experience, standing aside from most, participating only when it 'felt right' – as directed by 'inner prompting'. It's a concept often relayed in Buddhist teaching and represented by a still pool that we should refrain from throwing pebbles into, leaving the pool undisturbed and not cause ripples that would otherwise rebound on the far shore to return with at least an equal force to be confronted with.

The process of stepping out of the mire is not magic, it's just the same old need to refrain from interfering with God's Will – Apparently it's been that simple ever since time began, something I needed to realise and align with before being able to break free. As previously mentioned, I often thought life was a big set up until eventually realising that I do have free will – not just to take part in decisions about my life before birth but throughout my life once I'd learned how to work with the laws appertaining to this physical plane and the universe that holds it.

Reading the signs – Being forewarned

The objectivity attained after years of looking at every aspect of my behaviour through a microscope, became an habitual way of looking at the whole of life and to me goes hand in hand with that elusive quality called detachment. One of the many gifts emerging as a result of this was the ability when called upon, to 'look into' the emotional life of others and gather a deeper understanding of the cause of the trauma they were suffering - though to do this effectively took many more years.

The physical body is seen from this perspective to be a conduit for energy which shows itself in various colours radiating at differing levels of intensity which, after observing and receiving constant feedback from students over many years, revealed a colour/health relationship through the linking of the more obvious and ever changing health issues directly with the intensity and mix of the colours seen. Generally speaking, it was found that the colours of those who have overcome or were well on the way to overcoming the debilitating effects of the Astral Plane appear to be more subtle and vibrant than those who haven't. I've also observed in much the same way how we all consciously or subconsciously react and interact with the colour emanations of others, which has provided much insight as to how and why many feel drained or conversely, energized by another person or a group of people - This branch of study continues with no end in sight as to the wisdom it may hold.

'Reading the colours' in this way provides a snapshot of a person's overall 'state of being' - usually accompanied with inner prompting as to how to respond.

Looking in a more discriminative way breaks down the feedback received into more specific health issues that could be emotional or psychological in nature, providing an understanding of the underlying cause of any discomfort being suffered. As a result this 'insider knowledge' often helps me gain insight into a person's present day suffering which often has its origin in a past life.

A prism displays a rainbow of the seven major colours when sunlight is shone through it. This mimics what the Ancient Wisdom says is one of the main principle at work throughout the universe, that each of these major colours express a different aspect of creativity and that each colour has a distinguishing sound. Using the analogy of a piano keyboard, the colour-tones are in sets of seven and descend in frequency down to the densest level of creativity to manifest at this physical level. Our physical/emotional body is said to radiate the colour-tones through the Chakras - these Chakras displaying individual or collective colour-tones as we learn to increase our frequency by letting go and opening ourselves to become the colourful, free flowing musical sound that is our destiny when our being eventually merges with the cosmos to express those attained qualities.

Colour	Creative Effect
Red	Restorative
Orange	Penetrating
Yellow	Energising
Green	Balancing
Blue	Inspiring
Indigo	Releasing
Purple	Transforming

Figure 6 - Colours and their creative influence

More than colours to be 'seen'

When taking a snapshot of a student, in addition to seeing the colours as described above I also began to note that some had 'dull' or 'areas of shadow' [10] hovering around their being. Several more years past before realising that the colours and these shadowy areas were related, that they both indicated a resistance to life promoting energy - the less vibrant colours a sign of closed or partly closed Chakra's because life has presented difficult experiences and the shadow areas a sign that a past life has resulted in a resistance to certain experience being carried over into the present.

Insight often provides details of the particular type of experience, past or present that has led to this resistance to help the aspirant but from my perspective, the greatest benefit is derived from being able to assess any changes in attitude that may take place as a result of meditation practice in a totally objective way. As well as being able to give warnings about how a particular way of thinking has given rise to an illness, I can now give ongoing feedback as to how someone is progressing towards better health as they take steps to align with the needs of their Soul.

Any shadow or colour anomalies surrounding a person come into my awareness usually when in attunement with them with any feedback given only if asked, and only then with discrimination as many people tend to worry unduly. Every reading of this nature is noted to provide me with an ever deepening insight and a means to measure any progress made. If I do respond to what I 'see' then such response is nearly always included within ongoing conversations, impromptu explanations or meditations that may help to encourage the necessary changes to a person's resistance to life.

The Etheric field or body, along with its display of colour and any shadow that may be present, is to me the part of our being that carries life sustaining energy from the source and radiates it through every part of our physical body provided it's not blocked by the way we think. Its field of activity is able to be 'picked up' by a sensitive, though what's interpreted depends upon the level of consciousness such a sensitive has attained. It appears to the minds eye in much the same way as the magnetic field around the earth or around a magnet does when the lines of influence are plotted on paper for physical eyes to see, though colours or any shadows still evade detection by scientific instruments. This 'energy field' only catches my attention when I'm drawn in some way to focus upon it. I guess most schoolchildren have been shown how iron filings sprinkled onto a sheet of paper laid over a magnet gather along lines that arc between its north and south polarities. There's a similar field around the Angels that I've been blessed on rare occasions with 'seeing', and around every form of life - whatever its realm.

Even without our direct effort the pace of evolution is exposing us all to an ever increasing flow of energy which should be expressed, or used up, to ensure that it continues on its cyclic journey back to the source. If we do not use the available energy, block, or divert its flow, then an imbalance occurs that eventually shows up in some way. This, as you can imagine, will lead to a complex variety of 'symptoms' which, to a skilled practitioner, provide clues to the underlying cause. Louise Hay, (Hay L.) has written many books on the subject which give detailed explanations of the underlying psychological relationships to these symptoms. From this perspective, it would seem that illness arises due to energy being misdirected by the way that we think - instead of being allowed to do its job of maintaining the bodies overall vitality our thoughts may get in the way and cut off or restrict the energy flow. When I'm 'reading' someone, the aura appears to reflect this imbalance, becoming discoloured and/or showing itself as a shadow.

> **To me the principle of any successful healing should be based upon the release of conditioning.**

The shadow and its removal

When looking deeper into the cause of any perceived 'shadowy' areas the underlying cause that led to the blockage begins to reveal itself, usually the result of a long existing attitude which often owes its origin to a previous life. It would appear that only when becoming entrenched in a particular attitude or set of attitudes does a related thoughtform etch itself upon the Astral Plane. This in turn begins to affect the physical body the moment we are conceived in the womb, the new born displaying its less than healthy state as a shadow within its Etheric field to be followed up with physical symptoms should the individual concerned not embrace and disperse the debilitating thoughtform. The shadow appears in various intensities from light grey to almost black according to the strength of emotion distorting the free flow of energy into form. Recently I was confronted by a black, glistening mass attached to a family group I'd been 'led' into making contact with and was briefly swamped with very unsavoury emotions as I began to embrace, and subsequently absorb and not disperse in this instance, the effect it was having on various members of the family.

On the occasions I've been prompted, I've explained to those being 'read' what is seen in the aura in an attempt to stimulate feedback and to encourage a permanent cleansing. This 'seeing' allows me to know people on the 'inside' and usually provides feedback on the cause of any resistance to life, whether they originate in this or a previous life. As I've developed more confidence this has led to ever more insight and to giving better explanations that encourage the opening up and the moving on, provided I take care not to set up such 'seeing', allowing it to unfold naturally in synchronisation with a person's need and the blessings and help of their overlighting guides.

Literally detached thinking !

An experience that marked the beginning of being able to detach from my thoughts occurred when travelling daily between two London construction sites. On one of these journeys, thoughts were constantly whirling around in my head and I just had to stop my 'white van' and find somewhere quiet to sit, to hopefully still my thoughts.

As always when in need, a parking place appeared alongside the busy road that just happened to be adjacent to what I believed to be a public open space, though in my state of mind all that mattered was that I find somewhere quiet, and fast! Once parked I set off into the greenery away from public view and sat crossed legged with the intention of stilling my thoughts – again, thankfully, the gods were with me as the weather was mild and dry. I got far better relief than expected too - stillness yes, but also a detachment from what I knew to be my thought processes in a very graphic way - rising above my head as a cloud of spinning threads! It was as though each thought was leaving behind a dark grey trail like some aircraft do; only these trails were tightly woven and tangled within each other, appearing as a mass of wool spinning this way and that. Relief from my confused state was immediate – to be quickly replaced by feelings of humiliation as I found myself surrounded by a hoard of school kids! - Just a moment before, they'd been set free into their school playing fields for the morning break and must have raced each other to get a closer look at the hippie invading their school – I sported a very long beard in those days - open space indeed! - A few moments later saw me back on the busy road with a broad grin across my face and no doubt across the faces of the inner mentors who helped 'set me up'!

Love

Is love the gateway into the hearts of others – whoever they are?

Love, is the theme throughout Eileen Caddy's book: 'God Spoke to Me' (Caddy). Applying the advice she gives to my own life has provided proof of how love resolves every situation, whatever it is. From an esoteric point of view, the Law of love is the attractive force of the universe (Fortune, The Cosmic Doctrine), and maintains all life within its influence in perfect balance or continuously attempts to restore balance if disturbed.

As we learn to express love within our life it appears that we also emulate this great Law and likewise begin to draw the life around us into the same state of perfect balance. From personal observation, the most beautiful aspect of love is how it encourages human development in harmony with the whole of life.

A loving embrace applied to an uncomfortable experience, whatever its guise disperses energy that may otherwise sustain or worse still increase such emotional content to unbearable levels. With love, all thoughtforms, including those associated with uncomfortable experience, are relegated to the cosmic sea of oblivion unless they align with a need.

Love is the key to the inner heart, the gateway into the higher levels of being, and if we can remain detached and lose ourselves completely in our love of God, once through this gate, there seems to be no limit to the heights we may reach within the infinite corridors of life.

It is difficult to say exactly when I realised the need to generate a certain degree of love to open this doorway to personal and collective experiences of what is universally called 'oneness [11]'. Leading up to that moment there was a gradual build up of empathy towards life - the result of spending hours sitting in meditation which from the start began to stimulate the flow of love into my daily life. As always will be the case when anyone feels, sends or just becomes love, it's returned in abundance in a multitude of different ways.

Even now, with a developed ability to be detached, and with an extensive knowledge of 'self', debilitating thoughts still arise 'out of the blue' threatening to drain my energy should I dwell upon them. At the beginning of my conscious journey within I had no experience to protect me from the effects of the fears and doubts arising from these depths, I had opened Pandora's Box and exposed myself to whatever it contained – I'd made my bed, there was no turning back! These emotions were of course part of the healing process invoked as a result of persisting in my endeavour to become 'at one' with a Soul that was standing with open arms at the other side of this self-made barrier of fears and doubts. I had the feeling that Soul consciousness was always waiting for me to move closer and embrace its essence – that having sought and found the fabled 'Sleeping Beauty', the representative of all that is feminine within me - have awoken her to bring my being into balance, enabling me to move closer still to the goal of total oneness.

It's obvious to me now that I'd oodles of insight in the early days but didn't have the confidence to act upon it, needing instead to be taken along the road so far by the comforting words and advice given in Eileen Caddy's book: 'God Spoke to Me (Caddy)'. Acting on its wisdom it had a major influence on the practical management of emotions that were emerging from within me at that time. Eileen's channelled words were simple but effective, with sayings such as 'embrace', 'let go' and 'go with the flow' bringing instant relief as soon as they were adopted and applied within my life. Not only did debilitating emotions subside, but there was a major change in other people's attitude towards me too.

Though impossible to explain what 'oneness' feels like, it remained with me as an extended bubble of awareness long after experiencing a taste of it for the first time, periods that extended into permanency as the gait of the meditator became a habit. This feeling allows me to see life as an observer whilst being fully present at one and the same time, a place where nothing of the self gets in the way because I've adopted the habit of embracing and releasing any emotional reaction as it arises – the energy relegated back into its prime substance ready to be used again in the great wheel of life. It's this awareness that goes part way to answering the big question I have as to why love is so transformative – that all things embraced by love are drawn back into a state of balance - to a place where only perfection exists.

> **The simple recipe to dissipate the smoke screen standing in the way of my Soul unfolded - I just had to feel, show, and become an expression of love – why did it take me unnumbered lifetimes to realise this?**

Throughout history, devout students have done the same, side stepping all outer influences, they made a direct connection to the higher planes of being via the Soul well ahead of the rest of us - negating the need to return for yet another earthly round. The route I've taken has required at least the combined efforts of visualisation, inspiration, faith, objectivity and just plain old fashioned frustration, along with hours of meditation before a breakthrough was made! It was 'the work I needed to do' in order to move beyond the obstacles and conditioning I'd accumulated through the ages and into the inner sanctum of my heart.

It is said that 'no one can see the face of God and live' - Is this what detachment means – a dying of the self to enable the Soul to emerge?

Working away from home for most of the week provided opportunities to attend guided meditations held in various parts of the country. Trying out the more effective of these with the house groups focalised at home soon built up a portfolio of meditations to draw from. Many of the early meditations attended included dialogue that encouraged the 'Chakras' to open, followed by periods of 'bathing in the light' and ended with the closing of the Chakras for 'protection'. The facilitators of these sessions rarely gave explanations, leaving many questions in my mind unanswered - perhaps because my insatiable quest for knowledge could never be fulfilled? At one point I remember thinking that that no one seemed to have the answers – no wonder I drew increasingly on the inner source of knowledge, or had my guides been at it again, was it a cunning plan to have me keep and reinforce the connection within?

In the years since, I've modified and added to the portfolio of meditations, adding my own explanations derived after much research in an attempt to confirm the ever flowing insight from inner levels of being.

Chapter Ten – Karma - a name for insecurity?

Pandora's box

As referred to earlier one of the first meditations developed to present to students once they had shown a level of commitment was described as 'Pandora's box', a name borrowed from Greek mythology. It was given this name because of the success I've had in using it countless times as an entry point into the depths of the subconscious. Just as the myth foretells, once the box is opened, it 'releases evils into the world', which is, in relation to the journey within, a meditation student's first encounter with the 'inner world' and its store of repressed memories - a transitional stage for beginners to meditation who have managed to balance the emotions and are considered able to embrace the imagined fears that may be lurking inside 'the box'. From my understanding, the 'evils' referred to in the myth are the fears and phobias we have cast into the subconscious, that are too traumatic for the waking consciousness to bear, but which at today's level of human development can generally be looked at and embraced as part of a holistic healing process.

Visualising 'Pandora's Box' within a guided meditation, provides an opportunity for students to become aware of and release repressed memories from the subconscious to indeed release the evils lurking there but to also banish them for good – to rid the body of their hitherto perpetual contamination. Following the success with this exercise, more probing meditations are employed to take students ever deeper into the labyrinth of self to continue and complete the healing process before moving on.

It soon became apparent that after only a few sessions, students new to meditation became more expressive, emotionally and intellectually, with many changes in their lifestyle occurring after only a few weeks. Though taking many lifetimes to reach this threshold of this transformation, the simple act of reflection became the final straw to set many on the road towards enlightenment.

The results of these mediations also provided tangible proof to students and faculty alike that removing the smoke screen of the subconscious allows an expansion of awareness to take place and effectively increases the flow of energy into our lives as though a very real barrier had been removed – that as a result of this inner cleansing students begin to attract and precipitate a more balanced and creative lifestyle.

To remain connected on a permanent basis was the goal of everyone who had walked 'the path' before me – and it was the same for me - I needed to continue with meditation until my mind could be brought to stillness at will, to re-engage the mind when life demanded it or when underlying feelings prompted me to.

In the present day my thoughts are generally 'in tune' with feelings and hence I've found myself swimming more with the current of life or 'going with the flow'- it's much better than having my fingers wrenched from a particular way of life that's at odds with what's meant to be. Again, out of this process I was left with the distinct feeling that no one has any alternative but to do the same, to go with feelings or otherwise continue to live in chaos!

Thus choosing to align the self completely with the Soul was the only comfortable way forward. It was the only way I could be free of the constant chattering of my brain and be certain that all events that occurred in my life were 'ordained' - that I wasn't attracting some catastrophe or other with an unguarded series of thoughts – now where did I put the headache pills?

The 'Morphic Field' - A cosmic memory?

In recent research it's stated that there must be a store of memory beyond the brain with some describing it as the 'Morphic field'

(Sheldrake). This discourse bears out much the same conclusion I'd reached from personal experience and student accounts of meditations that were designed to recall memories relating to past lives. There had to be some form of mechanism for recording what was both remote from a physical brain and also accessible to it at the same time. Brains don't survive after death so how could memory from a past life be 'picked up' unless another means of storing memory existed? (Our brain decays on death and a new brain starts from scratch at birth so there must be a memory stick plugged in somewhere?)

Like many conclusions reached over the years, it didn't matter that I believed in the concept of the Astral Plane and its ability to store emotions – I'd connected to this store many times to gain insight and quickly moved beyond its sticky obsessions once the info' had been gleaned.

Astral Travelling?

At this point it feels right to introduce what is generally termed as 'Astral Travelling'. Many student's ask how they can develop the ability to do the same having heard or had read about it, that flying through space is something people can do when asleep. Connected by a cord to the body, it is said that we are able to travel wherever our imagination takes us - but do we actually go anywhere or is it a construct of the imagination?

As always seems to be the case, when contradictory explanations are being given about the same phenomenon it suggests to me that the source of the knowledge is coming from people at various levels of development. From personal experience, to move from place to place, all we need do, in the depth of a still mind, is attune to where we wish to go and put ourselves at its heart instantly! From the perspective of someone submerged in the controlling atmosphere of the Astral Plane their Astral body may appear to be 'tied' to the physical body by a cord that would in some instances need to extend thousands of miles instantly. Without wishing to degrade this requirement it would seem to me that there would be quite a tangle of cords, especially if thousands of Astral Travelers decide to visit a popular 'astral' destination all at the same time!

'Astral Travelling' is to me the simple act of moving awareness to another location, that a sense of 'oneness', developed in meditation, allows anyone to 'tune into' anywhere or anyone at any time. Having read many narratives on the subject it makes no sense to me of having to be 'tied' to a body with a cord or anything else during this process and looking into it further, it appears to be a person's fear of being completely detached from their physical body, that their anxiety is keeping them connected in some way. Because this fear is emotionally based, a 'cord' can generally be seen as extending from the Astral Body to the solar plexus of the physical body. Many of these emotional travellers worry about not 'returning' should the cord be severed - but how could they ever know? Do they assume that when a known Astral Traveller dies in their sleep that this has happened?

Many of those who Astral Travel describe the sensation of moving or flying, etc., which to me highlights their inability to move to a place or person as soon as they're 'put into mind'. They have not yet reached a level of consciousness where they have become 'detached' and 'Omni-present'.

Observing the Astral Plane 'from above', emotionally driven thoughts can be seen 'hanging around', attracted towards and becoming part of similar thoughts, adding to the clarity and therefore the potential that existing thoughtforms have to precipitate into form. Those who have set beliefs tend to 'tune into' and become influenced by these powerful thought streams that often relate to race, creed, family or other 'conditioned' groups, having added much of their own energy to help maintain them. Such people seem to find it difficult to break free should alternative beliefs catch their attention, or worse still, such believers may begin to oppress other faiths with equally powerful thoughts. Paradoxically, established thought streams could be a force for good if they become too overbearing and cause an avid believer to rebel against the controlling influences of their group to maybe change direction towards a more 'open' and freer view of life.

Should these thought streams push the believer into an unhealthy behaviour pattern it could apparently result in their devolution – a re-birth into a life where such behaviour is restricted or not able to be practiced at all. This interjection by overlighting mentors becoming in these instances, the only way to provide the obsessive with an opportunity to progress along a different tack. It's in these situations, that by the grace of God, obsessions are thwarted until a later time when the individual is seen to have developed the strength and wherewithal to overcome them.

Earth bound through fear or disbelief

As said before, the Astral Plane appears to also be for some, a stopping off place for people moving 'in' and 'out' of life; either beginning another earthly round or leaving for a period of rest. The Astral has also been observed as a place where many spend the whole of the rest period 'between' lives, finding themselves in what is often described as the 'Summerland' mentioned earlier and gravitating towards an area which best reflects what they expect to find. It's here where we can connect to those who have passed over with relative ease – those who have 'moved on' and into the greater reality can only be accessed via the oneness of being as the personality they knew has been absorbed into the greater of their Soul!

This 'pull' into the dream world of desires between lives is the acting out of the Law 'like attracts like' which not only takes us to our destination within the Astral Plane at the end of each life, it also draws our attention during meditation and in certain dream experiences unless we have developed a degree of objectivity and an ability to 'look' without being drawn in. This Law also acts as a gatekeeper to prevent students of meditation entering areas of the Astral Plane that are beyond comprehension.

The objectivity needed to 'see beyond' the Astral requires an attained level of stillness from its visitors that is completely unfettered by thought. Only then could I move through the various levels of the Astral Plane without becoming caught up in its many appealing images, and only then could I be receptive to the visions which lay beyond ready to re-establish perfection through the human hosts who overcome these tempting and debilitating layer of thoughts.

Intuition leads me into totally detaching myself from all preconceptions so that the greatest ideal will present itself to my inner life and as a consequence, influence my outer-life.

To help me climb out of the muddy waters of the Astral Plane I needed the help of all the techniques described earlier. Filling the brain with inspired thoughts (visions), channelled from above the astral, began the process of reconditioning outdated/habitual thoughts - releasing the old and allowing the new to take over became a continuous process. Uncomfortable experiences became less frequent when channelling more open-ended images into my thoughts which in time began to attract ever more inspirational moments into everyday life. Making time each day to be still, developing the habit of watching thoughts or impressions that arose within consciousness, ensured a continuous flow of inspired insights, apart from when I got fed up with the whole process and took time out.

This process of pushing out the old to make way for the new in our lives could be symbolised as a chalice offered up to the divine - to be filled with light, love and wisdom from above.

It is remarkably easy for anyone to visit the Astral Plane - simply by going to sleep! Dreaming is a doorway open to all but once entered we have no control on the experience unless we've developed the ability to be detached and become consciously aware during our dreams. As a novice meditator I became so thoroughly confused by all the many conflicting stories about what was to be expected of the Astral that it became a sort after experience to explore its malleable structure. As I became more experienced I realised that it was the last place to wallow in and should be looked upon rather than become submerged within such a sticky mass. Nowadays I can safely look through the eyes of the Soul and watch its illusionary emotions 'from above'.

Retaining some memory of pre-life experience was the foundation stone from which the whole of my life has been constructed. Though it's been full of trials and tribulations not dissimilar to others, this inner knowing did provide insight through difficult times whilst those around me cried out for reasons why. Giving words of wisdom in this respect led me to realise that people don't want to be told 'why' - the thought of being responsible for our plight is much too uncomfortable for most to bear.

Karma

'Karma' had a very real controlling effect upon my life by attracting experiences that were almost, but not quite, too uncomfortable to bear. (A good job we always have friends above who are watchful over our lives and making sure we are not overloaded, holding back much of my flotsam until becoming able to embrace and disperse it for myself). Hopefully, now that I've cleared the backlog I can handle everything life throws at me without creating any more ripples.

The behaviour patterns attracting the repercussions of this life have mostly gone, the visualisations of my mind now focussed increasingly on the streams of thought acting on insight emerging from within and as a consequence in tune with life. In effect the focus of my attention has moved to a position away from the Astral Plane to a level of awareness that is symbolically hovering above its debilitating layers, a level from which I can be of service by adding inspired thoughtforms to its malleable substance.

Becoming 'free' of the Astral Plane led me naturally into the arms of my Soul, and by association, into alignment with Divine will. This alignment brought a particular responsibility to make links with those struggling to break free of the Astral Plane's tempting thoughtforms which, at the same time had the effect of strengthening my objectivity. Having been stuck in the Astral Plane for far too long I'd worn out the tee shirt, now the feelings and attraction of the higher planes of being are much more appealing. The trick of commanding the events of the Astral Plane seems to be the ability to dip our toes into its sticky mass without losing a foothold on the bigger picture – to stay focused without being distracted from the work in hand.

With hindsight, this to and fro movement has been a necessary process of reinforcing an ability to stay aloof of such mind-numbing chaos so that I could tread its waters and be of service without getting caught up again. The veil between the Planes being more distinct these days, straying into the shadow of the Astral is hopefully behind me – aversion therapy of the spiritual kind?

It was explained earlier how a traumatic experience, to varying degrees, is often relegated to subconscious memory because it is too painful to remain in awareness. It was also explained that these hidden memories have a similar effect on general well being as conscious memory. This is further complicated in most people by having 'hung over' memory from past lives that also contain traumatic events to likewise cause discomfort. With the latter there is no apparent means of being able to bring such far distant memories into consciousness to were they can be dispatched and so they remain in many to gnaw at their insides.

Dreamwork

Awareness of this hidden agenda unfolded because of an increased frustration that 'other factors' must be at work in my life that were beyond my awareness and therefore beyond my control. This seeking for answers as to what they were eventually led to inner mentors taking charge and using the medium of the dream world to present to my consciousness the far distant causes that brought about such reactions.

On reflection, until I'd become able to rise above the influences of the Astral Plane there was no way I could be launched fully into its depths to remember or re-live traumatic memory. Neither could such memory be left to continue eating away at my insides, becoming ever more destructive the more empowered I became, (the paradox of drawing clear of the Astral Plane) - hence the appearance of mentors.

Dreams are one of the doorways into the Astral Plane, a door that gives access to all the thoughtforms stored there, including those from past lives. These thoughtforms can be as vivid as present day reality, if not more so, with all the attendant emotions intact.

The deep yearning that drew the attention and help of these inner guides also led to them 'kick-start' the dream world into unfolding/replaying particular experiences in just the right order to suit my understanding - 'Seek and ye shall find, knock and the door will open', and it did! It took several years to unwind some of the more traumatic memories but eventually the ghosts were laid to rest but imparted much insight and knowledge in the process. Always the same healing principle was to be followed - to embrace the uncomfortable experiences. The dreams recounted memories that were presented mostly in story book form - each and every scene in turn until little of the reactions they were causing in my life remained. After such a dream months were spent reflecting upon the experiences with understanding as to how these past experiences had sewn certain behaviour traits into the lifetimes that followed. In these 'special' dreams I found myself skipping back and forth in what I came to regard as a video record of my past history – apparently the only limitation to these sojourns being my ability to face and embrace the experiences being relayed.

There eventually came a time when the habit of looking, listening and embracing all that confronted me was established, bringing the realisation that I had finally cleared out all that I could in my present state of awareness and hopefully leaving nothing hanging around in the future to cause distress – tempting fate? Not when realising that no one 'up there' wants us to suffer but only to enjoy life – apparently we only ever bring discomfort on ourselves!

From these 'sleep time' journeys, the interpretation of dreams became an important addition to the portfolio of self discovery with students being encouraged to record in ever greater detail their own dream experiences after waking. Of course this 'cleansing process' unwittingly added another string to my bow – an ability to understand the meaning of dreams.

The usefulness of dreams

Of all the dreams I have had, one stood out way ahead of others – and took twenty years for me to realise its full significance. It was the first ever dream that I could 'blame' the inner mentors for instigating.

It was no coincidence that this particular dream occurred as adolescent hormones were forcing physical changes upon me. At the age of thirteen, on holiday with my parents, the dream was precipitated by the onset of feverishness. Suffering from a high temperature I just couldn't face eating the evening meal that day and made a swift retreat to bed, entering this life-changing dreamtime as soon as my head hit the pillow. There was no fear of being disturbed from what turned out to be a veritable nightmare as my parents had booked tickets for a show, and the last thing I would do is make a fuss and keep them from going. Anyway, I was accustomed to being left alone and in many ways it was preferable to suffering the uncomfortable feelings given out by parents should they be lumbered with someone to 'baby-sit'! (I've often marvelled at how sensitive many children are to their peers, making instant adjustments to their behaviour to save causing bother or to cause bother if so minded).

So the scene was set, in my delirium I couldn't break free from the half-sleeping half-awake stupor within which the dream had taken a hold. It began with me running for my life from a very real fiery dragon! Hour after hour, over hills and through valleys, the dragon kept its pursuit - quite apt considering we were staying at a hotel in Wales whose national flag boasts a red dragon!

In the early hours of this mid-summers day, as dawn began to show its dim light I finally made a stand - the dragon had tormented me long enough; I turned to face the foe and in that same moment a sword appeared in hand as I stood defiant in the path of this terrifying beast. The dragon came to an abrupt halt and immediately prostrated itself at my feet – the battle was won! The fever retreated as quickly as it had come and soon afterwards I was bouncing down the hotel staircase as if nothing had ever befallen me.

When I did eventually unwind the meaning of this dream I came to the conclusion that it both symbolised and prophesised my life's journey; a journey that has been one of taking in hand the 'beast within', facing the fears it represented to eventually take over its power and align it to inner prompting.

Another life-transforming dream was a replay of an event from a life previous to this and brought an awareness of the cause of many reactions and 'in built' motivations I have to situations in the present. I was about thirty years old when I developed a deep yearning to understand feelings of repulsion towards aggression in all its forms. In particular, seeking to understand why I withdrew into myself when witnessing ill feelings between individuals and groups. It wasn't a pleasant dream but becoming aware of this episode within another life allowed me to understand its purpose and reduce some of the energy draining reactions it was causing in the present. Standing in semi-darkness, night was closing in, I appeared to be dressed in the armour of the day – around about the thirteenth/fourteenth century AD, in France, but it could have been a battlefield anywhere in Europe.

There was an awareness of being covered from head to foot in blood, of being stood up to my knees in limbs and dismembered bodies. Around me was the sickening sound of flesh being slashed and pounded by swords and hammers. In my right hand hung a sword, in my left, a battered and bloodstained shield. The atmosphere was heavy and debilitating. I knew the scene to be a true record of a battle I'd been engaged in for several days. As I lingered within that sordid scene, the shouts of the battlefield gradually lessened into groans. The days of fighting had taken their toll and the will to win had gone.

As I stood back a wave of disgust, of sheer repulsion overwhelmed me. This was all so pointless, so futile, so against the core of what I knew life should be — what I should be. No longer could I raise my sword, I'd had enough and let it fall to the ground. Nothing mattered anymore, not even my life.

I awoke, no longer drenched in blood but in sweat. The battlefield gone, but the memories were not of a dream but of an experience as real as life itself!

Now I had my answers - not only that, I understood the reason why I stand defiant in the face of adversity whenever defending the principles of brotherhood. As my confidence has grown this defiance has mellowed to assertiveness and a dynamic objectiveness as my Soul is increasingly allowed to take the lead.

Do we have any choice - are we to suffer until we surrender to the principles of right thinking, right action - righteousness?

Dreams continue to be a major source of learning and a useful stage to witness progress - nightmares have become a thing of the past as I move ever deeper into the unlimited expanse of being and am enabled to look upon 'difficult' scenes with the same objective eye as those that are full of joy, to glean the wisdom they hold.

Chapter Eleven - *Shutting down the clutter*

Imagination.

The imagination is said to be one of the most important faculties a human being has. It's certainly been a major factor in my life, no doubt enhanced by childhood isolation and deliberately developed since as a stepping stone into higher consciousness. It was also put to good use in my career - assembling complex structures in my mind's eye as an aid to the design and planning of various construction processes.

Having a good imagination enables me to form inspirational landscapes which, when described in guided meditations, encourage the majority taking part to have feelings of restfulness, peace, etc. The landscape could be a seaside, on a mountain top, in a forest, or even a garden. The more spontaneous and Soul inspired meditations may display any one of an infinite number of 'heavenly' scenes to add to the possibilities awaiting the inner explorer.

Once students become able to relax into an imaginary landscape it also marks the time when they can be encouraged to move beyond and begin exploring a landscape presented by the Soul. Fifteen years ago it took approximately twenty weeks to achieve this goal with students new to meditation, nowadays the same progress is achieved in less than half the time. I cannot take the credit for this as I know that mankind is moving closer to a culture of self development with the tendency for people to be motivated to look into and resolve inner conflicts under their own volition.

One or two fledgling students, who think their thoughts are running out of control and find it difficult to develop an inner scene, quickly realise that such difficulty is short lived with a peaceful state of mind soon to follow should they resolve to remain with the process of becoming still.

When achieving a certain level of stillness whilst meditating my body is likened to being in a deep sleep but the mind remains alert, even more so than in normal consciousness.

I should think that everyone knows that remaining active in the world yet maintaining a calm centre is difficult. It became a fanciful idea to just walk away from my life, to leave everything behind, to throw in the towel, to join a group living an 'alternative' lifestyle. This wasn't to be, for me anyway, commitments ganged up to ensure that I remained with existing responsibilities - much to the relief of my family who began to fear what was to happen next as I'd turned into a 'hippy' overnight. Thanks to my family's support and patience this period did pass as continued meditation practice led me towards detaching from even these New Age glamour's and towards integrating an emerging awareness with existing commitments – to become at one with the whole of my life - and afterlife!

Opening of the Chakras - The new versus the old

It will be obvious to the reader by now that entering the stillness progressively heightens awareness and removes blockages that prevent energy flowing freely through the Chakra's. The resulting increase in energy led to much of what I had expected but other effects that I didn't. In particular I became very emotive in situations that I thought I'd come to terms with. Though this discomfort was easily quelled by embracing the nervous energy produced, I was left wondering why this was. I knew at this stage of my development that I'd just about emptied the store of repressed memories and was facing any fears that arose so the culprit responsible for the discomfort had to be personal preferences - I just didn't want to move out of my comfort zones. At the head of this queue was that of preferring to be a hermit but the increasing empowerment was attracting experiences that were forcing me into the limelight! Though I knew the practice of meditation was the root cause, I also knew that continuing with its practice would enable me to let go of every iota of conditioning and bring lasting joy and fulfilment. Conditioning definitely had to go otherwise I'd feel increasingly at odds with the needs of my Soul.

Conditioning thoughts, whether conscious or subconscious, had to be placed at arm's length before further progress could be made. The increased flow of energy effectively being invoked was empowering all thoughts to the detriment or benefit of me and everything I associated with. Even so called good thoughtforms had to go too as these also interfered with the 'grand vision'; only those associated with this vision were to be looked upon as acceptable.

More than a few aspirants have invoked 'energy' to move up through their being by various means at a faster rate than they could possibly cope with after reading or hearing stories about what enlightenment brings. Seeking instant results they spend countless hours visualising and beckoning this energy without taking time out to air their ever increasing awareness in day to day life and work, many become unbalanced in the process. This energy is potent stuff and needs grounding in whatever way is presented to the aspirant. Inner guides have a responsibility to ensure each of us are presented with the right experience at the right time and it's up to us to listen out for these inner promptings to ensure we adhere to their advice – they *do* know us better than ourselves!

I became acutely aware of this empowerment process when joining one particular group in which we were led through a series of visualisations that purposely opened up the Chakras.[12] Beginning at the base Chakra, and working up through the body, we were told to visualise a flower of a certain colour opening at each point in turn. From the instincts that were aroused at the 'base' we were led to the next highest where another set of feelings and sensations were empowered until each of the seven major centres had been 'opened'. These sessions were the source of much insight on what may happen when Chakras are deliberately and sometimes forcefully opened to cause the body to become 'energised' beyond the aspirants ability to cope.

From observation, exercises that encourage this are often responsible for many of the sudden mood swings experienced by seekers - brought on when repressed fears suddenly burst into the conscious mind.

Fortunately I had the time and opportunity to prepare for this 'kick back', the symptoms helped by retreating to inspirational writings and music. These always helped 'raise me up' from the depths when overcome by feelings of dread - a stage often pre-empted by the infamous 'dark night of the Soul'.
(www.drpokea.com/darknightsoul.html)

This history laden state of mind eventually became part of my history too when realising it was a 'set up' that helped to force everyone on this inner journey to take the only course they could when despair overran them - to develop the habit of seeking solace from within.

Chapter Twelve - *Moving on*

Detachment as a way of life

Achieving detachment was the beginning of a new phase of development. The veil between the conscious and sub conscious sections of memory became virtually non-existent and the gateway to higher faculties accessible as a consequence and granting free access into the next level of development. It was over thirty years ago that I breached this level of being, having entered on the first rung of a ladder that stretches into infinity. Most of that time has been spent consolidating my understanding of life and its inner workings with future progress dependent upon my ability to understand and assimilate whatever the inner teachers see fit to present to my consciousness.

The Astral Plane is the first one of these inner realms and as well as being fraught with danger can also be a medium for good. On the negative side there are stories of enchantment by Astral Plane entities that have been brought into existence and maintained by human thinking - Any group visualising together for a period of time on a specific outcome not only begins to manifest those images but also brings into existence entities that maintain them.

Becoming familiar with these entities provided a much expanded view of the physical plane and further understanding of how all 'levels' of being are interconnected - with fresh eyes, the mysteries of life began to further unwind, revealing how naturally they all fit into the grand scheme and help humanity succeed in its endeavour to return 'home'.

'Living in the now', 'being ever present' and loads more clichés refer to the state of detachment needed to break free of the limitations of life, none of them require we do anything more than stop interfering with God's vision - what I sense to be the prime vision for earth.

This of course goes against the grain of any person or organisation that is determined to achieve its ambition and meets with even more resistance if they are well established within society.

The attitude of 'not doing' had never been part of my thought processes before; in fact the opposite was true. I had, up to 'getting on board', been the sort of guy who would try to make it happen as soon as I perceived a task or given one to carry out. Increased awareness brought a greater focus to every aspect of my life and when achieving a level of stillness began to see clearly the direction I needed to take, relying on personal feelings rather than other people to guide me in day to day affairs. I even dared to stand back and allow a few feathers to be ruffled knowing now that others, no matter how close they were to me, needed space to test and flex their own muscles, (and to curse me for standing back and 'letting' it happen!)

Personal power symbolised as an animal

Often in meditation or dreams various animals and mythical beasts have 'popped up'. From my perspective each of these beasts represents a particular way of being and imparts much wisdom. The beast of my meditations and dreams has changed its appearance at various stages of development, from the dragon appearing at the dawn of adolescence, against who I stood defiant to claim the right to direct its energy, to the 'all consuming' Minotaur lurking within the shadowy depths of a pitch black cellar deep within my subconscious labyrinth that took years for me to approach and finally embrace; the emotions of fear this latter confrontation brought were far beyond any I'd had before but once faced, was likewise brought to heel to allow me free passage.

A more recent dream saw me stood on the head of a giant cobra steering its movements with reins; Though I'd taken up the reins voluntarily I was terrified as I've harboured a fear of snakes for the whole of my life, probably since the experience I had at the age of two when what appeared to be a snake slithered over my legs whilst I laid awake in my cot. To me the snake symbolises energy and the latest dream was indicating that I'd been given responsibility for guiding the larger than life energy that was now streaming through my being.

As before said, over many lifetimes of development the Chakras open progressively to allow an ever increasing flow of energy into our being and, because I'd deliberately traversed the depths of the subconscious I'd gone a long way towards clearing any blockages in the way.

Role playing the future

An emerging faculty of the inner journey is of being able to perceive what I need to become. These perceptions begin as feelings and progress towards unfolding, whether in life experience or in dreams, to challenge and test me way beyond anything that life would ever present. I have no option but to take note of what is being learned as such 'presented' experiences somehow indelibly print themselves upon consciousness to become a magnet that attracts an ever new way of being. Through this process I'm effectively forced into role-playing a way of life that eventually becomes my own way in the fullness of time. This 'Soul contrived' chain of events, from perception to actuality has become a major element of what is now presented to students.

The following is my understanding of the factors involved and the order in which we become receptive to the Souls influence:

a, Our Soul holds the 'prime vision' that has been guiding humanity towards its goal of perfection since the beginning of time

b, We can perceive, as feelings, whatever part of this vision is being 'shown' to us.

c, Should we seek to understand these feelings they will begin to unfold as symbols or perhaps as progressive scenes in meditation or dreams which provide an increasing knowledge of who we are and the role we can play to assist in bringing the latest instalment of the vision into our reality.

d, When aligning our life to the latest requirements of the indwelling Soul we also ensure that no unforeseen change comes upon our life unannounced, that we are prepared well ahead of any such change and step into the new as easily as entering another room in our home.

This process speeds up as we 'acquaint ourselves and work with the Soul through deliberately embracing stillness. Nowadays these feelings have, in principle, become the 'inner guidance' or 'sense of knowing' that is consciously guiding my path along a specific route with a series of experiences that could never be predetermined except by coincidence – hence the often repeated advice given to those joining in the personal growth movement - 'be spontaneous', 'live in the now' and 'go with the flow' to name but a few - in this way we are giving the Soul the best opportunity to take us on the shortest route home.

> **It occurred to me at this time that I'd crossed an unseen boundary and was beginning to express a way of life channelled direct from the Soul. The only thing I had to do was to keep going!**

The language of the Soul

It's relatively easy to perceive impressions emanating from the Soul with a still mind but not so easy to prove the effect these impressions have upon our life. But just as it took many years to understand the outcomes of journeys within the Astral Plane the same understanding unfolded with respect to journeys made looking through the eyes of Soul.

Meditation and dreams have provided the means to be shown what I need to see in a step by step process which is leading towards oneness. Moving ever closer towards this goal I'm becoming aware of the subtle changes this connectedness is bringing about. One of these changes is the movement away from observing various scenes, images, symbols, etc., towards an expanded state of awareness where I'm 'overlighting' the experience.

This overlighting has lessened the need to have a storyline to interpret and instead, connects me Soul to Soul to the person or group to provide a direct source of knowledge and feedback should the need arise. A link can be made with any other form of intelligence should I have the mantle of Soul consciousness to guide and protect me.

Meditation encouraged the attainment of a still, open mind, - an 'emptying' which included invocations that beckoned the Soul's 'take over' - invocations developed thousands of years ago to help turn the aspirants attention away from limiting carnal thoughts towards the more freedom promoting thoughts and visions of the heavenly realms. Invocations take many forms, from chants to rituals, etc., all help in the restoration of Soul attributes that are waiting to be awakened in anyone looking within. One of the first of these attributes, attained not long after achieving a still mind – was the effect my blossoming 'energy field' was having on others. I first noticed the subtle reactions in those I'd known for years - they began to react out of character, becoming competitive, emotive, fidgety, defensive, etc., whenever I spent time with them. No I hadn't suddenly transformed into a radiant being, but was responsible for the upturn of energy passing through my body that was without doubt empowering those around me through a process that could best be described as induction. ('Induction' is another of the universal laws). Many people in life have an aura of influence about them ranging from aggressive to gentle - it's our choice as to which influence we wish to develop but need to bear in mind that 'like attracts like'.

I've been aware for decades of a similar upturn in energy brought about when inner plane mentors have approached me – their aura always connecting with mine like a gentle caress which, in the early days, filled me with foreboding as at some level I knew I was about to go through yet another round of 'challenges' (or even a dreaded 'Dark Night of the Soul'). These days I look forward to their company, having been groomed into the letting go habit and have to some degree moved permanently into their 'Influential Field'. As I've adjusted to the energy streaming through from my Soul I've also learned to remain centred and open, displaying humility and sending out love to 'calm the waves' instead of making them, (in most situations anyway). This learned behaviour has to a degree lessened the adverse reactions some may have when approached.

I'd already developed an ability to tune into others at a distance, putting this down to extending my attention field into their 'space'. Now, with Soul to Soul connectedness I immediately attune to anyone moving near or to anyone focussing their attention my way. This development does have its drawback though – as with an increasing number of sensitive people these days, I do sometimes become overwhelmed with the baggage people carry around and the tendency they have for dumping it, (subconsciously for the most part), on any receptive shoulder.

This 'overlighting' by the Soul tends to catch people's attention just like a torchlight would in the dark, and seeking for further knowledge with regard to this phenomenon set me off on yet another round of contemplation. As always the answers were there like apples on a tree waiting to be picked and eaten to absorb the wisdom they contain. Understanding a certain level of cosmic law, the answers fell into place - the law of 'like attracts like' and 'as above so below' conspire as my Soul's emanations move over the energy fields of others and either announce to them the presence of a kindred Soul or act as a stimulation for them to 'grow'.

After many years of consciously seeking to align to God's will, I've passed an undefined milestone where I've become aware that I'm following a way of life that's increasingly providing the freedom to choose the way forward - albeit aligned to the needs of my Soul. It isn't that such options have not always been open to me, it's just that the options have become clear and relatively free of the emotion and the ensuing confusion that tended to cloud my decision making in the past. One practical application of this clarity is knowing that I have the choice to remain in the relationships already formed or to live in a community of kindred spirits! Such awareness is synchronised with the realisation that kindred spirits exist within everyone - all have the potential to suddenly break out into full bloom to join the merry band that is heralding the incoming 'New Age'. I do expect humanity to become a worldwide community of kindred spirits one day.

Visualising desires manifest only when they are also needs

Every step up in awareness brought images and concepts that needed to be understood and absorbed into my psyche before moving on. As covered earlier in this book, one major step in awareness embraced manifestation. Early attempts of manifesting 'the light' produced, to my amusement,* flurries of snow – perhaps I should have begun my practice in the summer months? My positives thoughts obviously worked a treat, but not the way I wanted - imagine the chaos brought into my life if I'd tried to manifest just one day filled with 'ideal' experiences, yet that's exactly what I was trying to do in the early days and making a complete mess of it – but I *was* learning.

These experiments carried out in my thirty something's brought to mind similar experiments carried out as a teenager after being handed the book: 'Bring Out the Magic in your Mind' (AI). Spurred on by results that could not have any other cause, I went on to adopt positive thinking as part of my attitude to life but as mentioned earlier, noticed that in many instances, the outcome was not always as expected. So where was I going wrong?

Attaining a detached attitude didn't miraculously flood my mind with wisdom but did allow a flow of insight having got the self out of the way and in this flow positive thinking became a necessary means of realising that my attitude to the task in hand had an effect on the outcome - but has a downside - it often led to other people's toes being trodden on! Of course it depends upon the degree of suffering to which a person is prepared to subject others to that determines just how rigidly they pursue an outcome that is personally orientated – a conundrum that provided the first clue to the principles involved in successful manifestation.

The disruption caused to our family life when proceeding with a major building project was enough for me to call time on certain positive attitudes. I determined that I could be positive only when all parties concerned were in agreement as to the way forward - but not always, as some things were 'meant to be' and others were not, effectively placing certain ambitions out of my control and certain feathers at risk of being ruffled, including my own!

In the end, positive thinking served as a sort of halfway house on the way towards the realisation that there were better ways to be positive about my approach to life with fewer detrimental side effects. Thus my journey eventually brought awareness of how effective visualisation was, especially when used within the stillness of meditation, though even this was not totally without flaws.

Focusing on this apparent inconsistency it was several more years before the cause became clear and ways to ensure success emerged. In conclusion the solution was to visualise 'needs'.

Visualisation works in a similar, if not identical way to positive thinking in that both approaches have to have a clear goal and sufficient emotion to drive that goal into manifestation. Even though both ways worked, neither could possibly take into account every contingency that may affect others in the pursuit of personal gain, even though visualisation was marginally better. A shift in awareness led to the understanding that visualising needs seemed to have dramatically more success in this matter than visualising desires, and when perceiving needs by attunement to the source within, I had 100% success!

I finally realised that the reason for the hit and miss success of my early life with regard to positive thinking was the fact that I was generally focused on achieving desires which only occasionally included needs

Establishing need became a fundamental element of lesson plans developed for the more formalised teaching presented at college. It remains to this day as an underlying principle when working with students and groups whatever the learning arrangements are. Asking anyone to write a list of needs as compared to wants produces amusing results with many realising during the process that most needs have already been provided with some finding it impossible to think of any needs at all !

From the changes I've noted in students work, and in the years following, the realisation that they can manifest their needs has provided the majority with the added confidence to step into and find fulfilment in a whole new way of life.

The success of manifesting needs flows naturally into an attitude of 'knowing all needs will be met' to become an all encompassing affirmation that attracts success in every venture that is in attunement with the Soul. It is also one of the most repeated statements in Eileen Caddy's book (Caddy).

'Knowing' something suggests an undoubted expectancy of the outcome - a very powerful affirmation that always succeeds.

Achieving a sense of knowing affects the outcome of the smallest and most trivial of needs and even works in a negative way - How often do you hear people say 'I just knew that would happen' when referring to a mishap! Yes, even mishaps can be a 'need' if the experience provides an opportunity to learn, which in this example reinforces the knowledge that we do indeed create the life around us!

There have been countless times when I've had the flash of an image of something going wrong just before undertaking a task I wasn't confident with – and of course, things did go wrong!

Ignoring a sense of knowing and not taking the 'right' tool for a job, has more than once led me to being upside down inside a kitchen cupboard cursing my disregard of intuition.

This was the beginning of yet another phase of awareness – in order to know that my needs would be met it had to 'feel right' and the only way this could happen was for me to 'tune in' and sense if it was 'meant to be'! It's not by chance that every task undertaken in the Findhorn Foundation is preceded by an attunement exercise in which the ideal outcome is invoked.

If it feels right – it's meant to be!

The needs of the Soul - Universal and all encompassing

My established attitudes of trying to make things happen eventually gave way to an inner life of 'just being'. Most of my time and energy is now spent on projects that align with feelings. Instead of throwing images into the cosmos motivated by personal aims I instead listened more to the still small voice within - the voice of my Soul.

Triggered by the adoption of an attitude of 'knowing' was a full awakening to the reality of the inner realms which both enhanced the memory I'd retained of pre-life experience and also integrated it into everyday thoughts at a much deeper level – its reality 'sank in'.

This brought with it the need to filter out what was 'meant to be' from what wasn't and helped to widen the gap between perceived feelings and emotional reactions. This has led me into speaking with a sense of purpose when the occasion arises, a way that is referred to on the inner realms of being as speaking with 'intent'.

This attitude did have the drawback of giving people a false impression of my behaviour – I'd only changed in so much as I was becoming more spontaneous in my reactions to situations and consequently less predictable. It was disconcerting to those close to me, for a while at any rate, until they got used to yet 'another' new me; I had to learn to be more sensitive as a result and not to expect too much from people, though there could be no real disharmony when responding to the needs of a Soul that is interpersonal.

It became essential to use this same philosophy when working with groups; consensus was soon reached once a group settled down and collectively attuned within, each to their own source of wisdom deep within, each discovering they could agree with the decisions made by others in the group without lengthy debate. In such sessions, it was also found that asking each person present to state their vision for whatever project was under consideration was a useful 'lead in' to group attunement – though everyone needs to speak from the heart for this endeavor to be a success

The conclusion I draw in this respect was that there appeared to be no barrier or demarcation between anyone at Soul level. That two or more people attuned together with the intention of reaching agreement instantly move into a consciousness of oneness – into what I perceive and describe as group consciousness.

I began comparing the holistic viewpoint of the group working at a Soul inspired level with the struggling decision making processes often encountered with the other groups I worked with that weren't and realised that my Soul didn't need to reach consensus - it came ready packaged. It was already connected to 'the network' along with every other Soul in the universe.

Whenever I become still I am tapped into this network and connected to every other Soul. Whenever I need to know the best way forward the answer is there and is perfectly synchronised to the whole of life. To me it's impossible to tread on the toes of others when tuned into feelings that are connected to this universal network of the Soul.

When moving into Soul consciousness I automatically 'went with the flow' which roughly translated is that of following the path before me even though it often means taking on board extra responsibility and moving out of my comfort zone.

Letting the Soul inspire

Looking into and associating with the 'latest' vision to unfold during a meditation had a noticeable effect upon my life and, as with all inner teaching, motivated me to share the experience with others.

This led to what is today the established routine of every guided meditation which begins ideally with a few moments of silence to allow the group to 'settle down' and become relatively quiet before a discussion takes place based broadly upon personal growth and development. This process helps to attune everyone to the 'lesson in hand', an attunement that usually invokes a group vision to form which can then be described and in many cases experienced first hand by many in the meditation that follows. This method of describing the vision presented during or just before a meditation session has proven itself over many years to be effective for the development of everyone taking part nomatter what level they have attained. As students progress, most reach a level where they're able to perceive and record visions independently.

Great effort had to be taken in the early days to ensure that perceived visions were not conjured up by the imagination of anyone in the meditation group and were indeed channelled 'from above'.

The effectiveness of this type of envisioning is no doubt due to the input of the 'inner mentors' who have and will always accompany each and every one of us, particularly in a meditation session were we intentionally open ourselves to their guidance. Observing these mentors at 'work' and connecting with their collective essence provides much insight and knowledge concerning their activities and how they create/channel the visions which are always tailor made 'for the moment'. These inner plane guides it seems projecting/fixing a topical 'vision' into the Astral Plane substance from where it may be perceived and interpreted according to the ability of each person taking part and the group as a whole – it's a process I've termed as 'envisioning'.

Guiding groups towards envisioning a particular outcome is a creative tool that is both effective in regard to manifesting needs and empowering for individuals and groups alike. It can be used as an aid to reach consensus if everyone involved attunes to the vision being 'presented' – the essential element here being the effort expended by each aspirant and their motive.

Insight is 'given' constantly during these sessions and has the effect of bringing Soul unification ever closer, particularly if the insight stimulates a reaction that stirs up the emotions of compassion, heartache, etc. The inspiration not only generates a closer connection to our Soul but also leaves behind a residue of effect that helps 'lift the spirits' of whoever enters the meditation room. It's confirmed to me why it's advised that 'sacred spaces' should be treated with reverence. Indeed we all know of places where we feel more than usually inspired, particularly at places of worship. 'Stored energy' (described in more detail elsewhere) can be, and often is a catalyst for life changing insight.

I remember being 'zapped' when standing on the altar stone at Fountains Abbey some years ago, but there are literally thousands of places that have residual 'good energy' topped up regularly by knowing aspirants and groups who purposely add their own bit of goodwill. Unfortunately there are also places that have negative thoughts 'left behind'! Intuition has led me, along with an increasing number of others, to help disperse these negative blackspots whenever and wherever they are perceived. I am also informed that we can influence a host of less than positive people to think about or carry out acts of good will just by spreading our inspirational thoughts and leaving behind 'good tracks' wherever we go.

Joy emerging out of tragedy

An inspirational story that raised my consciousness into the heavens and at the same time brought me to tears of heart aching compassion involved someone who'd lost her brother in tragic circumstances – killed when a light aircraft he was flying crashed. It was several months after his death when, as usual after a 'vision guided' meditation with a group, I asked each aspirant in turn to describe their experience. When it came to the sisters turn she described a very moving encounter – having met her brother in higher consciousness she could now move on feeling that all was well.

Newcomers to meditation may, at some point in their development, find themselves meeting with someone they have 'unfinished business with' – perhaps with close relatives or lovers who passed over without them having the chance to say goodbye or alternatively, with those they still cling to in some way - the emotions still harboured blocking progress on both sides of the veil.

There are often tears of joy expressed by those relating what has transpired and on this occasion I too was 'drawn into the encounter'. When listening to the sister describing the experience I naturally attuned into the consciousness of her deceased brother, feeling the emotion of the occasion and given no alternative but to share the thoughts that needed to convey to his sister. The narrative and feelings that were imparted described the moment of the actual passing over, that the accident, instead of being one of suffering as the plane crashed, was one of amazement as the brother became the observer of the event with a feeling of being strangely detached and free – He just wanted his sister to know that, rather than her continuing to think he'd suffered during the final moments of his life. He related that he had felt none of the fear associated with such an event but had been launched into a state of freedom beyond description that he said had continued to grow ever since! Needless to say that I had felt those tremendous feelings of joy too which left me with tears streaming down my face as I passed on what the brother had so earnestly wanted to relate.

As previously explained, thoughtforms generated by human minds accumulate upon the Astral Plane. In addition to these influences, other thoughtforms hold powerful archetypal images placed there by design, which are intended to influence the population at large by instigating/enhancing inspirational experiences of groups and individuals whenever they attune to them. Earlier I related some of the images brought into mind as part of my development – a python being the latest of these. My mind hadn't created the python but had tapped into a power source symbolised by the most appropriate representative of that power which is controlled/channelled by the guardians of humanity. The Cosmic Law of 'Like Attracts Like' had brought this power into my being with the integrating/initiating process played out in dreamtime because my waking consciousness was seen to be unable to cope with it. This step up in personal power was a direct result of aligning to the Souls needs and awaits anyone who seeks and then offers to help others 'return home'.

'Meant to be'

I've long since realised that the way I think today attracts the experiences of my tomorrow and as I've progressively stilled my thoughts these self created happenings have become less frequent. The added bonus to this is the realisation that more and more of my daily experiences are 'meant to be', (decided by the Soul), the direction I need to walk has become clearer as a consequence and my life infinitely more fulfilling. This realisation giving added impetus to achieve stillness at all times and the need to disregard the wealth of media bombarding every aspect of life, to just be an observer of life unless prompted otherwise – it's part of a growing responsibility of allowing the Soul aspect of my being to shine through. This is not dissimilar to what devotees of many religious orders have been required to do for centuries but nowadays, with all the distractions of modern life, an increasingly difficult task to achieve, or was it always so difficult?

We are all free to use our thoughts however we choose, with many using them for personal gain but with hindsight, these traits were, in my own life, an essential step on the way towards enlightenment, stimulating a change for the better after witnessing the distress I'd caused to those around me. And again, had both my parents not gone out to work I wouldn't have been alone in early childhood and have become as sensitive as I am as a consequence, nor would I have remembered my pre-life experience to the same extent, having worldly distractions instead for my mind to latch onto!

> **I am certain, as I enter the senior years of my life, that every experience laid before me was 'meant to be' and without them I would not be as far along the road 'home'.**

Without life experience there would be no stimulus to develop the wisdom by which I try to live by these days and which, at last, after many lifetimes, has provided the motivation to re-establish the connection within. It was indeed necessary for me to dip my feet into the depths of human emotions, to understand people to the extent I have in order to glean the wisdom to choose a more harmonious way.

Enlightenment?

Other enhancements to my life occurred too as my Soul moved towards its expression within my life. Witnessing deeds of compassion, watching a glorious sunset, listening to inspiring music, all and everything became much more joyful, tear jerking, fulfilling, etc., etc. Holding on to such feelings and reliving them in quiet moments became an added technique I used, and still do, to lift me quickly out of any doldrums trying to gain a hold and to help keep my consciousness chirpy.

It was springtime at the beginning of the invited takeover by the Soul, and whenever passing a tree in blossom or a display of spring flowers I became transfixed in a haze of joy, motionless, staring at a beauty I'd never really seen before, losing myself completely in the moment as my heart throbbed with ecstasy; I must have looked odd to passersby but I couldn't help myself and didn't care what people thought.

It took months of silent listening, before the initial breakthrough occurred and decades more before expanded awareness became part of who I am. The point of permanent transition was never recognised as one event but as a series of realisations that mostly came about after much pondering. Months of cramming an assortment of techniques into those early meditations to stave off the relentless nagging of my thoughts or to awaken me from bouts of lethargy definitely helped, but it was through shear frustration in the end that led to the very first experience, described earlier, of total detachment, a moment that has been indelibly etched into my brain cells - It was a breach made through the barrier of consciousness bringing a euphoric sense of freedom, joy and belonging, all at the same time!

Little did I know then that this first incursion would make future visits to the 'new land' beyond the Astral Plane easier to achieve. Many years passed before realising this new awareness was actually an experience of seeing through the eyes of the Soul – there were no guru's around to confirm or deny my progress, or even the still small voice described by Eileen Caddy – but there was a powerful association, a oneness with those on the inner planes, of knowing what I needed to be involved with and what should be disregarded. There were also insights that could only be described as visions, snapshots of what life is always attempting to become. Many would say this ability was that of 'seeing' into the future but to me it's simply seeing what has always been there.

And there is more

From close observation it seems to me that a number of individuals who, after attaining a level of heightened perception, are more than happy to remain at that level with no wish to develop further; to me this is an acceptable level of achievement only if it represents the full potential of their present life. However, in most instances I can see that it's a fraction of what they could achieve and that they should continue with self development for as long as they are able to.

Many of these 'contented travellers' were born with the 'gift' unaware of the effort expended in previous lives to earn them with more than a few using their gift to impress others rather than using it to further their own development. Among these are a number of psychics, mediums, clairvoyants, fortune tellers, and the like, with whom I've had close contact with and have had the opportunity to 'tune in' to see the level at which they operate gain such insight.

These conclusions arose after being present to witness scores of 'readings' taking place in a Spiritualist Church that I became a member of for over three years and saw first-hand the source of what the practitioners were 'perceiving' and relaying to their clients. In the majority of these sessions the reading was a description of the thought forms that the client themselves had 'fixed' in their imagination and which were being sustained by the emotion they were naturally expressing as a result of losing loved ones. Though readings such as these does provide a measure of comfort to the client, it does tend to encourage many practitioners to think there's nothing more to be perceived or learned from the encounter. In the greater reality, sons and daughters may become fathers and mothers or sisters and brothers in a following life with every possibility of a husband or wife in the present life becoming the stranger down the street in the life that follows!

At every level of achievement I'm informed there's a higher level waiting in the wings for the day when the old is released. Not being able to see above the level they have attained until inner yearning parts the veil, the Astral Plane with its many layers of self created illusions continues to keep imprisoned many who meander through its corridors.

At the lower levels of achievement, fortune tellers and the like will only 'see' the illusionary thoughts of mankind and usually those which tend to present scenarios that match what they, and their clients expect to see - many of these perceived scenes express humanity's fear and guilt. The glamour seeker's personal stuff as well as the seekers, may also distort 'readings', giving an outcome that can be totally unreliable, misleading and in a few cases damaging to people's wellbeing.

Being motivated to forever seek out the truth, the temptation of being attracted off the 'path' to practice some of the acquired abilities regarded as glamorous by the world at large was never an issue; I was determined not only to achieve a state of detachment but to remain in that consciousness until it became a normal way to look at others and the world as a whole. I did have the advantage of having experienced detachment many times during the early months of life which, although not fully engaging with life at the time, did imprint certain ways of thinking into the neural pathways of my carnal brain. This must have provided the deep resolve I have not to be distracted off the path by 'exciting pursuits' like many of my contemporaries - I had 'the knowledge' of what lay beyond, awaiting to be brought down into my life once I could comprehend the images perceived.

From observation many Astral Plane images are transitory and are continually changing in response to the individual or collective thoughts of humanity, images that would, from experience, tend to influence my mind if I entertained them. It wasn't until I'd detached myself that free passage was gained up through the Astral and into the 'detached' and thoughtform free but feeling filled Plane of Soul. In this elevated plane, these feelings became visions filled with symbols that hung like apples on a tree falling into my receptive consciousness as I attuned to them, requiring only objective translation by an ever struggling finite brain before the inherent wisdom could be gleaned – a wisdom which to me is the universal language of God.

At this 'higher' level, the relayed wisdom unfolds a storyline to provide an ever increasing knowledge of life and its inner workings, leaving imprints in consciousness that can never be forgotten. Interpreting the symbols for the wisdom to become evident took years to understand which was helped considerably by having to work at unfolding the meanings behind the many and varied results provided by students of meditation. I can now understand, further along the path of development, why some people hear words, meet with various beings or have visions in addition to the general flood of insight available to all - each one as valid as the next.

When learning to drive a car I needed to focus on each and every action until such time as driving became automatic. In a similar way, having repeated the 'tuning in' process hundreds if not thousands of times in an effort to understand the outcome of meditations and dreams presented, my consciousness has now learned how to 'read' them almost without thinking to become an instant 'knowing' of the storyline and its inherent wisdom.

> **Anyone can express 'the knowledge' – it's just sitting there, waiting for someone, anyone, to listen, to take note and learn how to interpret what is being said!**

Selling my wares, losing sight of my Soul

It's tempting to market the various attributes that meditation has promoted, particularly in the present day when people are more than ever looking to the 'spirit world' to take away some of the woes and anxieties of life - but it just doesn't feel right. I've taught a number of students who were already established as clairvoyants, mediums and the like, with many more students eventually joining their ranks to 'sell' their wares. The only advice ever given to these is they should always respond to inner prompting - if it feels right, it is right. If someone is in need of their counselling or healing, their paths will cross in perfect timing with that need!

The objectivity provided by looking through the eyes of the Soul has allowed insight into the 'knowledge' contained in everyday affairs, a place where it's always been but remains undetected amongst the flotsam of a busy life. When caught sight of, this 'knowledge' stands out like a beacon and often leads to a new way of thinking, taking me by the hand along a different path of experience - this knowledge often displays itself in an abstract way and is often upturned when we are prompted to talk to a stranger or find ourselves looking through a borrowed magazine.

The Souls objectivity increasingly influenced the intensity of experience I was having in meditation, allowing me to move closer to other expressions of life on the inner levels – to the very source of the knowledge being perceived. This led naturally to sharing consciousness with these 'others', to become 'at one' – to effectively join minds and see through their eyes the 'stepped down' visions they are collectively and constantly, channelling into human consciousnesses.

Chapter Thirteen - *Into which reality*

The attributes of raised consciousness

It's at this point on my inner journey, having been set free within the realm of Soul, my path forward is now determined by what is needed of me and not what I need of the Soul. Perhaps this doesn't sound like a very glamorous end to the journey but being of service is the most dynamic, demanding and fulfilling role I've ever had! These divine images streaming down into my being, burning their tracks into consciousness, are simultaneously impressed upon the Astral Plane, around which the physical elements are commanded to mould themselves and which consequently help to speed up my development and influence those I interact with

Changes in my life have confirmed the effectiveness of meditation and have reinforced a belief in the whole process - the feedback sparking off a positive cycle of intent that has become self-sustaining. Envisioning is now a natural part of life and I no longer need to go into the silence to 'connect', as my Soul 'speaks' via feelings at any time I'm moved to take note. It must be mentioned here that I've met scores of individuals born with this ability, including many successful business people who are fully attuned to the 'inner wisdom' - Though most are not conscious of the fact or would want to give it credence it becomes obviously true when looking closer at the work they do. I'm also aware of many others who could quite easily activate this innate ability - with a little prodding!

I've been led into developing many 'gifts' on my journey within and am reminded of the biblical quote: Matth. vi.33.—"But seek ye first the kingdom of God, and his righteousness, and all these things shall be added unto you."

It's always necessary when envisioning, to raise consciousness to a level above the Astral Plane by stilling the thoughts to ensure that the Soul is the source of inspiration/insight. Access into the Astral Plane is gained by thinking or dreaming, access into the Higher Planes is gained when becoming 'still' – empty of self.

The path to raised consciousness

Raising consciousness to other levels of being with the resultant 'unveiling' is shown symbolically by the following diagram:

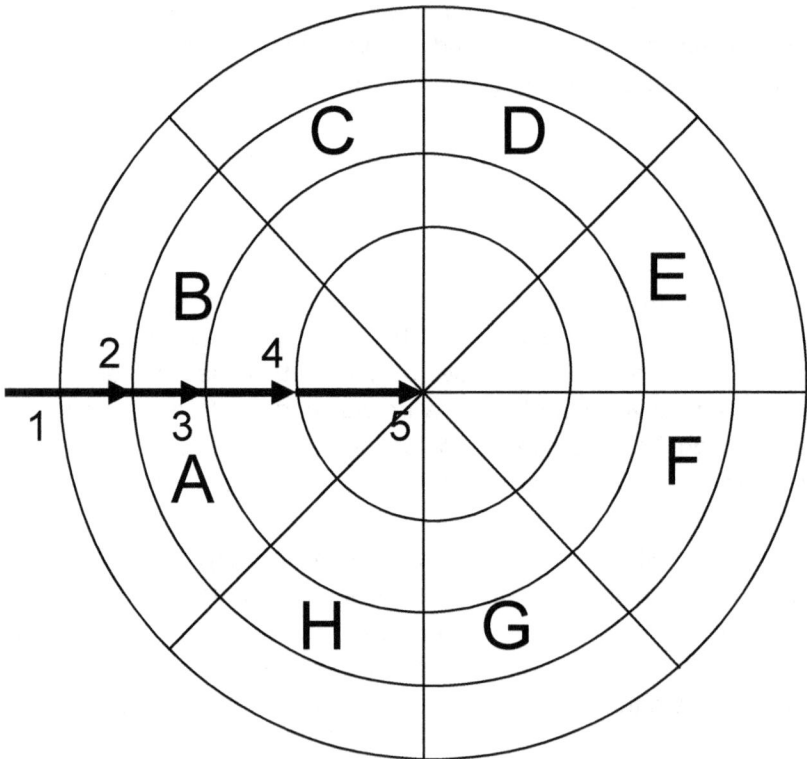

Figure 7 - The path within

In Fig (7) the arrow indicates the 'journey' – the movement towards 'detachment' and consequently Soul consciousness, a journey beginning at the outer circle (1) and moving towards the centre, (5). The journey progresses between sectors A & B, moving symbolically towards the 'centre' and closer to all the other sectors C to H as consciousness develops, eventually becoming 'at-one' with all the sectors shown when reaching the centre.

By representing other forms of 'life' by the letters clockwise from C to H it is seen that as awareness develops, these forms, normally hidden from consciousness, gradually come into view - becoming the 'many mansions of God' perhaps? This diagram could also be used to explain how an awareness of the different ways of expressing spirituality develops.

An experience that will perhaps give a little knowledge of these 'other' ways of being and how they reveal themselves took place during a week's stay at the Findhorn Foundation in Nov 2007 at a Resource Person gathering. This visit, in hindsight, marked the turning point of a major shift in awareness from the personal to the interpersonal level. My close relationships were in the process of being 'thrown up into the air', to land in a completely different arrangement and as a consequence, and probably by design, enabled me to become more open to change – hiving off yet another layer of resistance to the greater life.

Having visited the community on many occasions I'd resolved, to help me attune to the gathering as soon as possible, to include early morning meditations and walks in the Findhorn Garden and surrounding area. The 'encounter' with an otherworldly being occurred on the third day of my stay shortly after entering the garden for the early morning walk. Moving into what is called the Chakra Garden via the lower gate at Cluny, the figure of 'Pan' was standing in my way, arms folded, greeting me with his stern demeanour demanding to know what I wanted, only to burst into laughter at my equally stern resolve to be there!

Laughter also when two of the group, after relaying the story over the breakfast table later, followed in my footsteps the very next morning anxious to catch a glimpse of the same being - tracing my route step by step and watching intently at every move I made for signs of a 'sighting'. Needless to say nothing was 'seen'. It never is when things are orchestrated!

The atmosphere of Scotland's far north and at Findhorn in particular, seems to lend itself more easily to 'seeing', helping to maintain Findhorn's reputation as a special place to 'be'.

Equally inspiring were the overwhelming feelings experienced when returning to Findhorn in the early hours a day later, to be greeted by the majestic image of an Angel, well known to the community as the 'Angel of Cluny' overlighting the main entrance to the accommodation. A blessing indeed after an evening of intense sharing and reconciliation off campus!

Both these aspects came together on the final day which led to me 'suffering' tears of joy for several hours - Clarity of direction, of purpose and a total release as the Angel of Cluny grasped my being during a mid morning workshop, taking it into the heavens where a vision was presented that took three months for my finite brain to unwind and comprehend.

Most people look within at times of severe stress, turning away again when life becomes easier to bear - a fact highlighted during the war years, when apparently churches were filled to overflowing. It's for this reason that many of the exercises taught in the beginning stages of meditation are geared not only towards the relief of stress but also to provide an opportunity to have a life changing experience that hopefully encourages newcomers to continue in the practice and develop the habit of 'looking within'.

This combination of benefits certainly produced the desired effect in my own life, with an initial interest in meditation developing into a lifelong vocation that became cemented in place because of the feelings of peace it brought. It could be said that the stress of 'outer life' had served its purpose and that turning within to find respite was meant to be! The heartache and frustration experienced in the outer world certainly made it easier to align with my Soul as new and more peaceful thought processes were established and then reinforced.

Knowing needs are provided

Knowing that needs are provided is a powerful invocation that side steps most of our day to day concerns, enabling us to experience an increasing level of joy in our life; It's also a powerful way to invoke a speedy entry into the higher planes of being when we can 'know' that we are expressing Soul consciousness whenever entering 'the silence'.

This powerful invocation instigates the provision of psychological as well as material needs and helped me overcome the tendencies I had to being a recluse. Eventually it became an attitude of mind that continually assures me that every step I take is exactly the step I need to take.

Material needs have also been provided since absorbing this mantra as a way of life, allowing my overlighting Soul to work through me to create positive thoughtforms upon the Astral Plane which attract and manifest any need I may have - sometimes even before becoming aware of it!

Another effect of 'knowing needs are met' is that any fears or concerns are immediately brought to mind to be embraced – I have no doubt these days that any experience that stimulates the emotion of fear must be needed as an integral part of my development and therefore can and should be accepted without reservation. This led to me being more content and dynamic in letting things 'be', focusing attention on the responsibilities before me instead of worrying about what the future may hold. This new way of being increasingly clarifies the steps I should take and in what order.

As said, it became easier to re-enter universal consciousness following the first occasion because my mental faculties had experienced how to 'be' and after several more sessions I could 'tune in' whenever prompted. It is obvious to me that many people must be born with this ability which added to my belief that past life accomplishments are never lost - that as humanity evolves, an increasing number of individuals are carrying over into the present life the 'earned' ability to 'be still'.

Interpretation of dreams and meditations

I've always felt it necessary (17) to have students record and then share each meditation experience with the rest of the group, both to become aware of the many diverse experiences people have and to give me the opportunity to provide the students with feedback. This feedback definitely helps students begin to understand and interpret the meaning of their meditation experience. Most recorded accounts appear fragmented, but with a developed objectivity can be threaded together to provide a storyline that reveals the wisdom it is conveying. This reviewing has become an important part of the 'awakening' process and helps aspirants establish/reinforce a direct connection to the source of their life, deep within.

Getting my head around some of the experiences presented for explanation was one of the most difficult parts of the teaching process but also the most important to overcome. Initially it was impossible to find common denominators but eventually general factors did emerge once I began to stand back and take an overview of the dozens that were milling around in my consciousness at any one time - reviewing and responding to thousands of outcomes produced by students eventually made sure of that. 'Tuning into' each student in turn to give a response that felt right required a Soul to Soul connection to be made, a connection which provided a direct insight and understanding of the wisdom steering the impressions into their consciousness. The communicating medium is to my mind the Soul's equivalent of the Astral Plane - a universally distributed intelligence which allows consciousness access to any part of its 'field'. Soul to Soul communion via this 'inner network of light' seems to have no boundaries to anyone who genuinely seeks 'knowledge'.

Symbol	Relating to
Pools, lakes, rivers, the sea, etc.	Emotional content
Swimming over water	Mastery of the emotions
Flying over water	Emotional aloofness
Swimming under water	Indulging in the emotions
Drowning	Overwhelmed by emotion
Trees, Mountains, etc	Growth, Strength
Flying	Emotionally detached
Underground, caves, etc	Exploring the subconscious
Fire	Transformation
Death	Re-birth
A baby or young child	Opening the door to the Soul

Figure 8 - Symbols common to both dreams and meditations

Attunement

It's essential for me to remain 'attuned', Soul to Soul, whilst any explanation is being given otherwise I run the risk of the intellect taking over. It's the same process involved whilst writing this book - I have insights or visions into what I'm trying to explain and need to stay 'in tune' until what's written feels 'right' before moving onto the next paragraph.

'Attunement', as I understand it, is the dual act of focussing on and taking a reading of any aspect of life by becoming 'at one' with it.

In the objective stance that is essential for attunement to be successful, it becomes relatively easy to 'read' various views of life by seeing and feeling its essence. Afterwards I'm left with an impression which remains, not obstructively so, within consciousness for as long as I give attention to it. For a period I was entranced by all the inspirational feelings that abounded in ordinary things such as flowers, trees, rivers, the elements and of course, people! Nowadays, when a need arises my attention is drawn to 'look into' a person's 'state of being', to connect with their Soul, sensing and taking whatever action is prompted. This ability has led to an understanding of such things as how herbalists match plants to cure particular ailments or how scientists uncover the trail that leads to a new discovery. This process of attunement could be likened to that of tuning into one of any number of TV programmes, each broadcast on a different frequency.

Extending 'Soul to Soul' links made with students I began 'looking into' other aspects of life other than human. This proved to be vast area for exploration and study which included the more subtle realms hidden from physical sight.

Of course what came next was expected – a boatload of extra responsibilities   attracted   automatically   whenever   expanding awareness. This flow of responsibilities began as it always did with a period of 'training' and confirmed yet again that someone 'up there' had a hand in my development. This pattern had shown itself many times with regard to spiritual development, a sequence that began with the realisation of a new concept, followed quickly on its heels, as soon as it was seen that I'd embraced it, by the lifting of yet another veil. Because I'd opened myself to its influence, my Soul had become a fully enrolled, interactive guardian over my affairs and whilst bringing an increasing awareness, had up to this point, also regulated the intensity of experiences according to my ability to cope. It was obviously 'seen' that I could now cope with an extra turn of the screw, an act that exposed my consciousness to the full spectrum of whatever problems needed to be resolved without the filtering that was usually applied to protect my psyche – warts and all ! I was no longer just picking up images from one student at a time but every image from a multitude of sources and instantly began to feel the pressure! – I could handle one or two depressed individuals but not a seemingly unending stream of depressing thoughts coming from the ethers surrounding me!

It would seem that the 'absorbing and embracing habit' I'd developed to disperse my subterranean baggage was now to be extended and used to help 'hoover up' the baggage that was overpowering others – many others!

For about a year I tussled with these new and extended responsibilities without a clue at the time about what was happening - I only knew that it felt right and that I should keep going despite the often overwhelming waves of dread that swept over me from time to time. Little by little the swings of emotion settled down to allow a constant connectedness within and the realisation that I'd been pushed into connecting with my Soul at an interpersonal level. This in the end was the only means of respite.

This latest development of what I regard as spiritual attributes was running hand in hand with every other 'happening' in my life and its difficult to determine chronologically, the sequence in which these the many experiences and consequential developments occurred, except to say that they all conspired to place me in the right place at the right time with just enough experience to cope with the next round of experience being presented.

This period became the crossroads where I chose never to turn back. The moment when guides, masters, angels, etc., all began to take note that another family member had returned home and pulled out all the stops to ensure that I didn't turn away – or run away! The bridges were indeed burned. It turned out to be, as it always does after stepping out into the unknown on trust alone, a magical episode filled with a cascade of 'out of this world' experiences that did indeed ensure that my feet remained firmly within the perimeter of my new found *'home'* - the home I had left to make my way in the world a long, long time ago!.

My very first Angel!

The height of this new phase of 'learning' was marked by an encounter with what I realised much later to be an 'angel'.

It was the summer of 1984, when working on a refurbishment project in a recession hit industrial area close to the city centre of Sheffield that I began to experience yet another round of deep seated anguish. With hindsight, I know now that it was brought on by my developing field of awareness picking up the general mood of the locality, back then I assumed it was 'just' another round of inner cleansing.

These feelings subsided after work, but returned with greater intensity when returning the following day. This carried on for several weeks until one bright sunny morning the feelings became unbearable - I literally had to walk away from the job, out of the confines of the construction area and into the adjacent derelict city streets! I couldn't think straight; neither could I talk to anyone, nor even carry out the simplest of routine tasks. (The last time I'd felt like this was when leaving behind my wife to be to go back to sea for another tour of duty!) Even though I had responsibility for the project I needed to get away, to effectively leave everything behind. Carrying what seemed to me to be the burden of the ages on my shoulder, I walked around and over the dust and rubble in the streets outside the site that had been just a few years earlier, a world famous stainless steel making district but which now, appeared war ravaged.

The feelings remained - God wasn't to come to my aid on this occasion as he had so many times before. These feelings were mine to deal with, my responsibility. Was this part of an expanded role on the pathway towards God, to take full responsibility not only for my work but also for all the feelings in the atmosphere around and about? Eventually thoughts of work began to drag me back from the depths, even though dread was still my companion; I knew I had to go back. My work was before me, as it is for everyone. Somehow I needed to embrace the dreadful feelings, to love them better, to transmute and lighten them, to stay with them until they had dispersed. My fate was sealed. I felt I had no alternative but to return to my responsibilities and taking a deep breath, I set off back to the workplace.

The security gates loomed large ahead of me, and so did the dread. Where are you God? - Have you forsaken me? - I sighed deeply and entered through the gates.

Lost in self-pity, walking round the last corner to face the entrance I was suddenly confronted by a glorious fountain of colour - a shimmering rainbow of colours, radiating outwards from a form I'd never seen before but knew instinctively to be an angel. Eight feet tall and six feet wide the majestic and benevolent form lifted my depression immediately, a smile returned to my face, my God hadn't forsaken me after all! - How could I have ever doubted? - The angel showered me with love and healing and I entered a moment of ecstasy......

I'd never experienced such a phenomenon before and had only read conflicting stories about angels. Now I had my own experience to draw upon and what an experience - I was restored to fight another day, ready and waiting for another battle, onwards forever! Heads turned as I danced back into work .... God does love me after all !

Group unification

Even though meditation sessions were now guided spontaneously by whatever vision 'presented' itself, feedback from students over many years has provided insight into the way we pick up or give off images between each other when meditating together. This feedback also fine tuned my sense of discrimination which provided ongoing confirmation of what I was being 'shown' and if anything was getting in the way. Because of this sometimes tedious interaction, which at a more developed stage is not only useful but essential for promoting 'synergy', I've needed to keep certain students apart. On occasions almost identical scenes have been experienced by up four members of a group in any one meditation session, making it difficult to assess individual progress. Moving certain students apart did help.

Another challenge of group meditation was that of having to learn how to discriminate as to whether the visions arising in my consciousness had been distorted by conditioning, either my own or by anyone in the group or even by an entity external to the group. This was easy to achieve by remaining in a detached state of consciousness when meditating alone but difficult when in a group setting. As the group's focaliser, I needed to be receptive to whatever was presented and spent years working to understand the different forms of 'interference' from a multitude of sources.

Universal thoughtforms influence everyone

The ever increasing sensitivity beckoned by entering the silence develops all the potentials a human being has with many of these 'gifts' tempting aspirants off the path of development.

Humanity has had many idols to worship which have been created from the longings of thousands of people, their collective aspirations having precipitated the needs of the age. The wheel of life continues to move forward and has reached what is considered to be the 'Golden Age', an age when peace on earth is ordained to prevail - the next instalment of the unfolding vision. Humanity has much to overcome on its collective journey if it wishes to meet with the timing of this edict – perhaps not surprisingly, preparations are well under way and success is assured even though most can't see it!

Ceremony and celebration play an important part in generating the emotional energy that 'sets up' and maintains the more powerful thoughtforms upon the Astral Plane which in turn influence human behaviour well beyond the boundaries of the groups and communities that had a hand in creating them. Positive thoughtforms of this nature have an immeasurable effect in helping to raise human consciousness. It's important to remember that the Astral Plane is just the recorder of human thought and perpetually attempts to bring them into form no matter whether they are positive or negative. The enhanced feelings of joy and connectedness experienced are the result of connecting with that part of the Astral Plane storehouse which 'hold' joyful thoughtforms, our earthly celebrations adding to it and encouraging its ever expanding expression across the globe. (Not all thoughtforms are detrimental to human development.) In preparation for this coming golden age many of us are engaged in promoting goodwill and feeling all the more joyful for doing so – the barriers between the realms thinning as a result, and bringing closer the day when paradise is restored!

Living the 'life within' was longer a matter of choice, I became, as much as I was able to be, an expression of that life, moving to the second rung of a ladder that stretches to infinity. It is to me the only way to be – at one with higher consciousness, ever growing since I'd had that original timeless, space less experience in meditation, had tasted the possibilities and had now had begun to make them my own.

My Soul knew I'd developed to a level where I wouldn't turn away and had, it seemed to me, deliberately 'turned up the heat' to burn away any residual resistance to being an 'open channel' but that wasn't the case – after all, I had volunteered!

There was no time to waste – divinity is a perfect recycling organisation – as soon as someone's able they're whisked away to be put to work. My task was, as explained in greater detail earlier, to join the merry band engaged in embracing and dispersing the great storehouse of negative thoughtforms within the Astral Plane – no wonder I became swamped in waves of emotional dread - along with a mixed bag of other stuff that continued the process of stretching and pummelling my consciousness.

In perfect timing, several like minded Souls joined the ongoing meditation group at this time, supporting and assisting each other within the world wide network of light to collectively form bridges /doorways between the various realms to ease the dispersal of the untoward atmosphere holding many Souls in stasis. This work continues unabated, the latest post declaring the release of many with a corresponding lightening of the debilitating atmosphere affecting many within the physical realm at this time.

Chapter Fourteen - *The next milestone*

The attraction of the group

Just like the phoenix rising out of the ashes into the freedom of flight, it seems to me that every human being is destined to find a way out of suffering by realising the freedom that can only be found in the self sacrifice that unification demands. It's the only conclusion reached after many experiences since my launch onto the 'new age' circuit to share experiences with others on the path - it's a storyline that's been repeated throughout history. I've found that the longing, and seeking, to belong to the greater human family, to be an almost universal reaction within the 'awaking' process. This 'awakening' seems to generate and develop the awareness that we're all part of each other – the same family, an awareness that can only be attained it seems, when we let the Soul shine through.

> **Only when taking part in group activities did I feel that my emerging awareness was being served. Only then did I feel that the inner drive to express divinity was being assuaged – and oh - the joy that such sharing brings!**

The greatest upheaval caused by this unfolding need was to existing relationships; from the viewpoint of my spouse, family, and friends, I was spending more and more time with 'strange' people and groups[13] - and for many years found it almost impossible to explain why! All I could say was 'that 'I needed to follow my heart' or similar statements that only made matters worse. I knew without a shadow of doubt through this period, that the journey must continue – that I had no alternative. The feelings of connectedness within went beyond any religious doctrine to a point where nothing could be placed in the way of the unfolding revelations streaming through from within, the feelings of oneness that I'd found and was establishing as a new way of life.

The inner kingdoms

To me, meditation is about getting to know the self, and by association gaining an increasing knowledge about the whole of life and its many kingdoms, including the many levels of being. It's an awareness that's limited only by my ability to understand what is 'seen'. A list of the 'gifts' pressed upon me on my inner journeys, stretching as far as my understanding will take me, is given here to provide a little insight into what is often regarded as glamorous to the outsider and as an irritation and tempting distraction to 'travellers on the path'; distractions that could add many 'lifetimes of delay[14]' if allowed to get in the way.

The 'Gifts'	Common name
Recalling memories, including those of past lives	Regression
'Connecting' to other life streams	Attunement
Picking up/sending thoughts	Telepathy
Helping people to 'open'	Healing
Communicating with other realms	Channelling
Seeing what people expect to happen	Fortune Telling
Seeing what people fear, and are attracting	Fate
Seeing what is 'meant to be'	Prophesying
Seeing beyond 'seeing' – 'Knowing'	Oneness/detachment
Reading the signs of conditioning	Palmistry/Reflexology, etc
Seeing people as 'whole'	Encouraging personal development

Figure 9 – Some of the 'gifts' awaiting a 'still' mind

The table above indicates the order in which I became aware of 'the gifts' – not necessarily the same order of unfoldment for everyone.

A Kirlian photograph of a leaf with a part missing shows the leaf to be whole with regard to the energy field that supports it; looking at the same leaf with the inner eye also shows the leaf to have an energy field that is whole. These 'recorded' or 'seen' patterns are to me, created by thought that is eventually clothed in form by elemental beings. When any part of a life form is removed at the physical level, whether a plant, animal or person, the energy field is still there, intact because the thoughtforms that precipitated the life form remains – for a while longer. To me a 'reading' is taken of the Etheric shell of the form, the underlying pattern that brings into being and maintains the life.

'Elemental beings are the worker bees of the nature kingdom and range from nature spirits responsible for individual plants and flowers to the more auspicious Deva's who overlight rivers, lakes, forests, mountains, etc., and have responsibility for the nature spirits on their patch. On more than one occasion these Deva's have demonstrated delight when I've either made to run away in fear or have conversely, embraced them – they have always been around to attune to (or tune in to), but first I needed to put the self aside, (fear, belief, etc., etc.) Of course there are departmental heads overlighting all the realms of life - Angels who have specific qualities and responsibilities, radiating their influence under the dominion of God - their role is to hold and maintain the 'prime vision' at every level of being.

The importance of what I later came to know as attunement was not apparent following the initial 'break through' in meditation, it was just taken on board as a growing ability to 'see into' things – objects and life forces – in whatever dimension they existed, bringing into awareness a source of knowledge that seemed to be unlimited and exhilarating! Initially, 'tuning in' gave feedback that took the form of a feeling which provided insight for my intellect to assimilate as and when it could. Each new insight entering my awareness usually began its journey towards its understanding with an experience that drew my attention. For example, I would be drawn to a book, a person or a place and find myself focusing on it in such a way that revealed things I'd never noticed were there before. I've spent hours, weeks, month's going over 'old ground' since with a single minded attunement that has gleaned knowledge I've overlooked many times before.

Whenever my attention is drawn to someone or something these days I'm quickly drawn into deep attunement; it's a very real melding that's beyond intellectual busy bodying.

When 'at one' I'm attuned to a level of consciousness in which the mind is still and has become a receptacle for insight – an open 'channel', 'detached'. Could this be the symbolism of the 'Chalice' used in religious ceremonies - a cup empty of self to be filled with wisdom?

An explanation of being 'in tune' reminds me of the sixties when trying to find Radio Luxembourg on my transistor radio only to have it frustratingly drift in and out of clarity just when the latest No.1 record was playing! It always amazes me to think of all those different stations broadcasting simultaneously on different frequencies with ideally just one able to be heard at any one time. There's apparently no limit to what I or anyone can tune into, the only requirement seems to be the ability to remain objective so that a 'reading' can be taken without interference and then be able to understand what is perceived. I've noticed too that the variable tone heard when 'tuning in' my old fashioned radio is similar to the varying higher pitched signals I 'hear' within my mind when others are tuning into me – yes, Soul communion is definitely a 'two way street'! My understanding when attuned to Soul Consciousness, is that I'm connected into what I can only describe as a 'Collective Consciousness', an omnipresence that allows channels of communication between all levels of being, the connections limited only by an ability to both tune into and understand those levels; just like an old fashioned radio tuner, without knowing the frequency of the transmitting station it remains hidden from view – the frequency making itself known only when we act in response to feelings and direct our undoubted attention its way to uncover its secrets.

'Seeing' is generally the name given to the way a Fortune Teller 'looks into' or attunes to someone or something and relates what is 'picked up'. Clairvoyants do much the same and generally relate what they 'see' as being 'told from Spirit'. Both have the potential to be genuine at whatever level they perceive from but to me these are only two of many ways of 'seeing' waiting as gifts to be developed further, unless distracted before reaching the alter stone of the inner sanctuary.

Talking to people these days I've found myself focusing on what they say with such intensity that I become 'at one' with them, to 'know' them from the 'inside'. This focussing or 'attunement' is apparently a practice that stretches back thousands of years[15]. Most people these days attune to others even in the briefest of encounters - reading 'body language' along with the way people are dressed, but fail to connect at a deeper level having satisfied the conditioning of their carnal mind. Should they be so moved they would be open to the possibility of becoming 'at one' with almost everyone they meet, needing only to remain objective and non judgmental thus 'allowing' attunement to take place.

William Zorn wrote an excellent book (Zorn, 1968), which gives a definition for attunement: 'Attunement on the substance, form and rate of change of a thing brings an intuitive knowledge of it. - you come to know the object's true quality, expression and purpose'.

Just as William Zorn predicts – through attunement I 'see' people from the inside and glean insight as to their needs. It's now the only way to relate to others, to nature, to anything that presents a mystery to be unfolded. The whole of life is available for scrutiny provided that I am quiet of mind enough to use the utility that comes with Soul awareness. My 'awakening' was an expansion of awareness that embraced anything and everything, bringing the insight that nothing is separated from anything else that all life 'is as one' and that attunement is the means by which my consciousness could move around within this oneness in the twinkling of an eye! Attunement to my own being is available in exactly the same way; my physical, mental and emotional counterparts open to having a snapshot taken to know my ongoing needs. This quality presented yet another world for exploration and perhaps provides some understanding of how experienced people in any profession develop a 'nose' for getting straight to the heart of the matter.

A mother's intuition with regard to her newborn has obviously developed through an attunement to the foetus growing within her body for nine months. Continuing after birth the mother is naturally able to know the baby's needs, not just its physical needs but also its psychological and spiritual needs too if she is sufficiently still.

The most important part of the journey within was getting to know who I am and needing to embrace everything 'in the way' - loving whatever came into awareness to enable the knowledge that lay just beyond to become within reach. This was the alchemic love described earlier which balanced the lower body with the upper, causing the gateway of my heart to open to provide access into the inner kingdoms of the Soul. From that moment, my ability to link with others via Soul consciousness blossomed.

From my perspective, entering into this collective consciousness can be achieved by anyone via the gateway of their heart, and whenever groups of such achievers undertake a task together, just like bees in a hive, each person in the group tends to undertake the right action at just the right time. Obviously our guides and mentors upon the inner planes of being are always connected in this way. This collective consciousness though suggesting restrictions of some kind, paradoxically, provides an unlimited state of freedom that surpasses anything we could ever experience at this physical level.

Love - Opening the gate beyond the veil

When connecting to those who have 'passed over' love is always the key to its achievement. Feeling love for a close friend or partner who is between lives opens up a connection through every boundary, allowing a sweet embrace to take place whenever the need arises. Neither time nor space seems able to separate a bond that has been formed out of love. From personal experience it's possible to follow a loved one's progress well into the plane of Soul provided grief is set aside and feelings of love held uppermost. This 'arms' length contact does provide one of the most joyous experiences I have ever had and have been able to facilitate for others. On many occasions I've been given the heart warming task of leading groups and individuals through 'the veil' to provide both hope and inspiration - helping to remove the fear of death in the process and if granted, rekindling the bonds between lovers that have been parted for a while – confirming to all that love is everlasting.

From time to time when people meet they instantly 'connect' or 'attune to' each other at a very deep level, a phenomenon that is apparently due to having had a close relationship with each other in the past - Just imagine how many partners, children, parents, siblings, etc., we've all been closely associated with after the passage of many lifetimes - love is never extinguished!

When observing/listening to demonstrations by fortune tellers, psychics, mystics, seers and the like, it soon became clear that the authenticity of the experience is limited to a level akin to the practitioner's level of development. This conclusion was reached after many experiences of 'tuning in', knowing that the impressions or feelings that become 'available' to me are limited to the level at which I'm able to pick them up and understand what is perceived. Over the years, as my perception and understanding grew, so too did my ability to assess the various levels of attainment reached by others in relationship to my own.

This assessment provided the insight to know that if a practitioner of one of these 'new age arts' has evolved only as far as the psychic level, the reading will be limited to Astral Plane illusions emanating from the client and/or others in the room or from those who are close by. Alternatively, if the practitioner is working within Soul awareness the readings will be more open ended and more likely to carry wisdom in the words spoken and in time, prove to be helpful to the client's development.

When consciousness is attuned to the Soul, communication with every aspect of the known universe becomes possible too and puts individuals in a position to become a channel for the benefit of humanity.

Being an open channel when not 'in tune' with the Soul, allows communications from any mischievous entity that may be 'hanging' around in the Astral Plane. This is the classic background to those who are trying to impress their clients and who are themselves still bound up within the Astral Plane. As always it seems, determining what is reality and what is make believe is down to how 'tuned in' we are and to what degree we are connected to our Soul – to feelings and not to emotions.

Looking again at Figure (4) showing the symbolic relationship between an individual and the rest of life; Are we limited or partly closed off by our beliefs as symbolised by the circle / broken circle, or are we part of the whole where nothing is kept from awareness?

About ten years along the road of self development I began to be concerned that I would not be able keep up with the ever increasing demands upon my life. With hindsight this upturn of activity was a direct result of invoking personal growth which attracted a build-up of experiences with the sole purpose of pushing me towards the goal of detachment and a step nearer home. 'You don't get 'owt for nowt' the old Yorkshire saying goes – thirty five years later and I'm still going through changes necessary to maintain detachment.

Had I known how long it was to take to be completely free of self, would I have persisted? – Of course I would - it's taken countless lifetimes to get to this point - one lifetime is just the blinking of an eye by comparison! At least now I've begun to develop an attitude of continuous change – to enjoy the moment and not fear the future.

Of course I was primed and ready to begin the next phase of awakening that couldn't begin until a level of detachment had been attained - a phase that took me into other realms of life apart from our own.

Inner plane entities

These 'other' realms included those in which our guides and mentors reside, freely providing a source of knowledge the moment we tune into their aura whenever they near. There seems to be no limitations placed in the way of anyone seeking knowledge in this way, taking only a brief embrace for it to etch itself upon consciousness, to become our knowledge the moment we express it within our life.

These inner plane embraces often lead me into reading particular books, taking part in workshops, and have even led me taking to the stage, which to the old me, would have been viewed as cranky but with inner plane insight I've been encouraged to forge onwards, both with research and with action. Nowadays there's no hesitation when given the thread of something in this way - it provides the motive to go head long into seeking all the related knowledge I can get my hands on.

Similar threads that led me further into the diverse nature of the 'hidden' life of evolved humans, angelic beings and nature spirits to name but a few with each unfolding their own hierarchy of sorts. There's also a mixed bag of 'other' apparitions waiting to tempt the novice that are generally constructs of human imagination which I've learned to disregard or have had to banish according to the dictates of inner prompting. Yes, there are aliens too – apparently each and every one of us has a connection to one or another 'ET life stream' prior to having a go at this earthly one, 'visiting' the earth for a few millennia to go through its 'very physical' training course. Our space cousins 'hang around' at vibrational levels slightly out of phase with our own; perhaps many of these 'visitors' will eventually 'descend' to this material plane if their path dictates? These ET's should be looked upon as less evolved but harmless because the source of their motivation is apparently aligned to that of Divinity – free will is granted only to those seen to be ready to descend into matter, those who have passed the entrance interview, and for that reason humanity is regarded as being slightly more evolved but initially, less trustworthy!

Contact with faeries

An outing with my family to Rosemarkie, a small fishing village on the Black Isle, in Scotland, unfolded an unexpected experience with nature spirits, a life stream hidden from 'normal' view.

I'd been planning to take my family walking at a place called the 'Fairy Glen' on the outskirts of Rosemarkie ever since reading the account of two well known characters from the Findhorn Foundation - Roc and Peter, who had purposely visited the area some years earlier as part of a successful effort to reconcile man and nature. In its heyday, the Fairy Glen was the main feature of the garden on a Victorian estate long since neglected and left to overgrow for the most part except for a meandering pathway. The Findhornian's had made a visit to Rosemarkie to make contact with the nature kingdom - a story which had inspired me to retrace their steps long before returning with my family on this particular Sunday afternoon. We started out along the winding footpath leading from the car park at the eastern end of the village into the neglected but renowned beauty spot.

From personal experience I knew that the place was 'alive' - I'd sat in quiet solitude on a previous occasion invoking the Glen's 'overseer' in whatever form it would take. On that occasion it was dusk, the atmosphere quickly became ominous and overbearing and the strength and majesty of the being beginning to show itself proved to be too overwhelming, causing me to make a hasty retreat - no doubt an act that gave rise much mirth within their world!

I remarked to my wife Katherine, a few steps ahead of me on the walk that day that if anywhere we were more likely to meet with fairies here than anywhere else – Her response was a disbelieving glance accompanied by stifled sniggering – she was well aware of my 'silly' beliefs.

Half a mile further on and we were well into the Glen. The children had disappeared into the distance and we followed in silence about twenty paces apart – I brought up the rear; suddenly Katherine began stepping about in a most unusual way as though playing hopscotch!

I kept silent … and at a distance, watching in sheer fascination when realising nature spirits were about her! They appeared to be swirling and dancing at random around her feet. Needless to say I was giddy with excitement by the time we reached what was a glorious waterfall with Katherine's face a picture of bewilderment. - Katherine didn't relate the story of her enchantment - not until several days later, when she obvious' felt that her embarrassing encounter could safely be revealed. She had ridiculed my 'fairy stories' for years and was now confronted with one of her own!

Figure 10 - Waterfall at Rosemarkie

The 'Deva' of the upper waterfall – Rosemarkie 1986

Encounters of the Inner Planes

All the encounters I've had with 'entities' from other realms, move in and out of awareness spontaneously and only then when able to switch off from day to day concerns - of course the other necessary ingredient is a deeply developed empathy for nature. It's this connection through the heart centre that also ensures the overlighting protection of the Soul is engaged when entering non human dimensions. These conditions of entry ensure that the kingdom of nature is only ever empowered by our entry - their life force enhanced and brought into greater activity to help restore the 'ideals of life'. – Do you believe in faeries?

'Other' apparitions encountered between the physical and the elevated planes of Soul depend upon the prevailing motive of the meditator. Those seeking after glamour may attract unsavoury entities that are always seeking to perpetuate their existence with 'human energy', whether it is being cast 'abroad' without discrimination or directed via the Soul to manifest needs. When used for selfish ends any imbalance caused will need to be compensated for at a later date, causing much delay to progress that would otherwise be made.

The motive behind the 'seeing' always determines the type and quality of intelligence that I could and can attune to. Remaining detached ensures that I am completely free of personal desire during attunement sessions and that whatever 'I get into' is the result of inner prompting, though keeping a state of detachment is easier said than done! It was twenty years or so before it dawned on me that I'd been led through a sort of apprenticeship which had taken up a good part of this life and an undetermined number of previous lives to accomplish the 'right attitude'. It must be remembered however that this is my particular route home – everyone travels a slightly different path but all paths lead back to the core of being. The journey takes as long as it takes but we do have the promise that the gate will not close until every 'lamb' has entered the fold!

Understanding the impressions imparted to my consciousness when making contact with 'ascended' beings has always been restricted by my ability to understand them, but in the same way that the student's descriptions of meditation experience revealed their wisdom, so too did these lofty embraces become easier to understand over time. These beings have always presented the 'right' step to take on the pathway home, helping to raise my awareness as fast as my understanding would allow.

It was in this way that I became increasingly focused on 'higher plane' contacts, intent on opening my consciousness to them as easily as they could open to me, with a major 'step up' in this attribute once the point of no return had been reached - the point when continuing to progress along the path of self-development became infinitely more desirable than turning aside. As always, this was observed 'from above' and led to the consolidation of the many new relationships being formed across the different planes of being as well as helping me move closer to establishing a sense of security based upon 'living in the now'.

This was also the period when bringing into line the dragon of flesh was joined by an attitude of deliberately stepping aside to allow the Soul to guide my day to day affairs and caused as a consequence, my life to become less demanding and more peaceful - but it definitely was not the end of personal development! - As always the Soul was more than one step ahead of me and had already prepared the ground for the next page of my life to be turned. To this end it effectively blocked all attempts I was making to gain employment and forced me to settle down into what's unfolded as a period of deep contemplation.

Moving into this phase of development I didn't know what the next page of my life was to reveal even though I had a constant stream of insight - the signs and symbols coming through were far beyond my understanding at the time but with hindsight it's become clear that I'm moving into a closer affinity with Soul consciousness, a closeness that is bringing an awareness of how I'm beginning to co-create at this level. I am also aware that that this movement is drawing me closer to becoming a 'Christed Being' but first I need an undetermined period of time to adjust to the rarefied atmosphere of the Soul - a process, which as far as my knowledge serves, has never been explained as to how it effects a person's day to day life.

In describing this effect I should explain that my present perception of the Soul is of an androgynous and interpersonal being that is connected to every level of life within the known universe. My first introduction to becoming identified with the Souls 'way of life' began over five years ago with the realisation that I'd moved into a transpersonal attitude somewhere along the way leading me towards becoming totally objective in every 'situation' - the self taking more and more of a back seat. Included in this transition was a marked step up in receptivity - a quality that represented the feminine aspects of my consciousness and without its balancing energy in place would block further progress. From a present perspective the feminine aspect of my being is the receiving station that is receptive to the insight channelled through from the Soul and the masculine aspect empowers these perceived visions with emotion to become thoughtforms upon the Astral Plane.

This process of identifying with the Soul in this way is seen as enabling me to move into and 'activate' the Soul in much the same way we activated the body of flesh at the beginning of time. Not so long ago, the Soul was seen as my guardian, a being that overlighted and guided every step I made, but now, just as I was getting used to letting myself be led by this larger than life being, I'm finding myself being launched into the new responsibility of becoming at one with its guiding light and of having to be directly receptive to a multitude of 'other' sources of life.

In this way, I have moved closer towards giving birth to a new life in service to God – the Christ Child[16] has begun to stir!

The apprenticeship called life

After several years of learning the basic skills of a chosen career it was many more before I became proficient. Somewhere along the way a point of development was reached when I began to 'tune into' a wealth of wisdom associated with the profession which resulted in a boost of confidence and the realisation that I could stand side by side with mentors! What I didn't realise at the time was that I had tuned into a store of thoughtforms upon the Astral Plane relating to the trade which had been established over many lifetimes by past masters, thoughtforms that are forever being added to by fledglings like myself whenever reaching the peak of ability to extend the possibilities of future generations

It's been a similar learning process on the inner journey but instead of beginning with a chosen career it began with a belief and was followed up with years of research and much contemplation, becoming ever more attuned to a wellspring of knowledge relating to the source of my life, the Soul. It was synchronised with a developing transpersonal attitude leading me to become aware of a group mind of infinite proportions. This attunement wasn't to a collection of thoughtforms created by humanity but to a series of events waiting to be revealed to my receptive consciousness as and when I grew in understanding.

It proved to be a very dynamic and ever present group, and in consciousness I had the impression of being sat around a table of sorts at which I was accepted as an equal member. I could only ever describe this group as a club made up of those who had trod the pathway home long ago and were there to give more specific and direct guidance to anyone who searched deep within and had reached a certain level of achievement. The same blessings await everyone who puts aside the self, who realise they can never reach journeys end without the support and encouragement of others at every level of development.

The main difficulty on this inner 'journey' is that apprenticeships or training programmes of any kind are not available under the heading of 'enlightened being' other than the traditional method of retreating from the world to reside in a spiritual colony or community. I had no intention of abandoning the outside world and turned instead to the countless books that are available to read on the subject. Many of these were found to be contradictory and forced me to fine tune my intuition and discriminate between what 'felt true' and what didn't.

It was this gut feeling, connecting to this inner club, the 'kingdom of heaven within', that eventually appeared to be the only real help anyone on the path ever has. If there was another way I certainly haven't found it. My path has led me through a 'supermarket' of many religious organisations, books, people and experiences, leading to a unique combination of 'opening' that would probably be unsuitable for anyone else – something that has been confirmed from student feedback and from life experience.

The conditioning of childhood has had a major influence on my life but only scratched the surface compared with the powerful undercurrents that have been my guide since turning within. It's this inner contact that leads me to advise that each individual should follow their own prompting, to follow a route that feels right for them. It's the only way through the subconscious labyrinth - to move from group to group and book to book as the need arises within them, just as I have. We're following the footprints left by the ancients who found 'nirvana' long ago!

To maintain the momentum of development and not fall back into what is by comparison, the mist of a mundane existence, I often needed to ensure my thoughts remained inspired. Though I continued to 'go within' and re-experience the bliss to be found there, after each visit I was left with a growing discontent at not achieving more and found myself needing to bring that bliss into my everyday life, permanently!

Avid reading of anything remotely spiritual was a boon and is a well known phenomenon to everyone at this stage on the journey, a stage that broadened my understanding and knowledge about the God that was moving out of his throne and becoming more personal, becoming a quality, a principle, rather than a person.

Following gut feeling was to me taking responsibility for aligning my will to this God principle which eventually proved to be the 'right' way and the only way to enter deep into my heart where the door opened to the inner realms. This was not the doorway to the readily accessible Astral Plane, but to a plane of being that forbids entry to any consciousness concerned with self. – I have tagged this realm the 'Plane of Soul' and consider it to be the first level open to any human consciousness that has achieved an ability to be detached from the flotsam, good or bad, hanging around in the Astral Plane. Achieving detachment, even for a few seconds allows instant access into this inner sanctum and is from my perspective, the nearest thing yet to my concept of God. It is here were inner plane mentors and their storehouse of knowledge has so far proven worthy.

Belief in God was never an issue as the concept has shifted constantly to match my understanding.

Communion

The depth and width of my relationship to the 'Elders' on the inner planes continues to grow apace with an understanding of their role and the way I communicate with them. Communicating at their level of being is more of a shared consciousness than an arm's length conversation these days with the feelings transposed for relating to others generally expressed in fluent dialogue without having to purposely take time out to meditate.

Living 'in the moment', is an important qualification to allow this communion to take place. A detached and open mind can be the only receiver. Having this hot line to an infinite source of wisdom also brings with it a constant understanding of the reasons for any changes in my life and always these days, removes any resistance to 'going with the flow'. As I moved into this attunement it's like being absorbed into a greater whole and is a 'challenge' to be exposed, warts & all, to enlightened beings looking deep into my psyche. A side effect of this two way exchange of feelings is to be bathed in love!

Those who have the motivation to pursue personal development to its ultimate conclusion will be rewarded with a heightened sense of discrimination and an ability to disregard much of the flotsam lurking in and around their consciousness. This led, in my experience to an attitude that is increasingly focused and single minded, making the inner world as real as the outer but retaining very clear boundaries. In the normal course of events, and particularly with the subject and vocation that is meditation, students become teachers in their own right, learning from their 'connection' within to become aware of the part they can play to help others to reach the same level of awareness – onwards and upwards to include everyone as the pyramid grows!

Up to this point I've described the steps I've taken on the path towards expanding awareness, a path that's proved to be a safe way forward without any of the pitfalls other routes sometimes bring upon the traveller. It is a route that leads to mastery over the Astral Plane allowing the achiever to use its malleable substance. This journey within may seem boring and monotonous to many, but those who remain true to their inner self will find the rainbow's end as surely as day follows night!

Chapter Fifteen - *Glamorous side effects*

Beyond regression

Recalling and by that very action, refreshing memories of before birth, not only helped release the fear of death but also unveiled memories that led to a deeper understanding of who I am. These pre-life sojourns stretched my mind across the sands of time, across many lifetimes of experience, to overwhelm the fears of a previously restricted outlook.

It is now realised that all past memory is accessible, but just like going into a library or undertaking a search on the internet I do need to know a little of what I'm looking for or am given via inner prompting. Without this 'starter for ten' to attune to I become swamped with confusion or led into a cul-de-sac that comes to nought in the mass of memories stored since the development of the thought creating faculties of humanity. With a thread of information, not dissimilar to the open palm of a hand presented to a Psychic, I'm enabled to attune to the track that eventually leads to the memory sought.

The need to research my past was brought about by a deep desire to understand why I reacted as I did to specific experiences. This desire not only led to an attunement to the causal event but in many cases instigated one of the many dreams I've had throughout my life to provide the answers. These long past events could have occurred in any of my lives, (or associated lives), since time began, memories that were etched upon my mind in such a way that every detail could be replayed in dreams and be remembered on waking to provide much food for thought. All 'unresolved' memory remains within the recording mechanism of the Astral Plane to be retrieved and banished as we develop.

To help students who wish to understand more of themselves by uncovering the past they're asked to record any behaviour pattern that doesn't appear to have been brought about by the conditioning or experiences of their present life. The resultant list is further diminished if they are encouraged to focus attention on any the behaviour patterns they feel uncomfortable with. As it did with me, this exercise tends to stimulate a reaction in life or in dreams that relate the cause, a process that also helps to ensure the student's own past is attuned to and not someone else's.

Telepathy

Most people can recount experiences where someone has either phoned or crossed their path within a day or so of thinking about them. There are those too who have had the thought of someone and have gone to the phone only to discover when lifting the handset that the very person is on the line - Is it coincidence?

To help reinforce a belief in our latent abilities I've often had students carry out the experiment of instigating a contact with someone by simply visualising their image and keeping it in mind for a few seconds. Attention on the subject needs to move away from the person when reaching a level of knowing that they will be in touch. It doesn't take long for the magic to work, an outcome that has been beyond comprehension to more than a few!

Like all experiments of a similar nature, to get the best result it's important to remain objective. Another experiment is to have someone make you a cup of tea or some other trivial act by simply visualising the deed being carried out within your imagination. It is again surprising to many how quickly someone rises to the task without a word being said. It's a useful technique for implanting ideas that if verbalised would lead to objection, provided of course that any endeavour is prompted from within.

Often we volunteer our agreement to be influenced when watching or listening to advertisements or when aligning ourselves to the rules of a particular group. These examples demonstrate how the media can affect our thinking when entering into the 'field' of their established thoughtforms. From observations and after reviewing student's work, most people influence others automatically. The conditioning we're all subject to from birth is almost entirely due to the influence of various peer groups, e.g.: parents, teachers, creed, nationality, etc., reducing only when the individual develops objectivity. If this level of 'stillness' has been developed, people can more easily choose to act according to how they feel rather than be influenced by others.

I've often used archetypal images in a guided visualisation to help students, particularly those new to meditation, to have a deep and meaningful experience to help provide a level of motivation to continue with the practice of meditation

Responsibilities of revelation

A certain level of detachment is needed before 'seeing' can be relayed responsibly – thus the practitioner begins to wield the two edged sword of discrimination.

Indiscriminate 'seeing' may lead to recipients focussing too much attention upon the information given with a very real danger of reinforcing the negative images they may have had a hand in creating. In worst case scenarios, threatening thoughtforms, held at bay by the grace of God, may be tipped into form by the process of suggestion. Relaying everything that is 'seen' may sometimes bring about events that would otherwise have remained harmlessly suspended and eventually dissipated into the sands of time. Conversely, there are occasions when such 'seeing' works for the good by confronting the individual or group with their very worst fears, shocking them into embracing and dissipating such thoughtforms before they manifest into form – though it's difficult to prove the success of this action other than to the 'sensitive'.

The world wars are an example of thoughts of jealousy, hate, domination and the like precipitating into form, and from observations made of the storehouse of Astral thoughtforms there's still a need at this time in human development for an increasing number of world servers to neutralise the debilitating thoughtforms still in creation which would also allow the formative space to be filled with more life enhancing visions of perfection always attempting to stream down from above through such individuals.

When In a detached state of mind, consciousness is 'at one' with Soul consciousness and if attuned to, brings into awareness various aspects of humanities unfolding journey,

Fortune Telling

As explained in 'seeing' there's a form of divination that involves perceiving images 'floating' around the Astral Plane. These images are either the result of human thinking driven by emotion or archetypal images placed there to inspire humanity and draw it ever onwards towards perfection.

Fortune telling in its most positive aspect presents an opportunity for people to embrace and disperse the fears that are relayed to them, knowing that the removal of such fear no longer attracts it into their life. Practitioners could also give out descriptions of inspiring influences that encourage joy into a person's life.

On the negative side, should the fortune teller not be able to tune into the inspirational levels of the Astral Plane and instead only 'see' and go on to describe the more debilitating images that surround a person it could have a devastating effect by becoming a catalyst that brings any associated fear into their reality.

The choice to go to such people for advice is ours, but personally, if looking for comfort or security, I would seek out the seer of the higher planes of being – a being who is beneath our very own skin – our Soul!

> **Any forecast for the future beyond the present moment is transitory and subject to change. Only the ones that inspire and uplift, as part of the grand vision of perfection set up for mankind at the beginning of time, remain constant and unyielding - to become reality as soon as we begin to believe.**

Prophesy

Worldly forecasts or what are to me visions of perfection can be perceived at any time by anyone with a detached frame of mind, a forecast that provides awareness of what's 'on the horizon', i.e.: what is ordained and cannot be changed – a forthcoming reality waiting to be embraced and absorbed into our way of life.

Change naturally causes great anguish and upheaval when it lands on our doorstep unexpectedly, but the unexpected can be alleviated to a degree when developing this objective sensitivity. Tuning in and 'reading' the signs and symbols – some of which indicate coming changes that are well on the way to becoming manifest in form, provide the opportunity to prepare for and to meet with them gracefully.

It became obvious that I must have attracted just about every experience into in my life by the way that I thought, reasoning that most of these thoughts were the result of conditioned thinking in earlier life or indeed in past lives. Louise Hay, in her series of books, states that 'all disease begins and ends with the way we think' and that 'illness is treated by changing or modifying attitudes to life experience'. Statements like these are not easily accepted, especially by those who are locked into a perpetual spiral of suffering. In psychologist Gill Edwards' book 'Living Magically' (Edwards, 1991) she says much the same and presents easy to understand exercises that promote new attitudes with visualisations encouraged by both authors.

Concluding that I was the cause of any discord in my life was in direct conflict with an age-old belief in forecasting the future – How could the future be fixed and foreseeable if it's subject to the fluidity of my thoughts? I was left with the knowledge that all the 'hanging' thoughts of the Astral Plane are subject to change, and the only certain future we have is the one that is above this level but also able to use its substance to bring about change - hence the archetypal images referred to earlier, vision of 'perfection' presented to human consciousness which are constantly radiating from the source of all life. Being detached was the first requisite for seeing with clarity within the confusion of the Astral Plane but it took many more years before I could make sense of and begin to interpret the images that presented themselves to my consciousness. In recent years my consciousness has naturally and increasingly shifted its focus towards the source of the radiations and provides impressions of a collective vision that can only be added to, that these building blocks of paradise may suffer temporary delays caused by the growing pains of human consciousness but are so very far above and beyond our interference that the overall plan for humanity is bang on schedule!

Presently, such 'seeing' provides a vista of peace and harmony that is pushing its way into form through the disintegration of existing thought streams that have hitherto held them at bay since the humanity began to think creatively. Creativity that aligns with this incoming idealism is of course infinitely more successful.

The principles of oneness as applied to an individual's life now need to be applied universally if the expression of energy in all its forms is to be prevented from drying up. For example, finance institutions need to align with the laws of manifestation in much the same way as we do as individuals - currency should be used to provide needs and once determined should be released without fetters to 'allow' the need to be provided - it should never be stored unless that too becomes a need. Today, the world markets are in turmoil because those principles have been disregarded with institutions trying to hang onto and manipulate what funds, commodities and raw materials they have. To me our perfect future is assured and it's only a matter of time before the grasp of those who are holding onto old behaviour patterns are gently or forcibly released.

It should be born in mind that our universe is circumscribed by a set of laws that were set up to protect us from the chaos beyond .We apparently chose this earthly experience because we wanted to learn how to live within those laws and enjoy its benefits, to eventually graduate it's limitations to become at one with and help expand its grand scheme.

From the conclusions reached, when relating anything to do with prophecy I'm referring to the ability to foresee influences acting upon my life and others from two perspectives. One is of a future born from the womb of conditioned thinking and thus restricting and throwing into chaos the possibilities of what tomorrow may hold, the other is from an open ended point of view, predicting a future that can only ever be perfect.

I am of necessity forever taking snapshots of my life, assessing how much influence I've had in attracting day to day experience as compared to how much I've stood aside and allowed my Soul to take the lead. It has of course, become more economical to follow the Soul's lead in the matter - 'seeing' that it will eventually get its own way – no matter how long it takes, so I might as well give in now unless chaos has become more attractive!

As an aside, this process of letting go and effectively removing tinted glasses, provides an increasing opportunity to observe and understand 'other influences' acting upon life as a whole.

> I do try to pre-empt changes 'perceived' from 'above' by taking positive but sometimes uncomfortable steps into the new - I've realised that this, in the long term, is the easier route. The Bible's 'Prodigal Son' also realised this, as I'm sure everyone will eventually - to 'tow the line' and 'return home'.

A note on what the future holds?

Increasingly I've been asked to explain to students why they attract experiences regarded as burdens. From my perspective, having had to look deeply into such debilitating forces in my own life, the general cure for this malady is for the sufferer to embrace them with all the strength they can muster and if need be, to beckon help from above in any way they can. In many instances, the reason these experiences have become unbearable is due to the student/aspirant invoking change and not realising just how much 'work' is involved in the 'letting go process' once the changes come on stream! Many are advised to back off for a while, to stop invoking growth in this way, to step back, re-group and gain strength before advancing again. By embracing uncomfortable experiences when they arise, the emotional energy expended in attracting the experience is released into higher levels of being where it's dispersed/re-cycled. It loses its effect at this higher level where it is absorbed by the love we have generated and the vicious circle of cause and effect is broken or becomes less severe.

From my point of view, the Soul is now universally presenting itself to each and every one of us, stimulated by a general movement of people beginning to make tentative steps towards becoming 'whole' – to look within, a movement motivated by a need to know why life is appearing to become increasingly difficult to bear. Ever since purposely beginning the inner journey I've had the feeling that the 'Age of Aquarius' was stimulating this heightened sense of awareness to humanity whether it likes it or not. It's a feeling confirmed through working closely with so many people at the inner levels of being for so many years. This global influence it seems has brought to the surface debilitating psychological reactions and a consequential search for answers and also the cure!

It's a strange paradox of today's world that the healthiest of people are not immune from falling by the wayside from time to time. I would suggest the predominant cause is humanity's resistance to the ever-increasing demands to 'grow' at this time in our human existence. A demand stimulated by the Cosmic Clock bringing the winds of change as its great hands point towards the Aquarian Age. An Age that is empowering every thought passing through the global and individual mind – for good or ill, an age whose beckoning was precipitated by humanities collective consciousness yearning for change, for an end to the suffering during the long, long journey that it's made 'in time'. Individuals are giving up the struggle and letting go because they no longer have the wherewithal to keep up – we've had enough – but here again the magic formula is applied as the 'letting go' allows perfection to creep in and balance to be restored!

Help comes from within

I've no doubt at all that heightened awareness is forcing humanity into seeking a respite from stress that is more lasting than alcohol or drugs can ever provide – a stress that is compounded by many new and confusing concepts entering into human awareness at this time, all of which need to be assimilated before peace of mind can be attained.

After a while it becomes obvious to the 'awakened' that they are being led along a path of self discovery uniquely tailored to their level of development, providing knowledge and experience that is perfectly synchronised to need. This is the battlefront where the individual is increasingly challenged to let go of personal aims and ambitions in favour of allowing wisdom to flood the consciousness from all manner of sources.

It may be a teacher from this or any other plane of being, a book or an 'in your face' experience, in fact any source that satiates the approaching Soul could be taken as part of the teaching that guides our footsteps.

Whenever an aspiring student stands aside and opens themselves to the inner realms, knowledge in visionary form, percolates into consciousness according to the their ability to perceive and interpret such visions.

These elevated visions, when 'brought down' into this plane, triggered by the opening of the heart centre and passing into mundane consciousness also have an infinitely greater influence upon the world of form than any other medium - one day soon they will reach the tipping point within the global consciousness of humanity to transform our world into a heavenly paradise in the twinkling of an eye.

Palmistry, etc, etc.

Palmistry also claims to reveal what the future holds; interpreting the lines that score the palm to put together a scenario that in most cases does seem to come true. Similar results can be had from reading heads, (phrenology), feet, (reflexology), and eyes, (iridology), to name just a few; all rely upon the practitioner's ability to 'read' the patterns imprinted on the body in a multitude of ways.

Over the years I've realised that such imprints relate more about the way we are conditioned than about the future - that the way we think has etched our 'attractive' traits upon the sands of time – and onto our genetic makeup via the Astral Plane to indelibly display the signs for all to see as we grow into adulthood.

Yes, such readings are quite accurate when it comes to predicting a future we expect because that is always what we are tending to attract unless we resolve to change nomatter what the discomfort. In a similar way psychologists can also predict what sort of life we will most likely lead just by noting our present behaviour patterns.

There is another factor at work in predicting which influences the turning up of cards (tarot), the 'right' swing of the pendulum (dowsing), the 'correct' layout of the tealeaves, etc, etc., Earlier in the book it was described how an experiment was carried out with students new to meditation when having them replace expected outcomes with those they preferred - essentially it's an experiment in positive thinking which proved to me, after many more experiments of this nature, that it was fairly easy for anyone to change the nature of an expected outcome and that similar changes could and do take place when using various methods of prediction.

'Tuning' into an intermediary such as the upturned palm or an object belonging to the person does provide a useful 'way in' as a less intrusive method of getting to know someone at a deeper level. (Amongst other experiences I observed and practiced this skill which they call Psychometry for a period of three years with members of the Spiritualist Church in Liverpool mentioned earlier who just 'happened' to be around the corner from the hotel in which I was staying - another of those miracles that led to bosses sending me to a Contract that was virtually on the Church doorstep!) Again, and reinforcing earlier deductions, the only true forecast that should ever be given about anyone seeking to assuage their fears about the future is one that encourages the release of conditioning and advises the seeker to look within to find the pot of gold that waits.

It is possible to cut straight to the chase (and reading the palm could be used as a go between), by attuning directly to an individual's Soul. When doing this with the objective of helping a person to understand their present life path it's usually possible to connect via the Soul to their personal history; these records, left within the matrix of the Astral Plane are a sort of blueprint overseeing the formation of the physical body in the mother's womb. At conception the blueprint is used by our Angelic overseers to bring together the elements needed to create our new body - warts and all, including the telltale marks on our palm, head, feet, etc., that reflect the 'state of play' of our thinking at the end of our last sojourn into this physical world.

A 'Soul attunement' also provides insight to guide a response that could be anything from advising caution to encouraging the use of inherent traits should they have a positive influence within their life.

This pre-life blue print also attracts the right conditions and experiences to enable the development process to continue from where it's been left off in the previous life but with, by the grace of God, one or two tweaks to help us on the way - always bearing in mind that the whole point of life is for each and every one of us to succeed in graduating beyond these physical rounds as soon as possible!

Generally, if we are to read a palm it would be better to err towards advising the subject to embrace any guilt or fear they may harbour, to forgive themselves in order to let the past go, to undertake to the best of their ability any task that 'presents' itself in the sure knowing that such advice quickens the journey to a life that reflects the peace and harmony that everyone eventually seeks.

Chapter Sixteen - *Healing*

Letting go of old wounds

Many students to meditation are primed ready to make changes to their life long before arriving at my door and just need reassurance that they are walking the 'right path' before disappearing back into the night. Others linger for months and even years in some instances; they have called by to receive 'the priming' before gaining the wherewithal to change. In all cases I can say without doubt that it's a change in attitude that brings about the healing which acts upon the inner levels of being, with confirmation showing upon the outer levels later. This confirmation appears in many different ways – a change of appearance, new relationships or even a new career!

Most changes in attitude can be encouraged in mundane day to day interactions - sharing a pot of tea, giving someone a hug, placing a hand on a shoulder or expressing a few words of encouragement all definitely help in this endeavour. These simple acts are a healing balm 'when the time is right' and if acted out spontaneously have an uplifting and fulfilling effect on all involved. Most of us can be involved in this interactive healing process which only stalls if our behaviour is premeditated.

> **Everyone knows that one of the greatest healing balms is a smile - aggression melts away, barriers are lowered, hearts open in its presence!**

Being able to 'see' has provided much knowledge about the efficiency of particular practitioners and the methods used. Observing their work over the years the more effective healer appears to be the one who responds continuously to the attitudinal changes taking place in their patient, 'reading' the effect they are having as a session progresses and responding accordingly.

Watching successful healers at work it can be seen that the majority treat the cause of the patient's illness and not just the symptoms. In this approach they appear to be actively encouraging life giving energy through the Chakra's. They chat to patients about various ideas/concepts as they perform their art - most times responding to questions arising, questions that 'pop' into a patients mind as they relax under the healers influence.

'Connecting' with the patient seems to be the universal key to unlocking many of the psychological blockages that have brought discomfort to them – initially encouraging a patient to relax, attuning to them and responding spontaneously to whatever is perceived is definitely the prime route to greater success.

An example of this in which I became a 'guinea pig' for a Healer was at a 'Mind, Body, Spirit' weekend during which I was invited to have my feet massaged (reflexology); relaxing completely into the process I began to understand without effort the meaning behind every word of wisdom the practitioner spoke, and the banter that followed without doubt, encouraged the release of many patterns of behaviour festering deep within my psyche. Several progressive groups use massage and other forms of healing as a means of helping each other to bond and release 'pent up' emotion which may otherwise remain as a barrier.

In successful 'healings', healer and patient are brought together at exactly the right moment, (a process often referred to as 'synchronisation'[17]). These, not quite by chance meetings, are to me the overlighting Souls of the patient/practitioner colluding to ensure they cross each other's path. At these times the healer becomes a catalyst for a spontaneous healing as the patient is tipped dramatically into a completely new way of looking at life.

The experience of my tomorrows were always being attracted by the way I think, but as the 'baggage' hanging around in my subconscious cleared so too did my life settle down to become relatively balanced, with the flood of uncomfortable feelings reducing to a trickle. It could be said that the attractive power represented by the outer covering in fig (11) lowered as I embraced and dispersed repressed memories – the centre, a representation of my Soul, became less shrouded, moving more into my awareness as a consequence.

The physical body - the shroud that conseals the Soul

Rebirth!

Figure 11 - Drawing back the curtains

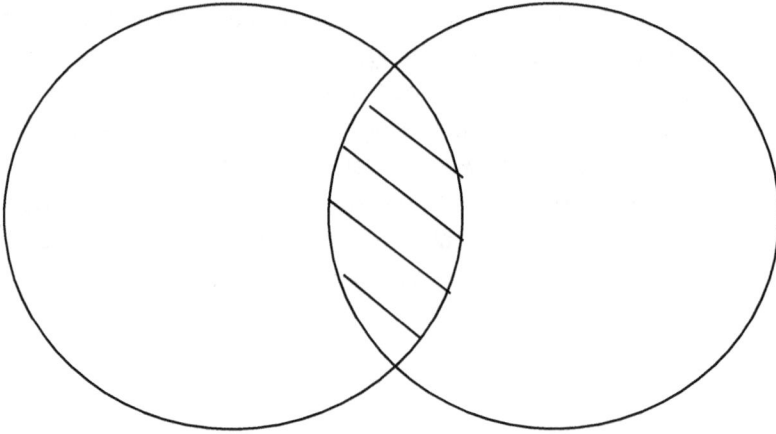

Figure 12 - Shared consciousness

In Fig12 the circles symbolise two people - the experiences they are compelled to share are represented by the shaded area. According to the law of 'Like Attracts Like' it's the proportion and intensity of this shared area, fixed before birth, which ties these two together. If the reason for this attraction is personality then the bond may last until such time as either one move into a detached frame of mind. Should it be unfinished business, their Souls may be seeking to resolve past differences in the present by playing out a bond 'at the right time' that is often referred to as Karma. Conversely, should a bond be needed to help develop either or both individuals, a similar tie, often symbolised by 'Cupid's Arrow', is formed.

Planetary pull - Habits are the death of me

Raising consciousness has had to become a habit to enable me to remain in a state of heightened awareness so that any risk of back sliding is less likely. It's turned out that meditation isn't a direct cure for all ills but is the vehicle by which illness is cured through an increased awareness of health debilitating reactions, their cause, and the means of embracing and dispersing the cause.

> **Becoming aware of debilitating memories as a means to embrace them became the first major milestone on the way to self healing – Remaining aware of the memory long enough to dissipate its effect was the next.**

In 'The Secret of the Golden Flower' Jung wrote:

'I always worked with the temperamental conviction that in the last analysis there are no insoluble problems, and experience has so far justified me in that I have often seen students who simply outgrew a problem which had destroyed others. This "outgrowing" revealed itself on further experience to be the raising of the level of consciousness. Some higher or wider interest arose on the person's horizon, and through this widening of his view, the insoluble problem lost its urgency. It was not solved logically on its own terms, but faded out in contrast to a new and stronger life-tendency. It was not repressed and made unconscious, but merely appeared in a different light, and so became different itself. What, on a lower level, had led to the wildest conflicts and to emotions full of panic, viewed from a higher level of the personality, now seemed like a storm in the valley seen from a high mountain top. This does not mean that the thunderstorm is robbed of its reality; it means that, instead of being in it, one is now above it.'

I've resolved to rise above and chip away at the segment drawn on Fig 13, for the rest of my life, hopefully accomplishing all that was intended as decided in conjunction with wise council prior to birth.

Initiation

Accomplishments in our development are said to be 'confirmed' upon the inner planes by a series of steps or initiations. Each time these occur in my own life seem to come after years of going it alone with a new set of ideas and concepts that take me far into unknown territory in so far as my personal life and endeavours are concerned. The initiation taking place once a particular these concepts have not only been learned but more importantly, absorbed into my life as part of behaviour. Often these initiations were said to be marked in the past by a mystical experience which the aspirant witnessed as an 'out of this world experience' – a step that seems to have become less dramatic these days as the average person is more open to change and tends to walk towards and through into the next level of development with no more than an understanding or realisation of the progress made.

Becoming detached has helped, enabling me to look more easily at every experience with an open mind, understanding and embracing new concepts to keep up to date with the Soul's development plan. This way of pre-empting 'life's lessons' has led to a closer alignment with the Soul and its needs, speeding up the overall process of development though I suspect this has made for a more demanding life if the stories of other like minded Souls are to be believed.

Self sacrifice for the sake of development

From deductions and having insight to draw from, it seems to me that many who suffer illness have 'chosen' to undertake the extra effort needed to accelerate personal advancement – 'getting out of the way' many lifetimes of struggle in a single lifetime perhaps? This insight provided the understanding that such people are equal to the more advanced of the race, that no one can be judged by outer appearances.

There are other influences too that act upon the whole race with respect to health and wellbeing - heavenly events throwing a proverbial spanner into the works to send everyone into a spin without there being any obvious cause - personal or otherwise. This I'm assured is the reason for many breakdowns in society as a whole and can affect the healthiest of people should they not keep up with the expansion of awareness expected as the physical plane moves relentlessly towards its goal of perfection – Could it be said that everyone 'in life' at this time in humanity's evolution has chosen to be here to help quicken our collective advancement?

A beneficial 'side effect' of expanding awareness was a marked increase in tolerance towards experiences that had previously been unbearable. The development of this non judgemental and accepting attitude was one that was seen as a weakness amongst many of my contemporaries and for many years kept any prospect of advancement at bay. This brought to the surface an inner battle between the beast of ambition that had been gnawing at my insides for many a year and a resolve to follow inner prompting that required me to be content with whatever life placed before me. Obviously it was a battle that was meant to be and provided the opportunity to overcome yet another obstacle on the 'path of return'.

Accident Blackspots - Banishing the gremlins

As mentioned earlier, I moved into an awareness of 'picking up' residual impressions everywhere, avoiding certain places and people, particularly when I began to 'scan' ahead and sense any foreboding atmosphere.

These days I'm better able to enter such arenas without my hair standing on end, embracing any 'at odds' energy with a wave of love that nothing can stand in the way of. From experience, radiating love helps to dissipate the effect the place has on others that pass that way. Love also expressed in this way to a person or group helps 'softens' any atmosphere - Would spiritualists and the like consider this to be a form of exorcism?

Dissipating my own 'blackspots' of subconscious memory was undertaken in much the same way - recalling every detail and embracing the past event and its debilitating effect to finally lay them to rest. These black spots were mostly 'locked into' another time and place, inaccessible until I'd developed consciousness to where I could traverse the planes of my psyche at will - to cross the landscape of the Astral Plane and to linger within its sticky essence without succumbing to any emotional content.

Being the plane of emotions, the Astral' held all my baggage in store - waiting for the day when I would return to negate the record. My experience in the years prior to that time of inner cleansing led me to believe that 'a journey' was imminent but I didn't have a clue as to what that would entail - my Soul did and was gently steering me towards building up a level of emotional objectivity through quiet reflection.

A personal revelation

Although taking many years to unpack some of the deeply buried 'baggage' within my subconscious, a routine became apparent from the start when I was summarily awakened after each dream excursion. This was to ensure the memory of the experience was not lost in the haze of 'normal' dreaming. Nearly always, when waking from these orchestrated sessions, I was awash with sweat and moaning loudly, causing much concern to my spouse! There's no wonder the Soul chose sleep to take me on these sojourns - If any hint of the trauma I'd experienced in sleep had entered a meditation I've no doubt the session would have ceased immediately with little or no progress being made.

These dreams occurred on average about twice a year for about ten years though with others I've talked to, there seems to be no set frequency. It all depends upon how much content there is to unfold and how well the mind copes with the fear, real or imagined, associated with the experience.

With regard to health and wellbeing dreams have served to consolidate my belief that life is about becoming aware of unresolved attitudes and taking responsibility for whatever is uncovered. In one experience, becoming aware of an attitude of attrition towards myself as a result of past behaviour helped me release it and move forward with greater confidence than ever before. I no longer needed to bow down to God because of feelings of fear and guilt. I had served my sentence and needed to take ownership of the present life and to let the past go.

Figure 13 pictorially represents the change that takes place as a result of embracing and releasing uncomfortable life experience – as the overlapping shadow attracting unwanted experience reduces there is a consequential movement towards true freedom and a more fulfilling life.

The subconscious shadow reducing

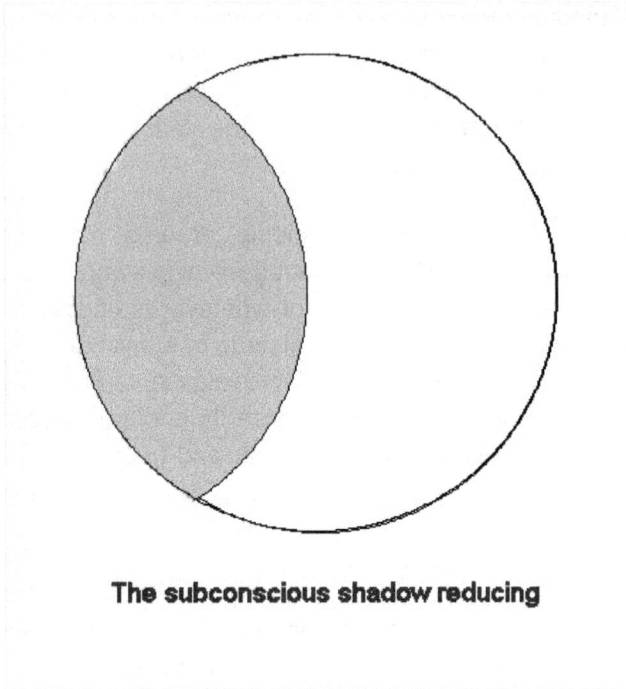

Figure 13 - The eclipse is over

Discrimination with love

Teaching and counselling for so many years has not only developed an ability to 'tune into' others but has also honed the skill of wielding the two edged sword of discrimination - to give out only that which is aligned with need, and this, as far as my understanding goes, can only be achieved by responding to inner prompting so aptly expressed in the cliché: 'if it feels right it is right'. I'm certain that an effective 'healer' will have developed discrimination to the same degree. I've observed many healers moderating the words that need to be spoken for fear of losing customers or because intuition goes against the grain of how they would normally carry out a 'healing'. In cases of doubt about the words to say I would always advise that love is the key – it opens the inner doorways and gives the healer permission to do nothing more than just to listen and respond to whatever they feel. A good bedside manner helps many in distress to 'take in' and absorb new concepts which begin the process of releasing lifetimes of conditioning.

It can never be repeated too often – it's essential that the healing process remains open to the flexibility of the 'moment', undertaken spontaneously, guided by inner prompting. It is necessary to be watchful against using previously successful techniques lest these override the needs of the patient and/or block out the essential guidance from within. The ability to be a clear channel determines my own effectiveness as a 'go-between' for healing to take place by providing the questions to ask and answers to give. When healing is given in this way the subject appears to respond more effectively which I can only put down to the healer /patient connection being 'Soul to Soul' with a powerful feeling of intent and purpose established as a consequence. This level of attunement obviously makes it easier for mentors and guides on the inner planes to communicate advice they may wish to give.

Observation has led me to conclude that the more successful of the techniques used in new age therapies are all engaged in easing the patient's consciousness into an expanded state of awareness. 'Healing' taking place as a result of an increased awareness and the simultaneous embrace of any reaction to that awareness.

Easing the way for change

Helping a person to raise awareness has become a well known factor of all successful healing sessions. In specifically designed meditations, students are encouraged to relax to the point of remembering and embracing all experiences that cause discomfort, with the aim of eventually dispersing associated symptoms. Recording and sharing the experience afterwards adds to its effectiveness, making the whole process one of the more successful forms of healing by encouraging the lowering of resistance to change.

Chapter Seventeen - *Perfection on the horizon*

Reflection on self brings healing

As before said, when in an expanded state of awareness it becomes possible to 'look at' (attune to) others and know how to respond. When this way of looking was initially used to 'read' students dreams and meditations it took days of contemplation and attunement before the essential message could be understood. Nowadays, after more than thirty years of dong this, an interpretation can generally be given to students whilst the account is being read – As many aspects of life, the more we exercise our inherent faculties the more efficient they become, a rule which seems to apply to spiritual development too.

There are many forms of life that can be attuned to and 'read', their discovery limited only by our lack of interest or perhaps by not wanting to because we have no belief in 'other worldly life' – the in-built ability to 'see' these other life forms remaining dormant until we do.

Being able to 'see' also leads on to becoming receptive to underlying visions that have apparently streamed forth from 'the source' since the beginning of time and which, in stages, urges humanity to return home to that source. It's an undercurrent to my life, and from what I sense is acting within everyone, that is constantly drawing us ever nearer to a state of perfection – with not a single person left out! One of the symptoms of this perpetual attraction is a feeling of discontent that everyone seems to experience from time to time. When perceived we either have a choice to align ourselves with these prevailing undercurrents or alternatively resist the changes that are 'meant to be' and suffer the discomfort of not doing so. Regularly communicating with like minded students and groups on the superhighway it's become easier these days to verify the latest instalment of 'the vision' that is presenting itself to human consciousness – are these the ultimate 'headlines from above'?

History teaches us that we are constantly evolving and that all we need do to confirm this is compare lifestyles of the past alongside the present - so where is life heading in the interim period - before we are absorbed into ecstasy?

The next instalment of 'the vision' for earth dwellers, 'heaven on earth', is already prompting its wishes through everyone and all we need do is listen, record, interpret and apply this inner prompting. In a divinely ordained way, the life we see and experience every day can only be created by human thinking and as we collectively open up to inner prompting and apply it to our life we also allow this vision to flow through our consciousness and increasingly manifest divine will into our reality.

By observation it can easily be seen how humanity is collectively attempting to move towards manifesting physical perfection which if the above is true must have already been, whether consciously or subconsciously, invoked and affirmed within human consciousness. Because this development is aligned to the grand vision it's a confirmation that we're moving in the right direction and progressively thinning the veil between heaven and earth; 'Knock and the door will open' it is said and we are knocking – big style!

This is perhaps the reason why there's an increasing need for healing – or more correctly – a need to release pent up emotions as the majority of us are being force grown to keep us up to date with the latest demands (and vision) for 'our time'. Those from above must have a weird sense of humour, for each time we catch up and seem to get our lives on track, along comes another boatload of change for us to deal with! In truth though, the enjoyment they feel, and often show, is from the changes we earth bound humans are making towards inviting in the dawn of the golden age much sooner and with less distress than was previously 'foreseen' from either side of the veil.

I can see the wisdom in humanity being held responsible for leading the way towards perfection, to invite back into existence through our collective effort, the fabled 'Garden of Eden', our true dwelling place. It's the only way we could learn the lessons of creativity, otherwise wouldn't God have frog marched us home like misbehaving children long ago?

Visions instigated at the beginning of time are at the head of the pecking order with respect to creativity, the only obstacle to this outcome being the thoughts of mankind watering the vision down or distorting it. Personally, many times since achieving 'alignment' with this flow of creation have I let my attention slip - resting on my laurels thinking that I've 'arrived' only to be knocked off the self made pedestal until gradually reinstating a 'connection' again. This 'see-saw' effect does serve to reinforce the attitude of being of service to life, to God, and helps to remove the stubborn stains of self-will. It also makes it easier to prostrate myself before the throne without absolutely anything getting in the way for 'no one can look at God and live'[18] - There are many interpretations to this statement but the only conclusion I can reach is that such death symbolically represents the standing aside of our mind, emotions and body. I haven't needed to turn my back on life to spend what I have left transfixed by religious icons but I have needed to respond increasingly to prompting from within to feel comfortable with myself.

Perfection is already here

I've discovered that, in sympathetic resonance to the latest instalment of the grand vision for mankind, my consciousness, along with everyone else's, can no longer ignore or thwart its influence upon our lives – we have it seems called the day forth when its empowering effect is magnifying our individual and creative abilities, good and bad, with the consequential effects acting out within our collective and individual lives. It's 'seen' from above that mankind is ready, that generally we won't destroy ourselves but will instead rise to the latest challenge, just as we are doing with the world wide action to reduce our carbon footprint, doing the right thing or at least trying to. God, just like any parent, does take into account our effort - even if it seems a little late. All that matters is that we eventually take responsibility as the 'prodigal son' did, and go home cap in hand, willing to do our bit – without any conditions attached!

My physical being deteriorates in proportion to how much I shut it off from the life giving energy streaming from above (or within). At birth, my conditioning, and consequently, my interference with the inflowing energy, was at its lowest level and therefore allowed my body to be at its most vital stage - I've had sixty odd years to increase the interference to this life-giving energy and its beginning to show! The major 'tug of war' within my consciousness rages between 'old age' conditioning and the ideology of the 'new age'. Which one will win the battle? - Only time will tell.

The prize of this battleground is of course heightened awareness and a 'quickened' body for whoever survives. Apparently the earth is having her vibratory rate increased too - the 'knock on' effect of humanity being prodded from above, expanding its collective awareness and causing the earth to awaken in tandem. We are all connected!

To my mind this quickening is confirmed by the increase in human development in every field of endeavour and not just in the scramble to be perfect, it's a measurable increase that always follows an expansion of awareness as sure as day follows night. The time scale for reaching the 'tipping point', where humanity enters into the more refined ethers of the New Age, is determined by a critical number achieving 'raised consciousness'. It has been said that 'no one knows the hour or the day' but what can be said from present evidence is that it's imminent – the curve measuring development against time has become almost vertical!

Each notch collectively or individually achieved in human development causes a corresponding quickening in the ethers as the universe responds to our call, placing on our shoulders yet another step up in responsibility towards the final goal of perfection.

Divine discontent is often attributed with being at odds with the general movement forward - deep feelings of needing to progress at a faster pace driving us ever onwards to expand our boundaries of experience even when our life appears to be fulfilled.

We all know that lights in our home don't come on unless we switch them on - and my being is no different. The life current needs to pass into it unobstructed if it's to remain healthy. I need to be 'switched on', receptive to life-giving energy for it to remain functional. I could if I wanted, limit and even stop the flow of energy to any part of my body - for example, if I lived in fear of overtaxing my heart and ceased to exercise regularly it wouldn't be long before my body was unable to function as well as it should – I would have effectively switched off the life giving energy to my limbs and would suffer the consequences – use it or lose it has to be the motto!

The obstacle of conditioning - Do it anyway

The challenge, as I get older, is to remain open to change and continuously flow with it. Without such a guiding thought or with a less determined one, that part of the body or my whole being would without doubt lose its vitality.

Because of childhood isolation I grew up with a severe lack of confidence when it came to taking part in conversations with peers or in public. The occasions when forced into doing so often drove me further 'underground' mainly because of people's reactions to my tongue tied efforts - at the age of twenty I still had difficulty speaking on the phone. Not until tuning into and aligning to inner prompting did this situation gradually change.

It's always been said that no one is ever given more than they are capable of overcoming and it was certainly true for me. I knew deep down my challenge in life was to somehow get beyond this barrier, to face the beast and embrace it – in this instance it was a very frightened animal! In perfect timing, meditation came along to strengthen my 'inner connection' and thereby my resolve which led to a confrontation with the fear, which was in this instance vulnerability. I began to deliberately step into situations that I'd previously avoided and to 'allow' myself to be vulnerable whenever I could. As my confidence increased so too were the experiences presented to test and strengthen it, including over thirty years of teaching!

> **So, what if I could attune perfectly to my Soul, open fully to the life giving energy streaming from the source - would I live forever?**

It would seem to me that the only obstacle to paradise on earth and longevity is the need for each of us to clear blockages to the flow of life giving energy streaming from deep within. If enough people do so it would not only bring perfection to these pioneers, but would also tip the scales and achieve perfection for the rest of humanity. Like a chain reaction, once the irresistible flow of change has begun, it will become an unstoppable wave with the veil between the planes disappearing in moments. I've often reflected on the words to be found in the 'Book of Revelations' were it refers to the 'the New Jerusalem descending from heaven' – does it relate to this moment in time, a time when the glorious vision for humanity is fulfilled?

New age therapies, old age cures

It has become easy to link people's attitudes to the diseased areas of their being in much the same way that Louise Hay (Hay L. L.), (well known in this field of knowledge), must have done. Becoming still and expanding awareness enhanced an ability I believe everyone has to notice the relationship between cause and effect acting out in their life. This ability appears to be the result of feedback to bodily senses, developed solely in my case because I believed it was possible and had the faith to persist until it became part of an ever-growing portfolio of a 'reality outside of conditioning'.

Our shadows block out the light

As mentioned in detail earlier, being able to categorise the various blocks to life-giving energy came about by 'reading' the shadow like patches hovering around those who are ill. After many more readings I'd developed an understanding of the relationship between the 'shadows' positioning and the related illness. In many instances the shadow appears long before an illness is apparent and in this way may serve as a warning to those with insight to make changes - In the stillness everyone becomes aware of the adjustments that need to be made for a healthier life but many haven't the strength or motivation to make them.

Perceiving in this way unfolds the whole picture of what has led to the malady along with the insight of how to respond. The 'shadow' acts like a communication conduit allowing me to tune into the very depths of the subject's whole-life story, relating it for them to remember and hopefully providing an opportunity for it to be embraced this time around, (this lifetime).

A major element of what students of meditation are encouraged to do is practice visualisations that recall, embrace, and release unresolved issues 'brought through' into the present life. What has proven to be interesting in this respect is how trivial most of these past experiences are when aired in today's world. No doubt in the age they occurred the person must have had a traumatic reaction to have automatically buried them so deeply within their subconscious. Some of these 'hangovers' may take several lifetimes to resolve and are far from trivial, both in cause and in the way the sub conscious memory affects them in the present day. An example of a repressed memory 'carried over' that is traumatic even when experienced in today's world was that of a mother who had no alternative but to watch her children starve to death. She had no means of providing food – herself dying of starvation shortly afterwards and taking with her the deeply entrenched feelings of guilt into future lives with all the attendant effects such guilt has on anyone. The main symptom suffered, the cause of which took years to uncover, was a lifetime of depression, with many attempts to end her life.

The cosmic clock is ticking

Placing people into environments to encourage self-reliance is one of many ways divine hands encourage development. It appears that we are all limited in various ways from the moment we are conceived to ensure that we achieve the goals set before us. Talents developed over many lifetimes temporarily suspended, with only the tip of the iceberg of abilities remaining to get us by until such time as we rise above all limiting factors and become 'at one' with the consciousness that is God – Is this the ultimate set up - but what about free will?

Just as we each attract a new life that reflects the way we think so too is each day presenting experiences reflecting the thoughts we have. As the cosmic clock moves humanity into the next astrological age, from personal observation, energy levels are intensifying the effect of all thoughts, conscious or subconscious and effectively pushing them into our reality. Energy and its free flow symbolise the water carrier of the Aquarian Age, and in timing with astrological events appears to be bringing change upon us on a global scale. I personally hold our American cousins responsible for this latest surge - whether right or wrong, those flower power people of the 60's, dancing for peace and love in the world were, from my point of view, a major catalyst that triggered this 'quickening'.

I've had to adopt a permanently flexible attitude to life because most pre-meditated plans change beyond recognition. Responding to moment by moment feelings and knowing that all will be well, works best for me. This new attitude also incorporated the shift in awareness from positive thinking, which only worked on occasions, towards the more open-ended concept of 'knowing needs would be met'. 'Living in the now' - allowing spontaneous events to unfold in tune with the whole of life – not just mine, have become the basis o f new mantras for me to repeat. I've no doubt that everyone will do the same sooner or later and as more volunteers 'join up' it is obvious to me that humanity will naturally move towards unity and peace as we collectively stop blocking the prime vision of perfection.

> **Of course this movement towards unity also brings us closer and eventually into constant attunement to others with all the associated benefits.**

From a personal perspective I've noted subtle differences in the vibrancy of my being as a result of moving towards 'oneness'. My journey has taken me through a series of experiences of varying intensity and duration tailored to take me by the hand, relatively unscathed, to the far side of the subconscious, into the summer-lands of being. It could not have been a pre-meditated route. It could only have been the result of choices made in alignment to inner prompting, each step guided by the unseen hand, which to me is the Soul and its unnumbered 'co-workers'. Temptations galore have presented themselves, and I've had to face each one with a measure of acceptance that such experience could only be before me because of the conditioned behaviour traits that attracted them.

Looking back, the simple act of listening and looking, and allowing energy to flood through a 'relaxed' body and a receptive psyche like never before has magnified every aspect of my behaviour, increasing self awareness at every level. Emotions of love, anger, jealousy, injustice, compassion, to name just a few, became larger than life, to confront and often overwhelm me. A major part of my 'training' has been the development of measured reactions to these enhanced reactions by giving full reign to some and none to others. It's become essential for me to experience every emotion in full measure, to feel the joy as well as the heart rending agonies.

It's been both a humbling and empowering experience, to realise my inadequacy at controlling life events and seeing how miracles are brought about by just surrendering to and expressing the higher qualities of being pouring through from my Soul. As a child, I couldn't express affection openly; After many 'uncomfortable' moments followed by much self-analysis and recrimination, I eventually learned to step back and respond to how I felt 'in the moment', to speak 'from the heart' – to at last experience the joy that a life is meant to be overflowing with.

The Kundalini?

Many books include instructions about how to raise the 'Kundalini'[19]; To me the main principle involved once a level of stillness is achieved, is that of attuning to and encouraging the vibrational rate of the body to be raised - the Kundalini energy moving up the spine in stages as successive levels of attainment are achieved. The trigger for this event on my journey within was that of listening intently to a barely perceptible sound emanating from deep within whilst at the same time generating an all encompassing feeling of love.

This heightened feeling of love must have been the alchemic ingredient that cleared the way for the latent energy of my being to arise. In eastern symbology, this rising energy is described as a coiled snake that is awakened and encouraged to flow through the body. This opening of the chakras is often described as mystical but to me seems more of a technical process, like clearing away the debris from a drainage channel to allow the water to flow. From what I understand the process of balancing the upper and lower chakras is shown symbolically in Fig's 14 & 15 as two triangles overlapping to form a star.

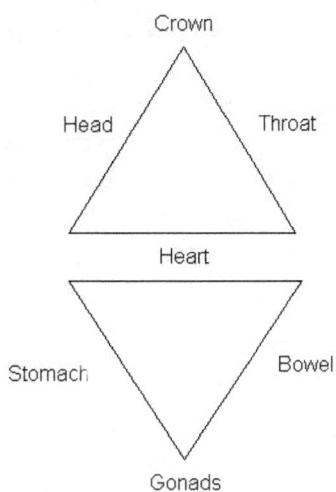

Crown

Head

Throat

Heart

Stomach

Bowel

Gonads

The upper and lower Chakra triads

Figure 14 - The Chakras

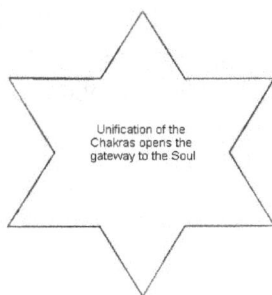

Unification of the
Chakras opens the
gateway to the Soul

Figure 15 - The Chakras unite

Awakening the 'snake', as the rising Kundalini energy is often referred to, is the goal of every aspirant but I would urge caution. The flood of empowering energy encouraged appears to intensify every behaviour trait including those that are negative far faster than would normally be the case. This often causes emotional and/or mental overload and leads, in some cases, to breakdown should a level of detachment not have been achieved. Such an alchemic awakening required that I had previously looked into and embraced every morsel of memory locked away in the subconscious to become free of potentially harmful reactions caused when becoming empowered in this way.

From firsthand experience of helping, and in some instances delaying many from reaching this gate of awakening, I would always recommend a gentle opening of the 'seals' to the subconscious, giving enough time for the 'inbuilt' Soul to lead the way one step at a time, apace with a person's ability to cope.

As an aspirant 'opens' through a feeling of self generated and all encompassing love, the upper and lower chakra triads, as symbolised in Fig 15, combine and the doorway to the inner sanctum opens deep in the heart – to become the star. This coincides with the Kundalini energy reaching the highest point of the body, the crown, to initiate illumination. This symbol also symbolises the mystical star of Bethlehem and the sign of the birth of the Christ child within.

Chapter Eighteen - *Manifestation*

Give to receive in abundance

From my teenage years I've continued to explore the workings of creativity, realising the potential of thought, especially when aligned to God's will with the result that throughout this book it is reiterated that tomorrow is a product of how we think today. Many people are aware of this phenomenon and make use of it by picturing in their minds eye /envisioning what they expect from life knowing that such thinking will attract it into this reality – but it does have certain limitations. Deliberately using thoughts to attract preferred experiences is to me an extension of positive thinking and can be used for any purpose which sometimes overlooks the needs of others.

I've come to realise that taking visualising to its next level and using it to focus on needs becomes a very powerful form of manifestation which also leads the meditator to become open to inspiration and guidance 'from above'. This new level opens up, if we remain receptive, to impress consciousness with powerful visions to guide our life from moment to moment should we have the volition. It is also at this level of development that aspirants are able to communicate 'across the many planes of being' should they be granted an awareness of the source of their attunement.

The Astral library

The electromagnetic storehouse of the Astral Plane is, as mentioned earlier, full of impressions left behind by creative minds from the far past to the present day. The pictures that can be perceived within the Astral are a conglomerate of human thoughts with individuals constantly adding to or diminishing them.

The thoughts that are ripe for harvest begin to radiate their good and not so good electronic blueprints onto the fabric of the Etheric Plane to begin the process of attracting the necessary elements to create the form.

I've concluded that the reaction time between a thought and its manifestation in form depends upon the intensity of the driving emotion and the success in letting go of any attachment we might have to the outcome. If the emotion behind the thought is fired with real and undoubted need and then allowed to be, the thought will quickly manifest into form. This process releases the thought or vision completely, to allow its transition across the planes of creativity. Those of strong faith do well at this juncture, they rely upon their God to manifest their needs and give it no further regard other than to have a grateful heart! – No wonder the Saints entered the gates of heaven long ago, never to return to the physical rounds!

Evolution or part of the grand plan?

In recent years humanity has become increasingly aware of how it is affecting the environment, but less known are the forces that originally created the environment long before the process of evolution even got started.

From what I've described so far is could be surmised that at the beginning of life on earth there must have been a vision in place that gradually attracted into manifestation the abundant fauna and flora that has evolved over time into what exists today - albeit the vision becoming distorted during these past few centuries by human consciousness.

At some point in history humanity must have evolved thought imagery to a level that began to interfere with this primal vision which was and is always attempting to hold life on Earth in perfect balance.

These evolving thoughts, effectively humanities collective consciousness, apparently began to build up thoughtforms upon the

Astral Plane which in turn manifested in less than perfect form. As ordained long ago to occur once we had developed our creative faculties, it seems that our individual and collective thoughtforms are to be allowed to take over the role of Earthly caretaker - after all, isn't humanity gifted with free will and the opportunity to train as a co-creators so why shouldn't we see the results of our endeavours – how else would we learn?

No need to worry though – we are apparently on schedule to realise our role and at the eleventh hour clean up any mess we have made and, even better than that, improve on the original model!

An interesting analogy of the process of manifestation is demonstrated at 'Mother Shipton's Cave', a tourist attraction at Knaresborough, Yorkshire. Various items such as soft toys are hung beneath a rocky recess dripping with water seeping through from the limestone strata above, the ground water having percolated through layers of rock, dissolving calcium on the way. This continuous soaking leads to the various items becoming incarcerated in stone after a year or two. The soft toy in this analogy represents the thoughtform and the calcium particles within the water the elements that are attracted to it to manifest the physical form.

Faith

Faith is no doubt the shortcut key to the inner realms of being and if driven by love opens the door instantly, though I'm sure those with such qualities passed through the sacred portals into heaven long ago - never to return!

Although my Soul has laid before me a series of experiences that would lead to that door I have, time and time again, turned away and disregarded the opportunity to enter until this life, and still I hesitated until becoming shocked into realising that heaven was closer to me than my breathe. It wasn't faith so much as being woken up to the fact that I'd been communicating with the heavenly realms since birth and had up to that time taken it for granted.

Those that seem to get away with it by flouting the laws of life are experiencing a short respite and sooner or later will need to replace every last stone they have dislodged but will in time join the ranks of the righteous – those that walk the right hand path. No one is ever judged either. It seems the objective of the principles that lie behind universal law is unity and in the fullness of time, it is said, each one of us will freely choose to prostrate ourselves before the throne, to rejoice in living a life of service and experience the joy of doing so.

It has been explained how prayer and affirmations can be used with real and lasting effect and will bring comfort to those who are in the throes of seemingly endless turmoil, (and I can give first hand testament to this.) Faiths around the world, and throughout time, have used any means to help bring about an early end to what is sometimes thought as the misery of life, which from my perspective is seen to be self-made if the law of attraction holds any significance. So here's to affirming 'peace on earth and goodwill towards all' – Amen!

It is by the grace of God that we are apparently saved from self-destruction when those above, who love and care for us, keep unwholesome thoughts generated by millions of human minds from discharging into form. Though there are exceptions, such thoughtforms are generally held back from manifesting their worst until such time as they are embraced and neutralised by the individual or group who created them.

Could it be true that Jesus saved humanity from further distress by embracing the thick atmosphere of the Astral Plane to effectively carry out a healing on a global scale?

Personal experience has taught me that I'm expected to do absolutely everything I can for myself, and having done that, can demand help and assistance from above. It's as though there is some cosmic agreement in place that responds to human dilemmas that we lowly humans cannot solve by sending in the 'A team. I've not been let down yet, though I've been pushed to the very limits of endurance – no doubt to strengthen my resolve to do better next time! It's obvious to me that everyone needs to become aware of their limitations and then move into an undoubted knowing that the whole universe is on hand to give support whenever we need to go beyond those limits.

Wouldn't it be a waste for the world to be destroyed for the sake of allowing a little more time for its prospective human caretakers to learn a better way?

Beyond the veil and into knowing

To promote personal growth I had to separate desire from need, an awareness that came after much heartache at watching those close to me suffer at my single minded attitude to life; an attitude focused on getting the things I wanted, an attitude that thankfully softened soon after beginning to meditate.

Students new to meditation are introduced to the difference between desire and need at an early stage and unless this is fully understood is seen to hold back development due to the continuing confusion filling many of their lives.

Increasingly, I began flow with life, to let it take me where I needed to go, finding that in the silence of meditation I could also observe my brain's activity and not be endlessly seeking to fulfil 'the next' project that attracted my attention.

Like any behaviour repeated regularly, 'stillness' has become a conditioned process as my brain now goes into 'silent mode' [20] whenever I have a few moments to myself.

It was becoming still that not only brought awareness of my needs, but also allowed them to flow, unimpeded by other thoughts that I would normally be having, to attract those needs into my life. This mindset further developed into one of consciously allowing my Soul to hold the reigns whenever prompted.

Most people exercise this wizardry to bring along their daily needs without realising it - In developed countries it's generally expected, without a moments doubt that food will be on the table and water will flow from the taps in our home. Further thought on the process reveals that such expectations are the result of decades of endeavour that automatically reward the believer with the needs of life. Eventually I reckon, everyone will realise there's no limit to the supply of anything we ever need - it's just our refusal to 'believe' this is possible and so continue to block the available levels of awareness that attract abundance!

Everyone needs an ideal environment to stimulate the 'return home' and most are surprised to learn that they were presented with that ideal at birth. The line between a need and a desire is very difficult to discern and realising that all the difficulties that life brings are 'meant to be' is often hard to accept. Confirmation of this is granted to anyone who returns in memory to the pre-life period when such decisions are made – and with our full blessing too! Before we are born the smallest detail is planned to ensure the best advantage is given to each and every one of us within the coming 'life period'. Meditation practice nurtured the stillness in which feelings were able to confirm this, helping me identify and follow the 'right path' whenever there was a choice to be made.

These feelings of rightness combined with a constant affirmation of 'knowing' needs were being met, kept and keep me up to date with whatever I need to experience - Remaining detached helps me to remain at a distance from unwanted responses and to refrain from interfering with this automatic process.

Visualisations fell far short of helping in the achievement of a sense of 'knowing' because there were too many distracting thoughts going through my mind, but once a measure of detachment had been attained such knowing became much easier to attain and proved to be more empowering, leading naturally towards the infinitely more successful way of manifesting needs which allowed visions to flow into my consciousness from deep within, from my Soul.

A benefit of detachment is the release of energy tied up in an age's long attempt to block out fear, guilt, etc., - an attempt that is futile in burying unsavoury experiences in the face of humanities relentless development. It is energy that is better employed in more creative pursuits but this distraction did serve a purpose – the tussle between the various factions of my being led to gaining mastery over the Astral Plane. If I hadn't won the internal battle I would have continued to be tied up in the Astrals illusionary influences and be denied the opportunity to perceive the untainted visions streaming through from the source.

Establishing an attitude of 'knowing needs were being met' has led me into a more fulfilling life because the source of the vision empowering those needs originates from the Soul. A source that always stood ready to press them upon me - even before birth. The Soul established my needs at the beginning of my existence by laying out a stream of perfect visions to attract the experiences I needed to stimulate the development necessary to find my way 'home', or at least to go another mile in the right direction.

As part of allowing the Soul to take the lead and to help reinforce the flow of abundance into my life I began giving thanks, not just for what I received, but also for what I needed – this helped to affirm an undoubted belief in the outcome. Thankfulness completes the circuit of manifestation, very similar to an electrical current travelling along a wire not being evident until the switch is thrown to allow it to bring to life some form of apparatus. The current had always been there, I just didn't believe it - once I'd stepped aside, the energy to manifest form was able to flow unimpeded.

> **Our thoughts today attract the experiences of tomorrow – As we become detached, our tomorrows tend towards being filled with what we need!**

The results of frequent meditation sessions had established increasing periods of calm within my life making it all the more apparent when disharmony erupted. It's this contrast of emotions that provided me, and probably every other student of meditation, with the opportunity to become acutely aware of the causes behind all reactions to experience. With this awareness I began to notice that periods of upheaval followed quickly on the heels of an emotional low – an obvious statement to make now, but it took a long time for such awareness to sink in.

Having the advantage of being able to pass much of the wisdom that drives the need to meditate onto students has drawn me deeper into the subject than would otherwise have been the case. This was aided greatly by having to review and update teaching notes continually. Similarly, working as a construction manager I've become acutely aware of how the thought processes of co-workers and students alike affect the work they produce.

The construction industry is an ideal medium for an analogy to be made. Nowadays most average sized buildings are constructed within a six month period and need managers who are able to perceive and envision the intentions of the design team, (or from my personal perspective, the needs of the Soul group). The client, architect, engineer, the contractors and each and every operative have images within their consciousness, both individually and collectively, that will ultimately influence the outcome of the proposed structure; even the local population can be influential. With most enterprises the visualisation process is well under way before construction begins, having been conceptualised, funded and plans produced well before commencement of work on site. After all these years of observation, it is to me very apparent when the vision for a project is substandard. When a project falters the culprit is almost always a flaw in the collective vision for the project. More often than not these days, the shortage of design funding has led to many projects being awarded to contractors with just a brief outline of the requirements, which places more responsibility on the contractor's shoulder to complete the vision. From out of this experience and spurred on by the principles underlying the need to meditate I'm a true convert to the idea of developing vision/mission statements well before construction gets underway by encouraging all those involved to attune to the needs streaming through from within.

Prior to experiencing the benefits that meditation brings, visualisation along with positive thinking played a major role in attracting all the things I desired, culminating in my twenties with the idea of making loads of money through the buying, extending and selling of property. Pursuing this dream it wasn't long before my life entered into its chaotic phase with the bank manager chasing me because I'd underestimated the cost of a building project I'd hoped would fulfil my dream. Initially it was exciting but I didn't take into account the effect it would have on my young family by forcing constant upheaval on them. Fortunately I had the sense to realise that I was putting in jeopardy the loving atmosphere that had been created in the first three years of our marriage and turned away from personal desires to those that fitted in with the whole family.

Positive thinking tempered by the needs of others

The visions I hold today begin as intuitive insights drawn from what I've grown to understand as being a collective thought of all those involved in its outworking – above and below; a perceived vision, channelled through the unlimited resource of my Soul, attainable only when consciousness is 'raised' – it's a process referred to above as 'envisioning'.

Raised consciousness is accessible only when deliberately standing aside from the self – akin to being like a trusting child along with the discriminating faculties of a grownup.

For many years I thought it impossible to progress further without ridding myself of stubborn behaviour traits. Being reborn seemed to be the only way to wipe my slate clean to return once more into the fold of life without the accompanying conditioning that is so difficult to let go of. I've since learned that such a route in no way negates the responsibility to deal with 'outstanding matters'. No magic is available to erase lifetimes of kneejerk behaviour - Only self-determination and the helping hand from those above to help clear the backlog, and only then when I had raised my head into the light to help myself.

Whether it's the result of attuning to the 'inner self' that the outer life is seeming to appear more chaotic by comparison, or whether the outer life is actually becoming more chaotic, the consequence is that it's reinforcing the contact I have with my Soul and is leading to insights / visions becoming clearer and easier to understand.

Detachment is a dynamic state of being that goes beyond positive thinking into a 'knowing' consciousness, beyond being reactive to the environment, to becoming its observer. This 'knowledge' does not belong to one race or creed but is universal and available to all, with people in the West adopting eastern philosophy more than ever before. My own journey within was kick started after a brief encounter with a teacher of 'Yoga' – a practice that's been around in the middle and far East for thousands of years.

Apart from the feelings of euphoria experienced when entering the 'void', the transition from a sensitive and positive person towards a detached state of being happened gradually and almost without notice - Only on reflection did the realisation dawn that I was no longer at the mercy of life's ups and downs. Meditation had introduced and strengthened a 'state of knowing' through the replacement of old attitudes with new ones that were unconditioned.

In the more advanced Meditation sessions, even the most compatible of groups formed from like-minded students eager to share and work together find it difficult to open up to the depth required without feeling vulnerable. I've put this down to the automatic surge in energy that moves through each meditators being as soon as they attune together – the Soul to Soul communion that is effectively invoked in this process appears to magnify every emotion.

The only ally I have is the certain knowledge that we're all in the same boat and everyone I've ever met is seeking the same sense of unity to satiate feelings of separation - to replace them with joy which the practice of mediation provides.

Encouraging students to move into an attitude of 'knowing that all needs will be met' helps them let go of the final barriers to unification - they had after all spent two years learning about how to do this but it requires an enormous leap in faith to achieve the last few furlongs.

Attunement to knowledge

When attuning to various sources of inspiration, I'm often limited to just looking, with an understanding of what I am seeing unfolding over the following day or so. It's the same when attempting to understand the essential message recorded by students – each student has a unique development path stretching from the beginning of time up to the present day with the result that the same meditation experience is described in a multitude of different ways. It is through seeking to understand the essential message they contain that I've been led into developing Soul to Soul communion.

All human life has at its heart a Soul through which a communication link can be made with other Soul or group Soul, provided that we first raise out consciousness up to its lofty heights. Love is the key to this communion and feeling is its language – feelings that may be translated into symbology, visions or words by our carnal brain according to its conditioning with regard to such contact. These contacts may also be made with Souls that have progressed well beyond the human rounds, to inner guides and masters whenever we are open to receive their guidance.

When making a connection to life forms that dwell within the bounds of the Elemental Realm, it's absolutely necessary to attune to and look through the eyes of our Soul as the 'go between'.

> **A strange affliction seems to take over everyone who looks within – the unity found encourages empathy towards the whole of life in all its many forms!**

Moving into a state of detachment included loosening the hold I had on personal likes and dislikes. Instead of judging others I began stepping back and relating to strangers as equally as friends whilst all the time moving towards a better understanding of the meaning of 'oneness'.

The more open and in love with life I became the more I gained access into its inner workings. It unfolded an understanding of how people can seemingly 'pluck' knowledge out of the air, or intuitively 'know' certain things without any more effort than that of 'connecting' with the object in mind. Working with the flow of this understanding it became obvious to me that such people were, as described earlier, 'tuning in'.

Group attunement seems to follow exactly the same principles but is infinitely more empowering. I think it can be assumed that family groups usually have no difficulty in attuning together where empathy exists between them – to me the result of many experiences worked through. Mothers have no alternative but to attune to the child developing within their womb – fathers too, if the relationship is close. Being in love with someone allows the individual unlimited access to 'know' those who they love – provided of course that they enter the 'silence' to perceive that knowledge.

A working group immerses every member within its collective soup to various degrees according to how open they are to each other. It takes literally years to encourage some students to lower self made barriers, with others always remaining an arm's length away. Often people feel vulnerable when others move into their 'space' and encouragement to work 'as one' needs to be done gently and carefully, apace with individual development. Just like enticing a timid animal to feed from our hand - only when they fully trust us will they risk all to move closer. This group process is often referred to as 'synergy'.

From observation, we determine our physical reality by constantly casting images into the ethers, but as we move into the 'stillness', an ever present vision of perfection takes over our lives, restoring balance and presenting the experiences we need – Imagine how effective a group can be if they all regularly attune together and respond to whatever prompting that arises.

Being in the stillness also allows anyone to share consciousness with those who have gone before, those who have achieved all they could at this level and have long since moved on to join the ranks of mentors upon the inner planes of being. Through a feeling of empathy we are allowed to make their experience our own, to share the wisdom they acquired long ago. We needn't suffer like they did and are given insight into the consequences of our actions when we become open to their prompting via the collective consciousness of the Soul.

Divinity offers an unlimited resource for those with an open heart through the process of 'melding'; I've placed much of my self-inflicted suffering into this Divine embrace to unload the burdens that conditioning insisted I carry.

Prejudice has never been a factor on the inner levels of being and whoever regularly enters this sacred space realises that differences just don't matter - the feelings of completeness and belonging crowd out every morsel of triviality.

Intuition informs me that as more people develop these same non judgemental attitudes it's 'effect' will help dissolve the barriers that ring fence the Astral Plane to become another factor helping to release the debilitating thoughtforms trapped there and their hold upon our physical existence – peace on Earth will ensue one way or another!

These *brief* Earthly rounds

My ever present task is to continue chipping away at conditioning to allow this physical body of mine to express the perfection that was envisioned at the beginning of time for all to eventually achieve – to let go and let the Soul guide my thinking! - 'I shall remain open to all possibilities at all times' has to be the mantra.

'Why are children taken from us'; a question that crops up regularly when discussing certain aspects of life.

With regard to those who have lost loved ones prematurely, who cannot accept that earthly existence is just an illusion, a simple explanation is that we never die, we only think we do – from where I stand we go for a period of rest and reflection after each life before moving onwards or back into this physical plane for another round. Our Soul pre-setting the milestones to be reached in any particular life and when achieved sometimes triggering a return to the greater life. Those who don't need to return have more noble work to undertake at the higher levels of being.

When we truly accept that that everyone is the same age, when it's realised too that our guiding Soul has chosen the Earth experience which has taken aeons to unfold, and when eyes are truly open to see the bigger picture, then, and only then, will it be realised that personal growth and development is all that matters! If our Soul chooses to vacate these experiential shells early because it's fulfilled this particular life's purpose then it will, despite our protestations. It is of course heart rending to lose someone close, but as the grieving becomes less devastating it may be comforting to know that the path our loved one chose provides the shortest route to the end of their development cycle. It will also be comforting to know that love is never diminished but only ever strengthened.

There are many 'grand reunions' within the heavenly realms, a time of great rejoicing when loved ones meet again to share their life stories, of the achievements made within the certain realisation that no one ever dies but keeps returning to this earthly school until all lessons are learned before graduating into the greater glory.

Life is one big 'set up' – and we chose it!

Born a 'blue baby,' a complete blood transfusion was needed which saved my life but removed any immunity I had in the process and making it a struggle to survive. Retaining an overlighting awareness of the reason for this struggle did nothing to relieve my young mind from the psychological consequences of facing near death experiences not once, but several times – a mix designed to confront me over and over with what is the ultimate fear of anyone's life – that of losing it!

On the one hand I had an awareness of the heavenly planes which provided consolation whenever I 'looked' its way and on the other hand a heightened fear of death as my bodily senses and primal drives to survive were challenged - a paradox indeed! This fight for life began at birth and continued for six months as I fought off multiple infections from the near isolation of a steam tent. This was the first phase of a 'planned' psychological set up that came to an end as my immune system kicked in!

From observing the life conditions and associated 'growth' of scores of students there appears to be any number of combinations to provide the right 'set up' for the life to be, designed to give an outcome to perfectly match the needs of each and every one of us. Much heartache would be alleviated if only the answers where sought within.

The paradox of being aware of both sides of the imagined battlefront has for the whole of my life hindered any thoughts of feeling sorry for myself - though I've felt frustration at not being able to blame someone!

Chapter Nineteen - *Soul to Soul connectedness*

Group consciousness

'New Age' author David Spangler wrote: 'Group consciousness is a sensibility born of the simple act of accessibility, the willingness to be there for another and to trust one's inner self into the hands of another' (Spangler).

> **As a part of my ever developing awareness it unfolded that I was already included in a group consciousness – we all are it seems. – Is this collective consciousness God?**

Experience led to my learning how much more creative a group can be in comparison to an individual – perhaps more so than the reader might think as from my perspective and what is confirmed by the outworking of Universal Law, the creative effect of two people working in tune with each other is much greater than both working independently. Perhaps the reason why a collective vision or Mission Statement is so effective when the whole organisation attunes to it.

When working in groups, each contributor tends towards self forgetfulness in favour of the group need with a consequentially raised consciousness gaining access to the much magnified energies of the higher planes of being to feed into the groups creative endeavours.

This self forgetful state of mind allows a merging of consciousness to take place into what is generally termed the collective consciousness[21]. To me this is another way for a person to become detached with all the advantages it provides. Being part of the 'Group Soul', as I've come to know it, increases output markedly when each of its workers 'fit into' a role that flows in perfect attunement to the organisation's needs because they have effectively become 'connected'.

The Increased potential of working together

The principles involved in group working have been adopted and developed by several organisations. The Findhorn Foundation includes these principles in every aspect of life within their community, an organisation I've worked closely with for over 35 years. At Findhorn, before any activity commences the participants gather for a few moments of quiet reflection to attune to each other with the objective of 'envisioning' the task in hand which is usually related by the 'focaliser'. The perceived vision is to me the main ingredient which encourages a successful outcome of the intended work and which is often part of the much broader and all encompassing vision that appears to be leading the whole community forward if my observations are correct.

Again, synchronised perfectly with ongoing development and an opportunity to further confront my reticence at entering the public arena, I was invited to facilitate ad hoc groups and representatives of organisations with the objective of encouraging the formation of their own group vision and subsequently a corresponding Mission Statement. This wasn't the intention when beginning this new venture. All I had in mind was to be of assistance in helping groups to work together - to help them clarify their needs.

Mission statements can be seen at the entrance to many high street shops and in the reception areas of many companies wishing to present what they perceive as their organisation's vision. Increasingly, many such organisations realise that such focused intent leads to increased prosperity, especially if everyone in the organisation is involved in its creation. If the company is large then representatives from each department should be encouraged to present their thoughts and ideas for the organisations future with the aim of reaching a consensus on the broad statements that can eventually be made with regard to an emerging or updated vision. The 'picturing' which takes place within everyone's mind during this process helps build a powerful thoughtform within the Astral Plane, and is especially effective if accompanied by emotive feelings, (the witch doctors of old must have had some idea this was a necessary ingredient). Emotions are the driving force of manifestation.

One example of this was when asked to help 'solve' issues concerning the future of a rambling manor farm. The occupying group needed to raise funds to purchase the property or face eviction. A group of several hundred, they had used the farm rent-free for several years and because of 'cut backs' the local authority needed to sell the property.

Up to my arrival they had failed to organise the group into one whole. Ideas had been floating around between various members of the group without reaching any decision about how to raise funds to buy the place. It became obvious when getting involved that the feelings of panic amongst the group were much enhanced by the large sums of money involved and the little time they had left to raise it!

Having as many of the group as possible meet in the largest room in the building, the first question asked following an attunement and a brief statement of need was whether they wanted the organisation to continue or not.

As the focaliser my task was both to ask the questions and record the answers, and to eventually work towards presenting a single statement for the whole group to agree on. It was relatively straightforward process achieved in less than an hour - they voted unanimously to remain in residence and had overwhelming enthusiasm for raising the necessary funds, with each person present stating clearly the part they would play. The agreed statement became the Mission Statement and helped to fix the vision into everyone's mind. - Within two months the funds had been raised – just one day before the deadline!

Once agreement is reached in this way there forms a tangible and irresistible flow of energy to attract whatever is needed which in this example, carried everyone forward on the crest of a wave – and with joy too!

> **Encouraging the fixing of a vision within the 'group mind' is one of the main outcomes of the work I've been guided to develop and apply over the years as one of an increasing number of individuals and groups from all walks of life doing the same.**

The potential results of such sessions is infinitely more dynamic and more lasting than many board room motions I've been involved with insofar as each individual is given equal status, with usually a unanimous 'for' when actions are eventually voted on. Decisions made during attunement sessions usually bring total agreement on every decision made as a powerful flow of insight through the group's collective consciousness is facilitated.

Insights and visions related to a group in this way are the foundation stone of any Mission Statement. Feedback of individual experiences after any attunement helps clarify the group's vision providing the empowerment to bring the need into actuality with little delay.

Consolidating my conclusions over the years, having observed, worked with and commanded construction teams for over forty years, I've noted that where the majority of co-workers align to a common vision or goal the outcomes are as good as they could be - but where a mood of discontent exists every aspect of the construction process becomes like a sluggish mill wheel that is difficult to turn, leading to many delays, obstructions and even poor weather conditions!

It became obvious to me that successful Mission Statements are those that have included everyone within the organisation in its production. It appeared to be the only way to ensure the emergence of a collective vision and leaves little room for dissention - How could anyone go against a vision they have been instrumental in creating? 'Third year' college students were encouraged to identify, research and present major studies on how organisations have not only applied the principles involved in creating Mission Statements but have gone on to use group consciousness in its day to day running. The concept of 'Partnering' uses these same principles in its outworking and is being applied increasingly within industry, proving time and time again that it helps to increase productivity and profit margins for the producer and reduced costs for the customer.

Having worked on 'Partnering' projects on a daily basis for many years has allowed me to observe the principles of group consciousness in action – or the lack of them! I've always ensured that the fundamental principle Partnering – to give both contractor and client an opportunity to express their ideas, has included everyone involved into the creative process. This method is to me an alternative form of attuning to the topic in hand without the sometimes objectionable holding of hands or the even stranger practice to some of closing the eyes and becoming still! Even though these more intimate acts achieve quicker and more lasting results I've realised it's more important to reach consensus and keep the group together rather than put people off the idea because they feel vulnerable.

Collective creativity – Knowing

Developing collective mission statements moves on from positive thinking inasmuch as students are encouraged towards losing any attachment to personal outcomes by becoming fully involving in the group process.

With any group, great strides in development are made when individuals tune into a collective vision. With a religious group; an 'attuned' prayer session with many people involved has the potential to be infinitely more effective than just one person praying. Group attunement will lead an organisation from strength to strength, particularly if a skilled facilitator keeps pre-meditation discussions focused upon the collective goal and free of individual scenarios.

Angels

Perhaps a strange concept for the uninitiated to grasp an established group will tend to 'attract' into existence an overlighting Angel depending upon the group's vision and its ongoing intentions. The 'Findhorn Angel' the Findhorn Foundations very own overlighting presence came into being in this way and is felt, and often seen, by every sensitive who visits or stays there. A similar manifestation overlight's our own meditation group most times we meet – I have no doubt that it's the result of literally hundreds of individuals over the years meeting together in the same place whilst maintaining the vision of 'service'. It is an overlighting being that may act as a group channel into other realms should the need arise.

Whenever any group meets regularly with clear intentions or a prevailing vision, it attracts elementals to create that vision in its appropriate physical, emotional or mental form or a combination of all three. Over time these nature beings become semi permanent and perpetuate the vision for as long as its creators continue to nurture it – and for a while afterwards too. If such a vision continues to be added to by an ever increasing number of individuals and/or groups, the number and force of elementals sustaining the vision attracts into existence an overlighting and independent intelligence, a sort of commander in chief which holds the vision 'in perpetuality' unless dispersed. This 'Deva' as it is generally referred to, oversees the work of its elemental workers but may in time have an overseer itself attracted into being whenever the vision aligns with Divine intent.

Every hospital I have ever visited has such a being overlighting the 'healing work' that its many human hands are engaged in. Places of worship and even some schools have attracted into activity these entities who without doubt ensure that the vision 'held' by the group successfully unfolds. Observing this process over the years has led me to understand that the whole of 'creation' must have been brought into existence in a similar way by an unimaginable collective of ascended beings creating 'the vision' in which just a small part is guiding humanity towards its eventual self motivated ascension.

My personal understanding is that a host of angelic beings, of various grades, were brought into being and are maintained through the work of creative minds that are aligned to the Will of God – a Will that is to me a collection of universal laws or principles that hold our cosmos in a state of perfection.

What was and is today equally fascinating to me is the way in which we seem to be constantly led into a close relationship or co-operation with the nature kingdom - perhaps more so than we think. It was years before I realised that as a child, whenever I'd pottered about in the garden I'd been responding to the life force of the plants that I had responsibility for. Most gardeners I know seem to do the same, though the language they use, describing themselves as 'green fingered' rarely gives acknowledgement to the fact.

I'm never satisfied with accepting what I've been told or have read until it's lain for some time within the reasoning faculties of my mind, there to be mulled over until confirmed by many other events, synchronisations and much head banging and it was the same with regard to the nature kingdom, – it took about twenty years to reach a level of understanding of how I communicated with these beings, the various levels at which they operated at and how they relate to one another. All that I had read and had been told sat like a heavy meal that was digested only after absorbing every scrap into my portfolio of understanding.

Not being a stranger to the world of crystals, (Geology was included as part of my college education and led to me becoming an avid collector of crystals and fossils), I jumped at the chance to take part in an attunement session to perceive the healing qualities which various types of crystals 'held'. With an assortment of crystals arrayed around a meditation room, almost immediately after the group entered into the 'stillness' I felt the presence of a very powerful being who I knew without doubt to be an Angel with responsibility for the mineral kingdom - a being with infinitely more 'power' than I'd ever felt before. At the point where the 'guided' aspect of the meditation ceased, leaving us in the stillness for a few moments to 'look into' the nature of each crystal, I hitched a ride with the Angel's consciousness and was taken on a wondrous journey of exploration. It was a journey that not only revealed each crystal's quality but also how each acted in unison to keep our physical bodies healthy. The outcome of this session became one of many that helped clarify just how the kingdom of nature knitted itself into this world and how the Earth can be the greatest healer of all, if we know how to attune to its vast array of life promoting energies radiating through its body …. and ours!

Restoration of planet Earth

Maybe it's the fear of 'Global Warming' that's stimulating change but whatever the reason, from my perspective humanity is beginning to take responsibility for the Earth, learning to work with nature and as a consequence allowing its life giving energy to flow again which will in time restore balance.

Apparently there's an astrological clock ticking away, a clock whose hands are moving around a Cosmic Zodiac of twelve signs, or arcs of time, each sign having an influence over humanity lasting approximately two thousand years. There's a level of development to be attained before the solar system completes its journey through the influence of any particular sign, with the heat coming on as the next sign begins to make new demands upon individual and collective development. Those not raising awareness to meet the new requirements are becoming increasingly at odds with life, especially now, as the Age of Aquarius is upon us.

The higher frequencies of the Aquarian Age is confronting stragglers with choices to make – Do they let go and join the merry throng or hang back and continue to exist in their own world, becoming increasingly isolated from life? Not that anyone has a choice - if anyone continues to shield themselves from its growth promoting influence they will fall by the wayside, to be returned further along the arc of time to continue their journey or be relegated to have another go within a different time loop. To avoid this, as life 'speeds up', it's essential we become aware of the process involved in 'growing', to become attuned to the will of our Soul and increasingly choose to allow ourselves to be directed from within – to 'let go and let God' - to listen to and respond to inner prompting and allow life to show us the way.

No one should ever feel unworthy of moving forward; perhaps thinking that there's too much ground to catch up on. We are all in the same boat and no matter how long we delay the day before aligning with our Soul it will still be waiting to take us onto the next stage of our journey. The moment we do try to make an inner connection, a host of beings will be at our side to 'lift us' out of the mire and lead us along a path that meets with our ability to 'grow'. Two people, living and working in the same surroundings may be separated by lifetimes of experience but find themselves drawn into an environment to work together for the purpose of stimulating further development. One may be stretching their capacity to cope with the experience and will need to remain with it for a lifetime. The other may be taking great steps forward, increasingly calling into consciousness their previously gained abilities to aid the assimilation of new experiences and moving on after a brief visit at an ever increasing pace.

The most important lesson I needed to learn this time around was to let go and allow my Soul to take the lead, with my childhood providing the ideal conditions to do this – though I didn't think so at the time. In the heady days of early life I consulted no one. I acted in a totally independent way whenever I could – After all I'd left home at the age of fourteen, lived in digs for three years and followed it up with nearly three years at sea, what else could people expect? In hindsight it seems that I was being prepared for the revelations that were to follow hot on the tail of youth and I needed to have the strength to 'watch' as the pressures of life increased. Life's 'training' eventually led me to perceive a better way forward and instead of wallowing began to deliberately let go of everything I'd put between me and the Soul. Living in poverty wasn't necessary but I did need to allow divinity to act through me. It took about twelve years before developing the 'right attitude' to pass through this phase - I have no greater security these days but I do have an inner connectedness that nothing can rend.

To my mind I've always thought the first paradox of life was created when we choose to 'eat the apple' – when beginning to do things our own way - I see this act as effectively shutting out the incoming energy of perfection which up until that time maintained our life in perfect balance. Like everyone, I chose to put layer upon layer of conditioning in the way which progressively blocked out who I really am and in so doing obscured what was being handed to me on a plate – I chose to do other things instead, which appeared to be more 'interesting' but which were out of balance with life.

This life is just the tip of the iceberg

Taking an holistic view, the students who have 'awakened' to their full potential and align to inner prompting have also begun to display a multitude of previously attained gifts that have lain dormant waiting for the moment when they 'opened the door' to their 'greater life'. It seems that we all have portfolios brimming with abilities attained during our 'travels through time' but none can be accessed until self-made barriers are lowered or removed altogether.

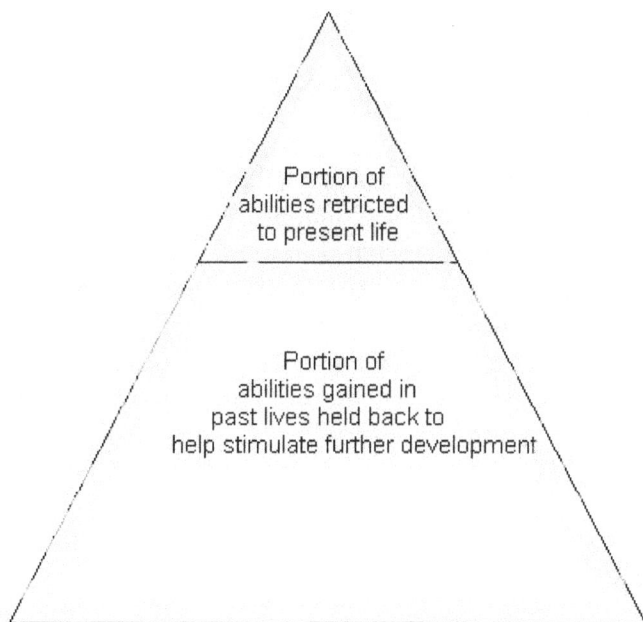

Figure 16 - The tip of the iceberg

Fig 16 indicates the proportional difference between the abilities we are aware of and those we are not. Many attributes lay dormant, waiting for the time when we consciously lower our barriers and expand our awareness.

Eventually even those dragging their heels will be forced to release the restraints they place on life as the energy flow into their physical vehicle increases. Our intellect, nomatter how developed, cannot think out the continually changing requirements of every moment but still we try; in our struggle to remain dominant, we cling to patterns of behaviour that are thought to provide security, becoming increasingly at odds with life until finally letting go and jumping onboard the train that takes us into a life of peace and joy!

On a positive note, the upturn in vibrational rate brought about by the incoming Aquarian Age is increasing our understanding and whether we are comfortable with it or not we are becoming aware of how our thoughts attract experiences into our life. It would be ideal for everyone to attain a level of detachment before the heat is turned up too much - the only side effect if that be the case would be a return to harmony and peace on earth with humanity becoming an open channel for visions of perfection to flow through our collective consciousness. Instead, many earth dwellers are struggling to let go, hanging onto what makes them feel comfortable, moving more and more out of balance as the 'increased' energy flow of the Aquarian Age, (the water carrier), manifests the very things we are trying to avoid.

Letting go of Karma!

I've reached the conclusion that not only are unresolved memories of the past stored within the Astral Plane but they remain there until re-absorbed by their creator by an act of love. These memories, until 'loved better', were a source of constant irritation within my subconscious and consequently within my life - irritations that could be referred to as Karma that attracted the conditions of this present life. This 'residue' from previous lives seems to continually draw whoever created them into increasing confrontation until 'looked' at and released. If I hadn't established a 'need to know' I would remain under the influence of this past conditioning.

Only after establishing an objective and still mind and after many more years of embracing whatever arose from the depths, did I come to know that any 'flotsam' still lingering had value and needed to be 'read' to glean the wisdom it had carried across the illusionary boundaries of time and space. Had I not retained the memory of the key events of my past lives, in my particular life, (not everyone is the same in this respect), I would only have a fraction of the motivation to keep moving forward.

We may suffer from an illness of the kind that inflicts our physical vehicle even as it forms within the mother's womb. In such cases a knowledge of the particular experience in a previous life which created the 'karma' would lead to some measure of acceptance of the present life condition and give an insight into the change of attitude required to help prevent its effect going forward into a future life.

We should be open to the possibility that nationality, gender and location may change with each life and realise the futility of prejudice in any of its forms – even prejudice directed towards the self. In this way I moved towards accepting the barbaric behaviour of my own past with the realisation that it was also helping me to accept and love others in the present. Our history books record that in the not too distant past, just about everyone watched as the latest person to be accused of being a witch was either tortured or burned at the stake. This has left in each and every one of us a stain of guilt that has, or will in time, stimulate a change of heart.

We do evolve. In ancient times human flesh was sacrificed as an offering to please or appease our Gods which eventually 'softened' to become the more civilised ceremony of killing a beast as the centuries rolled by. Today's act of presenting the prime of the year's harvest on the altar of the local church is all that remains - or is it? Each person's development is likewise tempered through time. The torturing of digresses of faith became progressively turned inwards to looking closely at our own weaknesses which, as a sort of side effect, led to some of us becoming self-condemning and guilt-ridden. These days we are encouraged to admit our failings instead of feeling guilty, to use the next opportunity that comes along to make amends instead of brooding about what we have done. When we do this habitually we break the cycle of cause and effect.

278

Chapter Twenty – *Adam, Eve and the beast*

In the beginning and at the end

The broad steps of development made on my journey through life have become clearer and more understandable over the years. From what's been experienced, read and perceived, these steps, or graduations of 'spiritual development' have been accomplished by countless others travelling the same path through the ages, it's a path leading us all back to our true 'home', the home that we left at the beginning of time. Though the reader will be familiar with some of these steps, it should be borne in mind that everyone has a unique history, one that often causes us to respond differently to others having the same experience. These steps may be presented in any order to that given here with much 'jumping' into and out of life to glean the right experience in the right environment in perfect timing with need and a 'blossoming' receptivity. A few of our brothers and sisters, needing just a refresher course to 'pass go' 'return home' after just a few short years, never needing to return to the training ground of the Earth to animate a gross physical body again – though they may return at anytime in their glorious bodies of light!

Creating the vision of a swarm of trainee creators descending into the dense elements of matter with the intention of subduing them appears to be a monumental task to my finite mind. I would also speculate that, because my senses cannot trace any tangible beginning to this process, the unfolding of the vision must have begun at the same moment the 'known universe' was brought into being.

From what I understand, human development is drawn out over a period of time that stretches much further and deeper than science has so far been able to prove. The 'prime vision' guiding the descent and the eventual ascension of humanity to complete its cycle of development which included the creation of physical bodies that had become sufficiently evolved to be ideal for 'incoming' Souls to procreate and develop a human colony with.

In synchronisation with this physical development, the Soul completed its transition down the Planes into matter through a succession of ever denser bodies to a level that matched, near enough, to that of the evolving earthly animal body. Though the Soul body was still androgynous and still needed to go through a process called the 'splitting of the infinities' - this splitting was a separation into male and female polarities, the 'making of two from one', that had to be achieved before interrelationships with the indigenous population could begin. (Adam and Eve?)

At this point of human development the Souls counterparts became separated and subdued by the new bodies of flesh through rounds of physical death and re-birth, a process that developed within these young Souls a deep, but remote yearning to become whole again - to forever seek to re-connect with their estranged 'Soul Mate'. This longing and the 'pure' genetics were in time spread across the globe leading to the next instalment of the 'prime vision' and its quest to enshroud the Soul within the beast of flesh.

From what insight leads me to understand, this scenario underscores much of the drama that is life – of lifetimes spent searching for the ideal spouse that could only ever be assuaged by developing the 'lost' qualities within ourselves, activating all the chakras of our being as we do so. Consequently, the design to have us all carry a taint of the Souls 'royal blood' in our veins has succeeded and has perpetually whispered its memory of a 'home' we once knew and are now beginning to return to through the gateway of our heart - to open when we let go and turn within to seek a solution to life's difficulties, a gate that leads definitely back to our eternal home!

The blossoming of the Chakras

Located near the bottom of our spine, the Base Chakra is often symbolised as a coiled serpent and has always been active, channelling the energy of procreation long before being mixed with the blood of any descending Soul. The animal instincts ensuring that only the fittest survived kept this particular Chakra in full flow, and only in later times, did we begin to express this force more creatively through higher ideals.

The next highest Chakra is positioned at the level of the bowel and is at the centre of a complex nervous system; this chakra is stimulated into full activity by the reactions we have to experience. Our brain was, after it had completed its evolutionary journey, conditioned to react instinctively to maintain its survival. Nowadays, in most people, it's a centre that generally responds directly to commands from our intellect. Over time these reactions and responses created what we refer to as an emotional body which was perhaps the first sign that we were more than just an animal - the more intense of these emotions began to leave their record upon the delicate electro-magnetic substance that permeates and surrounds both our body and the earth, an 'atmosphere' which is referred to here as the Astral Plane.

From my perspective it's at this point of development that the influence of the Soul began to make its mark upon the body of flesh whereas previously, only instincts were its guide. The developing emotional body beginning to, and increasingly attracting experiences that we reacted to, causing ripples to form and disharmony to ensue in the delicate balance of life around us. The 'Garden of Eden' became despoiled with these, our first acts of creativity; behaviour that tried to prevent anything happening that caused discomfort or distress. Life always seeks to correct imbalance – it's one of the cosmic laws included in 'The Prime Vision' and generally referred to as 'Karma' but to me it's a less personal attempt to restore balance – an extension of Isaac Newton's first law of motion: 'to every action there is an equal and opposite reaction'. It's a more subtle form of this action that I feel keeps drawing us back to the same experience time and time again until the day we become detached by embracing any residual emotive feeling; only then do we begin to leave the cause and effect cycles behind, stepping into other, ever more subtle cycles hand in hand with releasing personal desire. It is to me the same Law that draws us back into life for yet another round of climbing the ladder of development until the day we learn to live out our life in harmony with life around us.

As the emotional body fully formed and its related Chakra opened to the full flow of energy available to it, the next highest Chakra at the level of the stomach came into focus. This marked the beginning of a resistance to instinctual reactions as we held back from actions that in the long term would be detrimental to our development – for example, taking food from those who have helped to gather it would lead to isolation and probable starvation. Being the third Chakra, completes the lower triangle of forces acting through our being and serves to 'anchor' the Soul into the Earth's evolutionary process and also becomes the balancing energy to the upper triad of Chakras, when developed, combine to open the gate to the realm of Soul when embraced with the magic ingredient of love.

Symbolically, this third Chakra is where experience is 'taken in' and converted into wisdom through our interaction with life – Our stomach may be strong or weak depending upon the type and extent of this experience.

Still with the emotions but now expressed in their highest form through the heart Chakra - the next to come under the spotlight on the ascent up the ladder of accomplishment. In pre-history the heart centre was predominantly about the development of sensitivity to life experience.

The primitive mind, unaware of the consequences caused by harming others in the struggle to survive, left painful memories in its wake and loved ones suffered. Through time, and many similar experiences, these memories gave rise to new reactions that are often grouped under the heading of 'heartache' which stimulates qualities such as compassion and empathy.

In today's world, many people still suffer periods of emotional turmoil, not yet able to stand aside and remain 'centered' when confronted by experience that our past behaviour attracted - though at this level of development we may not be aware of these causative past actions.

The heart centre is the halfway stage of integrating the Soul into the reality of physical existence, with many still working to open it fully to the energy stream that is, and always was available from the inner realms.

The next highest Chakra that 'opens' in response to our efforts to be creative is positioned at the level of the throat; its flow of energy empowering the ability to be inspired, to link with ideals that help raise the individual above the carnal self. It's here where the quest to take life in hand and lead it towards more noble causes is stimulated to overcome behaviour traits that stand in the way of this.

Instead of 'accidently' placing thoughtforms onto the Astral Plane as a reaction to experience, at this level of development we are empowered to imagine and therefore we automatically create thoughtforms as we do so. We may to a degree use this inbuilt ability to achieve personal aims and ambitions. It's at this level of development that powerful thoughtforms are created upon the Astral Plane that may or may not be aligned with what is 'meant to be' and cause disruption on an increasing scale to the 'Prime Vision' that is guiding humanity towards perfection.

The highest Chakra within our physical body is positioned centrally within our brain and encompasses what is generally referred to as the 'Third Eye' which becomes active when the intellect is able to be subdued and its reasoning and envisioning abilities are aligned to the perceived needs of the Soul - the 'Third Eye' is an effective portal into and from the Soul.

As with all the lower Chakra's it's a process that takes time to unfold but once opened and then subdued in favour of Divine Will signals the final transformation of our being as the three higher Chakra's are activated to bring our being into alignment with the universal needs of the Soul.

From personal experience, at this level of 'activation' my awareness expanded automatically into what is often referred to as 'the void'[22]. This state of awareness stayed with me a little longer after each session until eventually becoming a permanent and natural state of being where I can generally choose to observe life and not be subject to its ups and downs. Feelings of oneness with life are also enhanced, leading me to become more connected with every expression of life.

A year or so after the above experience, when in the depths of a meditative state, I began to focus on 'inner' sounds that were barely perceptible. The sounds increased and after while began to intensify, reaching a point where a firework like crackling light was set off somewhere deep within my being that culminated in a sudden burst of light and sound that filled the inner screen of my mind. It was a little scary to say the least having never experienced this phenomenon before.

Thankfully, the brain has built in resilience to get used to anything in time and after many similar experiences the 'scary effects' quickly became little more than a faint buzzing whenever I chose to 'tune in'.

Unbeknown to me at that time, the moment that I entered the void, energy also began to flow freely through another Chakra point that is beyond the extremities of my body – the Crown Chaka. It was at this moment too that the love I had generated within my being to help make this breakthrough was also the unifying ingredient that also allowed that energy free passage through all the chakras simultaneously.

Had I not gone some way towards resolving many of the difficulties I'd had with life then they would have been magnified out of all proportion to become the demons that a few are confronted with when entering 'the void'.

Contemplation

Several hours a day for years on end were spent reading, contemplating, and meditating to help break down the monuments I'd built 'to self' and to develop the single mindedness necessary to move closer to the perceived goal of Soul unification. The more I managed to regain the long disregarded feelings of oneness I'd experienced before birth that overflowed into the early months of my life, the more the realisation of the greater life came into awareness with its unlimited potential when expressed in service to God.

Having made the choice to seek out and follow the dictates of the inner life, to follow inner feelings wherever they led me, I then needed to perceive, develop and establish some tangible form of inner communion to provide a permanent feeling of security; ironically, because this connection was being made to the realm of Soul, the security needed to be founded on constant change!.

It was the most confusing time of my life - perhaps it's the same for any aspiring individual who's chosen to walk the pathway home - the confusion was of not having the outside world to rely on for a sense of direction which leads many to turn aside. I needed the resolve to stand back, to allow the route 'home' to become clear enough to follow as there was no one to tell me which way to go, no parent or teacher to point the way, not even kindred Souls with the necessary experience were few and far between - only barely perceptible feelings. (Of course I did have untold numbers of ascended beings to connect to!)

It took over twenty-five years before releasing the need for material, emotional and intellectual security, to exchange it for a sense of belonging, an oneness that could only be found deep within. I needed to cross the gulf of insecurity, the no man's land of the intellect, to trust that 'feelings' were expressions of my Soul, the 'chip off the old block', the bit I'd inherited from God. I needed to stand alone, to become strong in that loneliness and not until then did I have the awareness that the whole of creation was stood at my side giving support and encouragement!

Having the patience to wait at this threshold was essential to allow feelings to become clear and more evident, I became able to step forward in perfect synchronicity with feelings, to flow with the stream of life – not doing so brought back confusion and a feeling of not belonging far greater than any that life could confront me with. I know now that the flowing stream of creativity has always been there – waiting patiently for every weary traveller on the path to step into its flow, its waters healing all 'aching limbs'.

Even with this life changing realisation there were times when following the path within made me feel overloaded at just how much I needed to change - I wanted to jump off the train of self-development at such times and wash my hands of the whole business. I've since got used to these moments realising that, paradoxically, taking time out, letting go completely of any attachment to even 'the path' is useful to allow the Soul to take charge and restore a sense of balance, and bring me down to earth – I didn't need to be a saint to walk the path. In time I learned to proceed without the baggage of personal expectations, moving more into an attitude of just being. This led to the establishment of an immovable intention to go on that didn't hold the risk of slipping back into old habits – an attitude of detachment where the only thing that mattered was to respond to the moment and engage fully with whatever is presented to me – 'if it felt right' of course!

Discrimination

Distinguishing which way to turn, from a continuous procession of choices that need to be made each day, has become much easier. The intellect that has ruled my life for aeons has generally receded into second place as I've paid more attention to feelings emanating from within. The experience I described earlier, where a mass of tangled tracks of limiting consciousness rose above my head, marked a significant step up in awareness. It in no way confirmed the battle had been won, though it was the beginning of the end to my intellect's control over affairs. I can also say, thirty years later, that I don't stand victorious over the intellect but now stand aside and observe its reactions without getting caught up.

This overlighting of the mind and therefore the body has provided insight into just how sensitive it is to the environment. I was made acutely aware of one aspect of this when completely out of the blue, my body became jumpy and on edge, with emotional responses to normal experience very erratic. I had all on to stay rational under this bombardment. As always seems to be the case when being 'made' aware of an emerging attribute, similar experiences followed and although strung out over a period of years my attention was drawn to the fact that earthquakes of various intensity were occurring a day or two after each of these reactions! It seems that other sensitive's were right when they said Mother Earth, or Gaia, had emotions and an intellect too - but much more so. It seems that any 'sensitive' worth their salt will pick up her moods, especially when so many of her charges are affected when she 'shivers'. Of course there were and are a multitude of other reactions too that have provided a constant source of tuition when it come to understanding life and what makes it tick.

If I were not steadfast in my intent to stay the course I would back away from being a world server and perhaps demonstrate my sensitivity in other less stressful and more lucrative ways. The level of perception I'm now experiencing gives insights that could easily be marketed as any one of many 'new age arts' - not that I'm anything extraordinary, on the contrary, feelings of self-importance have often led me down the proverbial garden path and into activities and displays that left me feeling separated from something I'd grown to love beyond anything else - uncomfortable feelings of isolation that are poles apart from the fulfilling and all encompassing embrace of the Soul.

On the odd occasion I've been literally pulled out of a developing situation only to realise much later why! One of these was after attending an evening gathering with a mixed group of kindred Souls in London. It was my first experience of a séance where two young women demonstrated an ability to change facial expressions and speak the words of 'spirit guides' - the ascended beings upon the inner planes who had under their wing one of the individuals in attendance, including me! I was greatly impressed and wanted to see and hear more but, just two days before the next meeting, I was transferred 'up north' with inner prompting confirming that such glamour was definitely not on my path at that time.

After many such experiences I've developed a chalk and cheese distinction between what is meant to be and what isn't. It is apparent that nowadays I'm 'allowed' to take part in one or two of these 'glamorous' associations as its seen that self importance has been mostly 'burnt away' to allow a sense of discrimination to be built up and to perhaps become more interactive with these inner guides should the occasion arise

Becoming

William Shakespeare's play, 'As You Like It', includes the famous line 'All the world's a stage, and all the men and women merely players'. The wisdom of these words can be seen unfolding in every life, and its implications, if taken seriously, help aspirants to stand back and observe how they themselves are performing.

We all begin our 'acting' career at birth by mimicking our parents or guardians; from the spiritual aspect, the purpose of this early conditioning it seems is to provide the best 'set up' to help an individual achieve their life purpose. This form of conditioning was absent from my life for the first six months due being confined to a steam tent but, as it transpired, another form of conditioning took its place to make it easier for me to watch and listen more intently than would otherwise have been the case – Because my thought processes were not tied up with the outer world as most infant brains are in the first few months of life, my Soul was able to establish a lasting influence in respect to having responded to its whisperings perhaps more than would have normally been the case.

The Souls influence came into direct conflict with everyday affairs, particularly with the entrenched attitude I had of trying to maintain job security. This attitude was definitely a detriment to 'becoming' though suffering redundancy four times and being forced into the uncertain world of self employment finally brought the awareness that impermanence is a necessary quality for every aspirant – an attitude of 'living in the now'.

This is what makes my life so full now – following inner prompting, being spontaneous, not knowing what will happen next, just trusting that all is well, that my Soul always sees the bigger picture and is leading me to my destination along the shortest possible route.

Realisation

I've always encouraged students to read through past notes knowing that it leads to the realisation of progress. This realisation is often a catalyst for a major shift in awareness as it is for me when reflecting on how far I have 'travelled'. This was a godsend as getting to know myself in more depth after jumping aboard the self development train unearthed all manner of flotsam that had been hanging around in my subconscious and made me wonder if I'd ever break free of these earthly rounds.

Previously it was explained how prevailing thoughts bring about or attract the experiences we have, and thus it wasn't surprising when looking back and realising the effect my change of attitude had already had on my life reinforced an already established belief in the universal law of 'like attracts like'.

Self-realisation is the companion on my journey through time – as I believe it is everyone's; to be achieved hand in hand with detachment in the process of becoming, towards the goal of attaining regency over the self, 'at one' with Soul consciousness. My ability to become 'at one' and channel through the Soul's needs into form awaits the moment of my acceptance of life's possibilities. The more I realise perfection, the more life around me changes to reflect that perfect expression of creativity, which ironically, has always been there!

Unification

What is remarkable about 'the journey' is the utter familiarity of having been down the road before. The memories of a long forgotten past that only seem like yesterday, not dissimilar to the experience of returning to a favourite holiday scene after many years' absence. Ironically, the feelings associated with deeper and deeper explorations within can also be a cause for concern for some as they can only be experienced when a person is totally detached, and here lies the rub!

Detachment, by its very nature requires me to step into a void, a place totally lacking any means for my outer senses to latch onto, a place where no comfort can be initially found in familiarity. A totally unknown territory confronting all first footers, a total lack of bodily senses causing all but the boldest of pilgrims to back off even before they've had chance to experience a taste of what is to follow. At such times the wise teacher slows the pace to allow a familiarity to develop within an experience that is devoid of outer sensations. Slow enough to allow the student to feel comfortable, to relax and let go of any fear that may be present or may arise. As soon as the journey resumes, familiar feelings of home emerge and become the carrot to establish the self-motivation needed to progress onwards and inwards!

Unification is a journey of developing then the bequeathing talents for all to use, returning to life what life has given to complete the cycle. This inner home has become, to all intents and purposes my permanent residence, full of love and creative possibilities, it's a stepping stone for future journeys into the infinite world of universal consciousness. My love of God has opened the door, from this vantage point I can explore the unlimited vista of wherever my Soul leads me, 'tuning into' and knowing every other form of life according to the level of my ability to comprehend what is within my field of awareness.

This new 'home' is the same home I apparently walked out of at the beginning of time – it's the famed Garden of Eden. It's certainly a haven of peace that holds its doors open to all who are able to put aside the self and raise awareness to its elevated levels through personal endeavour - and the best part is - we don't need to leave this world to taste its heavenly landscape, we just need to be still to allow ourselves to enter the silence!

Granville's 'awakening' in the 1970's marked the beginning of a quest to unfold a deeper understanding of life and its purpose. As an integral part of the journey, inner prompting led him into meditation, volunteer as a Resource Person for the Findhorn Foundation, undergo teacher training and to create and develop, during thirty years of teaching, a learning programme entitled 'Creative Meditation' – a course available nationally via the Open College Network. Now retired, Granville spends most of his spare time focalising group discussions, meditations, workshops and presentations. He also holds 'one-to-one' sessions for those wishing to clarify and strengthen 'inner connectedness'.

If any of these services are of interest or should you have any questions on the subject matter included in this book, the author can be contacted via any of the following media:

Web site: **www.stepping-stones-uk.com**

'e' mail: **lettingthesouldecide@yahoo.co.uk**

Bibliography

Al, K. *Bring Out the Magic in Your Mind.*

Benson, A. B. *Life in the World Unseen:.*

Caddy, E. God Spoke to Me. Findhorn Press.

Darwin, C. (1872). The Origin of Species.

(1991). In G. Edwards, *Living Magically.*

Fortune, D. *The Cosmic Doctrine.*

Fortune, D. *Through the Gates of Death.*

Hawken, P. *The Magic of Findhorn.*

Hay, L. Heal Your Body.
http://www.hayhouse.co.uk/events/218/many-lives-many-masters.

Hodgson, J. *Astrology, the Sacred Science: A Spiritual Perspective.*

Long, M. *Our Son Moves Among You.*

Quantum Physics. (n.d.).

Sheldrake, D. R. (n.d.). Mind, Memory and Archetype Morphic Resonance and the Collective Unconscious. *Psychological Perspectives .*

In D. Spangler, *The Rebirth of the Sacred.*

various. *The Bible.*

www.drpokea.com/darknightsoul.html. (n.d.).

Zorn, W. (1968). Yoga for the Mind.

---

[1] (Greek mythology) A box that Zeus gave to Pandora with instructions that she not open it; she gave in to her curiosity and opened it; all the miseries and evils flew out to afflict mankind

[2] The fear of death stands as an impenetrable barrier to expanded awareness – a symptom explained in detail later in the book

[3] Symbolised by the astrological sign of the Aquarian Age – 'The Water Carrier'

[4] Combined effort being greater than the parts

[5] 'A considerable body of research indicates that we register and evaluate stimuli that we do not consciously perceive' [Introduction to Psychology, 1995, Ch 4, States of consciousness]

[6] Surprises – these are the hidden memories which may cause reactions to experience. Deliberately entering the stillness helps us to become aware of these memories

[7] The beast referred to here is symbolic of the animal instincts that I was learning to subdue and guide in line with deific will.

[8] (Greek mythology) A box that Zeus gave to Pandora with instructions that she not open it; she gave in to her curiosity and opened it; all the miseries and evils flew out to afflict mankind

[9] In every person there is the potential to generate a feeling of love towards others. The act of embracing involves the deliberate awakening and projection of that feeling towards or into the situation as a healing balm that has the effect of harmonising all expressions

[10] Shadowy areas

[11] 'Oneness' is a general term referring to a state of being that is universal in nature

[12] Refers to a series of physically invisible doorways between the planes through which life-sustaining energy passes.

[13] As if to confirm the general direction that humanity is growing towards Abraham Maslow [1908-1970] introduced into his book published 1943, the concept of 'self-actualisation' as part of the hierarchy of needs. Carl Rodgers [1951] also came to believe that the basic force motivating the human organism is self-actualisation - a tendency toward fulfilment or actualisation of all the capacities of the organism. The individual chooses to grow rather than to regress.

[14] Our physical existence is referred to as a 'loop in reality' with each lifetime beginning and ending at the same moment but giving the illusion of time passing by having to live through a series of experiences within the dense and slowed down medium of this physical plane.

[15] Present day translations from Sanskrit writings that are at least 5000 years old describe the various ways of attunement.

[16] The 'mystical marriage' referred to in many new age publications concerns this awakening, blending and balancing of the opposing qualities of a person's being – quite a task if we remain either stubbornly masculine or feminine in our approach to life!

[17] Synchronisation, used in this context, refers to a popular new age cliché that describes how God schemes to ensure that certain people meet up at particular moments in time to share an experience.

[18] In John 1:18, the apostle wrote: "No one has seen God at any time." In Exodus 33:20 God said to Moses: "You cannot see My face; for no man can see Me and live." But Genesis 32:30 records Jacob as saying: "For I have seen God face to face and my life is preserved."

[19] Vital energy that Hindus believe lies dormant at the base of the spine until it is called into action, e.g. through yoga, to be used in seeking enlightenment

[20] One part of the brain stores commands that relate to repeated actions, i.e.: When driving a car for the first time every action undertaken is difficult but after a few lessons, if the actions are repeated often enough, they become automatic as the brain sends the commands subconsciously, enabling use to carry out the necessary function almost without thinking.